Ensuring the Integrity of Electronic Health Records

Ensuring the Integrity of Electronic Health Records

The Best Practices for E-records Compliance

Orlando López

A PRODUCTIVITY PRESS BOOK

First published 2021
by Routledge
600 Broken Sound Parkway #300, Boca Raton FL, 33487

and by Routledge
2 Park Square, Milton Park, Abingdon, Oxon, OX14 4RN

Routledge is an imprint of the Taylor & Francis Group, an informa business

ISBN: 9780367616052 (hbk)
ISBN: 9780367616038 (pbk)
ISBN: 9781003105695 (ebk)

Typeset in Garamond
by Deanta Global Publishing Services, Chennai, India

For Lizette, Mikhail Sr., István, Christian, and Mikhail Jr.
who continue making the journey of life worthwhile.

Contents

Foreword xv
Preface xvii
1 **Introduction** **1**
References 5
Additional Readings 5
2 **E-records Lifecycle Revisited** **7**
Introduction 7
E-records Lifecycle 8
Records Identification Phase 9
Records Standardization Phase 9
Creation/Capture Phase 10
Active Phase 12
Inactive Phase 13
Final Disposition Phase 13
Regulatory Agencies' Expectations 14
Summary 14
References 14
Additional Reading 15
3 **Data and E-records Lifecycles – A Comparison** **17**
Introduction 17
Data Lifecycle 18
Record Lifecycle 20
Correlation of Data and E-records Lifecycles 23
References 23
4 **MHRA Guidance – Revisited** **25**
Brexit 25

Introduction.....25
Data Governance.....27
Computer Systems Validation.....28
Requirements.....29
References.....39

5 E-records Integrity Expectations of EU GMP Inspectors.....41
Introduction.....41
EMA E-records Integrity Technical Requirements.....42
EU E-records Integrity Guidelines.....43
Expectations of EU GMP Inspectors.....44
Conclusion.....47
References.....48

6 Comparison of Health Authorities E-records Integrity Expectations.....49
Introduction.....49
Elements to Compare Guidance Documents.....50
Key Elements of Each Guidance Document.....52
Differences between Guidance Documents.....52
Consistencies between Guidance Documents.....54
Summary.....55
References.....56

7 Maxims of E-records Integrity.....57
Introduction.....57
Lifecycle.....57
A Measure of Validity.....59
Security.....60
References.....61

8 Vulnerabilities of E-records.....63
What Is Record Vulnerability?.....63
Protection and Security of Electronic Records.....63
Threats that Can Impact E-records.....65
Regulated Users.....65
Malware and Phishing Attempts.....65
Service Providers.....65
Unrestricted Access to Computers.....66
Inadequate Disposal of Old Hardware.....67
E-records Transfers.....67
E-records Storage.....67

Assessment of E-record Vulnerability, Risks, and Implementation of Control Measures 68
Case Study 69
Regulatory Agencies Expectations 73
Summary 73
References 74

9 CGMP E-records Risk Management 77
Introduction 77
Risk Management 79
Regulatory Agencies Expectations 81
References 81
Additional Reading 82

10 CGMP E-records Risk Assessments 83
Introduction 83
How Can E-records Risk Be Assessed? 84
Risk Assessment 85
References 87
Additional Reading 87

11 Security Service 89
Introduction 89
Computer Access 89
Password Policy 91
Audit Trails 91
Regulatory Agencies' Expectations 93
References 93

12 Defining and Managing Manufacturing Data 95
Introduction 95
Data Lifecycle 96
Medicine Manufacturing Operations 96
Identification of CGMP Record 97
Exchange of Data 97
Storage of Records 99
Protection of Data and E-records 100
  Transient Data 101
  Raw Data 102
Retrieval of E-records 102
Retention Time 103
Disposition of E-records 104

Summary ... 105
References ... 105

13 **Controls on Transient Data ... 109**
What Is Transient Data? ... 109
Protection of Transient Data ... 110
Regulatory Agencies' Expectations ... 112
Summary ... 112
References ... 113

14 **Digital Date and Timestamps ... 115**
Introduction ... 115
System Clock ... 116
Computer Clock Reliability ... 116
Digital Time-Stamping Service ... 117
Time Zone ... 118
Computer Systems Not Networked ... 118
Computer Clock Controls ... 118
Regulatory Agencies' Expectations ... 119
References ... 119
Additional Readings ... 119

15 **E-records Migration and Its Integrity ... 121**
Introduction ... 121
Migration Process ... 122
Automated Migration ... 123
Checklist for Data Migration ... 123
Regulatory Agencies' Expectations ... 124
References ... 124

16 **Ensuring E-records Integrity of Cloud Service Providers ... 125**
Introduction ... 125
Cloud Service Requirements ... 126
Selection of the Cloud Service Provider ... 130
Service Level Agreement ... 131
Periodic Audits ... 133
E-records Migration ... 133
E-records Accessibility ... 133
Regulatory Agencies' Expectation ... 134
Summary ... 134

References 134
Additional Readings 135

17 E-records Integrity in Hybrid Systems 137
Introduction 137
E-records Signed with Handwritten Signatures 137
Regulatory Agencies' Expectations 139
References 139

18 Technologies Supporting E-records Integrity 141
Introduction 141
  Cryptographic Technologies 143
Summary 147
  Cryptographic Technologies Apply to E-records Integrity 149
E-records in Storage 150
  Access Controls and Authority Checks to Computer Resources 151
  Audit Trails Control 152
  Authentication 152
  Security of the Electronic Signatures 154
  Signature E-records Linkage 155
  Time Controls 156
  The Uniqueness of the Electronic Signatures 157
E-records in Transit 157
  The Integrity of E-records in Transit 157
  Device Checks 159
Summary 159
Disclaimer 160
References 161

19 Integration Between Computer Systems and E-records Lifecycles 163
Introduction 163
Concept Period 165
Project Period – Risk Assessment 165
Project Period – Requirements 167
Project Period – Building, Testing, Documenting, and Installing 169
Project Period – E-records Migration and Computer Systems Release to Operations 170
Operations Periods 170
Computer System Retirement – E-records Migration 171

E-records Archiving 172
E-records Final Disposition 174
References 174

20 Miscellaneous E-records Integrity Issues 175
Introduction 175
Backup as a Service 175
Audit Trails Review 176
Introduction 176
Categories of Manufacturing-Related Audit Trails 178
Product- or Batch-Specific Data 178
Administration Events 179
System Activities 179
What Are We Looking for in an Audit Review? 179
Review of Audit Trail Entries 179
Guidance for "Regular Review" of Audit Trails 179
What Are We Looking for in an Audit Review? 180
Suspected Data Integrity Violation – What Do We Need to Do? 180
Testing Audit Trails 180
Databases Integrity 181
Retention of E-records – Verification 182
Introduction 182
Documentation 183
Testing Required Concerning the Retention of E-records 184
E-records Integrity in Wireless Environments 185
Introduction to Wireless Environment 185
Data Integrity in Wireless Environments 187
References 189

21 E-records Remediation Project Revisited – Medicine Manufacturing 191
Introduction 191
Remediation Project Fundamentals 192
Evaluate E-records Controls 193
Sample Project and the Evaluation of E-records Controls 195
Corrective Actions Planning 195
Sample Project and the Corrective Actions Planning 196
Remediation 197
Interpretation 197
Training 197
Remediation Execution 198

New Applications and Application Upgrade Assessments 198
Suppliers Qualification Program 198
Sample Project and Remediation 199
Remediation Project Report 199
References 199
Additional Reading 200

22 Designing E-records Integrity into your Practices 201
Introduction EU Annex 11 201
EU Annex 11 as a Computer Data Integrity Compliance Model 202
Supporting Processes Applicable to the Data Integrity Controls 204
Categories of Data Integrity Controls 208
Summary 216
References 216

23 Introduction to Data Quality 219
Introduction 219
Data Quality 220
Data Accuracy 221
Data Auditability 222
Data Conformity 223
Data Completeness 223
Data Consistency 223
Data Integrity 224
Data Provenance 224
Data Validity 225
Data Quality Design 226
Quality Control to Data 227
Summary 227
References 228
Additional Reading 228

24 Summary 229
References 230

Appendix I: Glossary of Terms 231

Appendix II: Abbreviations and/or Acronyms 269

Appendix III: References 275

Appendix IV: Things That Can Go Wrong when Validating Big Data Environments 287

Appendix V: Data Integrity for Analytical Instruments connected to a LIMS 293

Appendix VI: Data Integrity – EU Deviations 301

Index 315

Foreword

Orlando López is a well-recognized name in the realm of computer system e-compliance and validation.

Regulatory agencies have published many new or revised regulations and guidance relating to electronic/automated systems and any data created or managed within these. It can be quite a task following these regulatory documents and, even more so, to interpret them. At the same time, the regulated healthcare industry continues to increase their use of automated systems, for reasons of efficiency, cost, business need, and finally compliance. As a consequence, the integrity of electronic data/records is of paramount importance to industry, or else consequences can be dire.

This book is, therefore, a useful tool for those working in the field and those with just an academic interest. Orlando covers the subject from a variety of viewpoints: regulators, industry, suppliers, and technology in the 24 chapters of this book. It therefore definitely has something of interest for everyone.

Given that in the experience of regulatory agencies and many an auditor, the industry is still a long way from having full and commendable controls over electronic records integrity, this book should be an excellent aide to advance the state of compliance. I wish it all the success it deserves.

Siegfried Schmitt, Ph.D.
Vice President Technical, Parexel
March 2020

Preface

> Because the data have broad public health significance, they are expected to be of high quality and integrity.
>
> **US FDA, Pharmaceutical CGMP for the 21st Century – A Risk-Based Approach, Final Report," September 2004.**

Data integrity (1) (DI) has been one of the foundations of the Current Good Manufacturing Practice (2) (CGMP) principles for years.

As an example, the European Union (EU) Commission Directives 91/412/EEC (1991) and 003/94/EC (1994) in Article 9 item 2, and the 21 Code of Federal Regulation (CFR) Part 211.68 (1976) contain the requirements associated with DI in the EU and United States (US), respectively.

Falsification of data is considered by the regulatory agencies and competent authorities a critical deficiency to the regulated entity (3).

On the other hand, the information properly recorded is the basis for manufacturers to assure product identity, strengths, purity, and safety (4). The collected electronic records (e-records (5)) also demonstrate that the manufacturing process adheres to the CGMP, including instructions.

All data (paper and electronic) generated throughout a product's lifecycle must be accurate, auditable, in conformance with data definitions, complete, consistent, with integrity, provenance, and valid. This includes data generated during clinical or pre/post-approval stages.

Multiple DI citations during the last years have been reported by the US Food and Drugs Administration (FDA) investigators and European inspectors. A sample of EU Non-Compliance Reports referencing DI issues can be found in Appendix VI. Many US FDA Warning Letters (WL) and EU Non-Compliance Reports deal with serious DI violations.

DI questions have been and will continue to be the focus of many CGMP inspections. Consequently, the main international authorities and organizations – CEFIC, CFDA, EMA, EU Annex 11, EU OMLC, Health Canada, ICH E6, MHRA, PIC/S, SIDGP, TGA, US FDA, and WHO – published documents describing the regulatory expectations with DI.

Although all guidelines are not intended to impose an additional regulatory burden to the regulated companies, a lot of hesitation predominates the pharmaceutical industry on how to implement these requirements into the daily business and how to integrate suppliers' involvement.

The objective of this book is to provide solutions to the regulated user pertinent to the e-records integrity situations. Some chapters update the information provided in my first book about e-records integrity (6).

Data integrity refers to whether data is trustworthy. Just because data is trustworthy does not mean it is also useful (7). The usefulness of data is achieved by implementing data quality into the practices of data handling (8).

Each chapter in this book provides practical information to enable compliance with e-records integrity while highlighting and efficiently integrating worldwide regulation into the subject. The ideas presented in this book are based on many years of experience in the regulated industries in various computer systems development, maintenance, and quality functions. Based on risk assessment principles, a practical approach is presented to guide the readers around the technical, design, and testing aspects of the e-records integrity controls recommended in worldwide regulations and guidelines.

As in my first book about e-records integrity, out of the scope of this one is the behavioral aspects of regulated life science industries that knowingly employ unreliable or unlawful activities.

Enjoy the reading. If you have any suggestion for improvement or any question, send it to olopez6102@gmail.com.

Orlando López
SME – E-records Quality

References

1. Data integrity - The property that data has not been altered in an unauthorized manner since it was created, while in transit, during processing or stored. (NIST SP 800–57 Part 1).
2. Good manufacturing practice (GMP) is the minimum standard that a medicines manufacturer must meet in their production processes.
3. TGA, "Australian Code of Good Manufacturing Practice for Human Blood and Blood Components, Human Tissues and Human Cellular Therapy Products," Version 1.0, April 2013.

4. Wechsler, J., "Data Integrity Key to GMP Compliance," *BioPharma International*, 27(9), September 2014, pp 40–45.
5. An e-record is a collection of related data treated as a unit initially recorded in an electronic format that requires a computer system to access or process (SAG, "*A Guide to Archiving of Electronic Records*," February 2014).
6. López, O., *Data Integrity in Pharmaceutical and Medical Devices Regulation Operations*. (CRC Press, Boca Raton, FL, 1st ed., 2017).
7. Syncsort Editors, "Data Integrity vs. Data Quality: How Are They Different?" January 2019. https://blog.syncsort.com/2019/01/data-quality/data-integrity-vs-data-quality-different/.
8. MHRA, Section 2.7 in the "MHRA Data Integrity Guidance and Definitions," March 2018.

Chapter 1

Introduction

> Records should be maintained to demonstrate that the quality system has operated effectively and that the specified requirements have been met.
>
> **Australian Code of Good Manufacturing Practice for human blood and blood components, human tissues and human cellular therapy products, April 2013.**

DI is a critical aspect to the design, implementation, and usage of any system which stores, processes, or retrieves data. The overall intent of any DI technique described in this book is the same: ensure data is recorded exactly as intended and upon later retrieval, ensure the data is the same as it was when it was originally recorded. Any alteration to the data is traced to the person who performed the modification.

Any possible concern related to the reliability of data must be identified and understood for appropriate controls to be put in place.

The responsibility regarding accurately handling electronic records (e-records) and the integrity of such e-records lies with the manufacturer or distributor undergoing inspection. These entities have full responsibility to assess their data handling systems for potential vulnerabilities and take steps to design and implement good e-records governance practices to ensure that e-records integrity is maintained (1).

Since the publication of my first book about DI (2) in 2017, the information about DI in the regulated industry has increased by the multiple publications drafted and finalized.

The new/updated publications since 2017 are:

- Health Canada Good Manufacturing Practices (GMP) Guidelines, Version 3 (GUI-0001), February 2018
- MHRA, GxP Data Integrity Guidance and Definitions, March 2018
- Russia Federal State Institute of Drugs and Good Practices (SIMGP), Data integrity and validation of computerized systems, August 2018
- PICS, Good Practices for Management and Integrity in Regulated GMP/GDP Environments (PI 041–1 (Draft 3)), November 2018
- US FDA, Data Integrity and Compliance with Drug CGMP. December 2018
- CEFIC, Practical risk-based guide for managing data integrity, March 2019
- WHO, Guideline on Data Integrity (Draft), October 2019
- US FDA and MHRA, Data Integrity in Global Clinical Trials, December 2019
- IPEC, Data Integrity for Pharmaceutical Grade Excipients, April 2020
- OECD, Advisory Document on GLP Data Integrity (Draft), August 2020
- NMPA (former CFDA), "Drug Data Management Practices Guidance," December 2020

All guidance documents can be found at https://drive.google.com/drive/folders/1pB9XE29MuFpCBmNpQq0iG8RubmOCPe-u?usp=sharing

The industry has paid more attention to DI as a result of the regulatory agencies' publications. In addition, the amount of materials published by regulated users is massive.

DI continues to be globally a major concern to all regulatory agencies.

This book is divided into 24 chapters and 5 appendices relevant to production systems and quality control systems and pertinent to medicine manufacturers.

This book updates previous written practical information to enable a better understanding of the controls applicable to e-records. It highlights the e-records suitability implementation and associated risk-assessed controls, and e-records handling (3).

Chapter 2, "E-records Lifecycle Revisited," updates the electronic e-records lifecycle by adding two new phases to the typical lifecycle covered in the regulatory guidelines. These two new phases are related to the design of the e-records set. These two new phases are implemented before starting to collect e-records.

Chapter 3, "Data and E-records Lifecycles – A Comparison," discusses the correlation between data and e-records lifecycle.

Chapter 4, "MHRA Guidance – Revisited," is an analysis of the most recent revision (March 2018) guidance document of the Medicines and Healthcare Products Regulatory Agency (MHRA, United Kingdom (UK) medicines and medical devices regulatory agency).

The key expectations of EU CGMPs inspectors in the area of e-records integrity can be found in Chapter 5, "E-records Integrity Expectations of EU GMP Inspectors."

Based on a presentation I did in August 2018 (4), Chapter 6, "Comparison of Health Authority E-records Integrity Expectations," highlights the e-records integrity-related guidance documents published by Health Authorities only.

Chapter 7, "Maxims of E-records Integrity," discusses the e-records integrity principles applicable to medicine manufacturing operations. The lifecycle, the validity and fidelity, and the reliability of e-records integrity depend on maxims or fundamental rules for the effective handling of e-records integrity.

The vulnerabilities of e-records may be used to undermine the quality of records and may ultimately undermine the quality of medicinal products (1). Chapter 8 examines the typical vulnerabilities of e-records. The risk assessment performed at the beginning of a records handling implementation uncovers these vulnerabilities. Based on Chapter 8, Chapters 9 and 10 discuss the risk assessment and the handling, respectively, of e-records vulnerabilities.

Chapter 11, "Security Service," focuses on the security controls expected by worldwide regulatory agencies and competent authorities. Focal items include access control, password policy, and audit trails.

The required controls on computer-generated raw data in medicine manufacturing operations are discussed in Chapter 12, "Defining and Managing Manufacturing Data."

Transient data controls are discussed in Chapter 13.

Chapter 14 considers the critical issue of date and timestamping in digital environments.

E-records migration is the process of transferring e-records and related metadata between one durable storage location, format, or computer system to another. This subject is addressed in Chapter 15.

Chapter 16, "Ensuring E-records Integrity of Cloud Service Providers," provides the activities which the regulated entity and the cloud service provider must implement to safeguard the integrity of e-records.

Hybrid situations include combinations of paper records (or other non-electronic media) and e-records, paper records and electronic signatures, or handwritten signatures executed to e-records. Chapter 17 addresses the issues associated with records of hybrid systems.

Centered on information security, Chapter 18, "Technologies Supporting E-records Integrity," provides a broad overview of the cryptographic technologies that can keep e-records integrity for any CGMP-regulated activity.

Chapter 19 describes the integration of the computer system and e-records lifecycles.

Chapter 20 covers miscellaneous e-records integrity issues such as BaaS, audit trails reviews, testing audit trails, database integrity, testing the retention of e-records, and e-records integrity in wireless environments.

A manufacturing-related e-records remediation project is re-examined in Chapter 21.

My advice on how to design e-records integrity into your practices is offered in Chapter 22.

Data integrity refers to the trustworthiness of data. Evidently, just because data is trustworthy, it does not mean it is also useful. The usefulness of data is achieved by implementing data quality into practices of data handling. Elements to consider in data quality are presented in Chapter 23. The objective of this chapter is to modify the mind frame in our industry and establish data quality in our practices.

The emphasis in this book is e-records integrity in medicine manufacturing practices regulations.

To bring up to the reader additional information, this book refers to relevant regulations/guidance. Some descriptions are based on listed guidance, but judicious editing was necessary to fit the context of this book.

It is not the intention of this book to develop a standard for the regulated industry. This book intends to guide how the industry can effectively manage e-records integrity vulnerabilities and raise basic compliance in this area.

Except for the definition of DI, this book is consistent with the UK MHRA (5) and the Pharmaceutical Inspection Convention and Pharmaceutical Inspection Co-operation Scheme (PIC/S) (6) DI guidance documents.

The recommendations to implement e-records controls, as described in this book, are purely from the standpoint and opinion of the author and should serve as a suggestion only. They are not intended to serve as the regulators' official implementation process.

References

1. Russia Federal State Institute of Drugs and Good Practices, "Data Integrity & Computer System Validation Guideline," September 2018 (Draft).
2. López, O., *Data Integrity in Pharmaceutical and Medical Devices Regulation Operations*. (CRC Press, Boca Raton, FL, 1st ed., 2017).
3. Data Handling – It is the process of ensuring that data is stored, archived or disposed of safely and securely during the data lifecycle.
4. López, O., "Comparison of Health Authorities Data Integrity Expectations," *Paper Presented at the IVT 4th Annual Data Integrity Validation*, Cambridge, MA, 15–16 August 2018.
5. MHRA, "GxP Data Integrity Guidance and Definitions," March 2018.
6. PI 041-1, "Good Practices for Data Management and Integrity in Regulated GMP/GDP Environments," *Pharmaceutical Inspection Co-operation Scheme (PIC/S)*, November 2018, (Draft 3).

Additional Readings

Boogaard, P., Haag, T., Reid, C., Rutherford, M., Wakeham, C., "Data Integrity," *Pharmaceutical Engineering Special Report*, March–April, 2016.

MHRA, "MHRA Expectation Regarding Self Inspection and Data Integrity," May 2014.

Sampson, K., "Data Integrity," 2014. Update, Issue 6, pp 6–10. http://www.nxtbook.com/ygsreprints/FDLI/g46125_fdli_novdec2014/index.php#/0.

Chapter 2

E-records Lifecycle Revisited

Introduction

The e-records (1) lifecycle encompasses all the phases in the life of e-records from creation, use (including analysis, processing, transformation, migration, and so on), retention, archive/retrieval to final disposition. It includes assessing the vulnerabilities and the associated risks of impacting records and managing the e-records risks (2) during their lifecycle.

Even though multiple applications may access e-records in the same electronic storage device, e-records themselves have a lifecycle of their own separate from, but related to, the system lifecycle (SLC) (refer to Chapter 19). E-records integrity must be built into every phase of the e-records and computer systems lifecycles.

The conformity to data integrity starts from the Records Identification Phase. Chapter 3 in my first book about e-records integrity (3) covers the e-records lifecycle. In this second book about e-records integrity, the typical e-records lifecycle phases are expanded by adding two new phases. These two new phases are related to the design of the e-records set. These two new phases are implemented before starting to collect e-records in the operational environment.

The e-records steward manages the development, approval, and use of e-records within a specified functional area (4). The e-records steward is responsible as well for the security of the e-records residing in the electronic storage device (5).

E-records Lifecycle

Figure 2.1 (6) depicts a typical e-records lifecycle. E-records, as informational objects, have a lifecycle that begins with Creation/Capture, Active Phase, Inactive Phase, and Final Disposition Phase. Refer to Chapter 3 related to the association of data and e-records lifecycles.

The e-records lifecycle is needed to understand the controls necessary to effectively manage transient data, data, raw data, metadata, and records. Failure to address even one element of the data lifecycle will weaken the effectiveness of the controls implemented in the computer system and the e-data integrity-related controls.

Like the Conceptualization Periods in the SLC, the e-records lifecycle incorporates two phases defining the planning, requirements, and designing of the e-records model and the functionality to manage the e-records. These phases, namely, the Data Process Design Phase and Records Identification and Standardization Phase, are not depicted in Figure 2.1. These two phases come immediately before the "Start Boundary" in Figure 2.1.

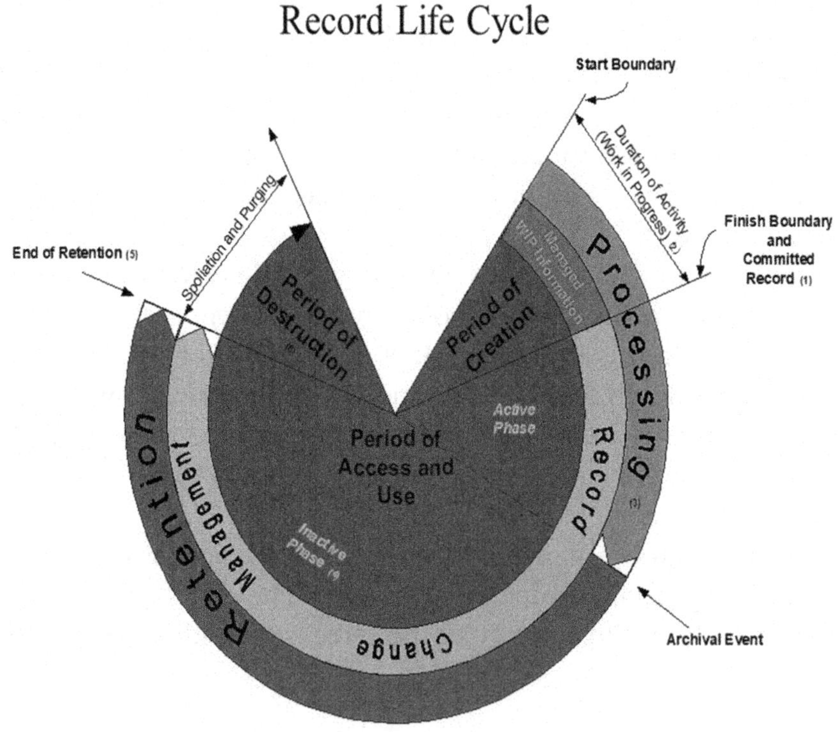

Figure 2.1 Record lifecycle.

Records Identification Phase

The Records Identification Phase of the e-records lifecycle is known as strategic e-records planning. Strategic e-records planning determines the information requirements of the function necessary to collect the e-records and implements a technology-independent set of techniques to arrive at a set of e-records and activity models that represent the CGMP process.

Current systems are analyzed for input, output, and processes (forms, reports, and code) to assess the feasibility of reverse engineering or reengineering.

The e-records models constructed act as a foundation for the development and definition of standard e-records elements. Thus, strategic e-records planning provides a framework where e-records become separate from their processes and constitute a resource independent of applications available for e-records use planning.

Strategic e-records planning is based upon the e-records requirements of specific functional processes performed in support of a CGMP process. Strategic e-records planning identifies the e-records required to satisfy specific information requirements most efficiently. E-records requirements can also be identified through fewer formal means, such as system change requests.

Records Standardization Phase

During the Records Standardization Phase, the information requirements identified through strategic e-records planning are given common or standard representations. Data profiling is the technical analysis of data to describe its content, consistency, and structure.

The Record Standardization Phase of the e-records lifecycle also addresses actual e-records values (items). There are many instances where the format and attributes of the e-records values must be standardized to ensure consistency across the regulated site/corporate. When e-records must be shared by more than one functional activity, the standardization of e-records values is essential.

Strategic e-records planning establishes common e-records values and provides a framework for standard e-records use. It is in this area that the lines between the standardization, acquisition, and maintenance stages become unclear. This is to say, once an information requirement is identified and the e-records elements representing that information requirement are defined, the e-records element domains may vary depending on usage.

The established standards will apply to information such as the authority for a specific instance of metadata, the preferred acquisition method and source for populating a database with a certain e-records element, the e-records' set owner responsible for the accuracy and/or integrity of the actual e-records values, and numerous other pieces of information. It is useful to view metadata as a type of controlling framework that outlines a broad set of rules to which the e-records of interest to an enterprise must be complying. The e-records administrator is the caretaker of this framework and its interface with the regulated entity's overall mission.

The final product of the Standardization Phase is the approved standard e-records and metadata, including e-records entities, attributes, definitions, and values.

The outcome of the Standardization Phase is employed to create the data flows to connect the data warehouses. Mapping the fields is essential to ensure that during the direct move, each valid e-record from the source is loaded to the appropriate target table(s), connecting precisely two databases.

Creation/Capture Phase

As described in the regulated authorities' DI guidance documents, the Creation/Capture Phase in the e-records lifecycle typically starts with the generation and capturing of data e-records, either automatically or manually (e.g., continuous e-records flow from a sensor, alarm event, or operator input during a process). The data can be imported from other sources, manually entered into the system, or linked to other systems.

The captured and transformed data is stored in defined fields (e.g., structured data). This action creates an e-record.

In a typical manufacturing environment, data generation and automatic capture mean that the data is generated by a sensor (e.g., temperature, humidity, pressure, and so on) and captured by a computer system (7).

After capturing the data, it may need to be verified and transformed to make it suitable for use in e-records. During the transformation, activities such as scaling, aggregating, and normalization are performed by the data acquisition system. The transformation may include user-designated data manipulation, including arithmetic operations and logic operations.

During the transformation, built-in checks (EU Annex 11 p5) are performed to verify the data after the transformation.

The data collected directly from manufacturing equipment and control signals between the equipment and a data server (e.g., Supervisory Control and Data Acquisition (SCADA)) may be regarded as transient and cannot be edited by reasonable means or reprocessed by a human user. Refer to Chapter 13, "Controls on Transient Data."

As an element of the e-records Creation/Capture Phase, the acquired data may be loaded into temporary memory. At the temporary memory, applicable controls must be implemented to ensure transient data accuracy and reliability. The interface between the originating computer system/equipment/manual entry and the data acquisition and recording systems shall be validated and, after validation, periodically checked for accuracy (21 Code of Federal Regulation (CFR) Part 211.68(b) and EU Annex 11 p5). The data, while in transit, must not be altered in an unauthorized manner. Any transformation process must be documented in the design document.

Because the data transferred during this phase is between equipment and computer, this interface should be qualified and checked periodically to ensure data accuracy and reliability. The accuracy and reliability of raw data depend not only on properly calibrated instruments and equipment but also on the integrity of the raw data produced by the recording action.

In situations where instruments/equipment cannot support expectations for secure access and administration of electronic data files, it may be prudent to implement a design strategy that will pass the collected data directly to a secure, "processable" environment for record-keeping purposes. In a typical manufacturing environment, the secure recording environment may be SCADA/Historian. An example of a remediation project applicable to the situation described in this paragraph can be found in Chapter 21.

This phase ends when the transient data is transformed and written onto durable media.

The data collected during the Creation/Capture Phase must be monitored. The monitoring of collected data is an element of the built-in checks per EU Annex 11 p5 and the US FDA Compliance Policy Guide (CPG) 7132a.07. It may include:

- Identification of missing data, inconsistent data, and deviations from process parameters
- Evaluation of significant errors in data collection

Any deviation must be reported and investigated. The root cause must be identified and a corrective and preventive action plan implemented (EU Annex 11 p13).

Active Phase

After the data is transformed and the corresponding built-in checks performed, there is a commitment to use the data and save it to a processing environment. The data is stored in defined fields as raw data (e.g., structured data). The raw data is used for its intended purpose as representing the activities it stands for. The raw data is capable of being edited from the time it is saved in an electronic storage device through to final disposition. In situations where data "processability" is extended into the Inactive Phase, access and administration will also need to be extended, ensuring controlled management of the modification to e-records.

To acquire a CGMP e-record, the data must satisfy a CGMP requirement. Besides, the collected data needs to be recorded immediately after the data is generated and transformed (21 CFR 211.160d), as applicable. Consequently, data is stored to prevent loss (21 CFR 212.110(b)). If the CGMP e-records are the first-capture records, the e-records are then considered to be CGMP raw e-records.

The Active Phase encompasses e-records that are kept and accessed for their intended purpose. Activities associated with the Active Phase are storage, access, processes (transforming and migrating), modifications, periodical reviewing, analyzing, reporting, migrating, retaining, backing up, and restoring.

In addition to the audit trail functionality during the Active Phase, change management may represent governance that controls editing or modifying the e-records.

Resulting from the criticality of the raw data, periodically, raw data within the e-records may be cleansed to correct inconsistent values after the use of the data. This activity must be suitably managed using procedural control and documented (e.g., audit trail).

The three key CGMP controls to e-records in storage compliant with e-records integrity are:

- Modifications to CGMP e-records must be recorded at the time of modifying the e-records.
- Periodic backups must be performed.
- Security controls must be established to all e-records storages as a means of ensuring e-records protections.

The process of managing records is the most active stage. This includes ensuring records are migrated and transformed as systems change, so the records remain usable.

Inactive Phase (8)

After the e-records in scope are inactive, superseded, replaced, and withdrawn, the Inactive Phase starts. During the Inactive Phase, the e-records in scope are ingested (9).

When acquiring or developing the electronic archive, it is expected that consideration must be given to the long-term retention schedule requirements for these e-records, particularly concerning accessibility, readability, traceability, and possibly any future processing needs through to final disposition.

Technical and functional requirement specifications for such electronic archives should include requirements for the long-term storage, preservation, management, and retrieval of their e-records. The set of requirements should include all the issues described in this section to ensure that e-records from these electronic archives can be archived in a manner that is compliant with all applicable requirements and industry best practices.

The key activities associated with maintaining inactive e-records are storage, access, periodical reviewing, reporting, transferring, retaining, backing up, and restoring.

Three key requirements to maintain inactive CGMP e-records are:

- The archiving process must include verification that no e-records and associated metadata are altered in value and/or meaning during the migration process.
- Archived e-records need to be verified periodically for accessibility, readability, integrity, and the state of security.
- Periodic backups must be performed.

Final Disposition Phase

After meeting the approved retention time, the e-records are tagged to discard and are physically erased according to an approved procedure. The Final Disposition Phase has a noticeably short event duration and includes content, metadata, audit trails, documentation, and any pointers to the e-record and connections to related records

Current good practice also includes, as part of a regulated entity's records handling program, a periodic practice to revisit the approved retention of periods of specific records as business, regulatory, or legal requirements change. It is important, from a legal perspective, to consider that e-record handling programs include defined provisions to suspend the execution of the purge process (including backup tapes) when records are part of a legal discovery process during pending litigation.

Purging e-records and paper records are the last steps in the record lifecycle. The reliable execution of the purging procedural control must be followed for the deletion of CGMP e-records (10).

Regulatory Agencies' Expectations

The regulated entity should know their data lifecycle and integrate the appropriate controls and procedures such that the handling of e-records will produce complete, consistent, and accurate records (PICS, "*Good Practices for Management and Integrity in Regulated GMPGDP Environments (PI 041-1 (Draft 3))*," November 2018).

Summary

The e-records lifecycle must consider all phases in the life of the e-records, from identification, generation, and recording through processing, use, archiving, retrieval, and (where appropriate) final disposition. Failure to address even one element of the e-records lifecycle will weaken the effectiveness of the measures implemented elsewhere in the system (11).

References

1. Record – Collection of related data treated as a unit. (ISPE/PDA), "Technical Report: Good Electronic Records Management (GERM)," July 2002.
2. National Medical Products Association (NMPA (former CFDA)), "Drug Data Management Practices Guidance," December 2020.
3. López, O., "Electronic Records Life Cycle," In: *Data Integrity in Pharmaceutical and Medical Devices Regulation Operations*. (CRC Press, Boca Raton, FL, 1st ed., 2017). pp 39–45.
4. Department of Defense (DoD) 8320.1-M-1, "Data Standardization Procedures," April 1998.
5. EudraLex, The Rules Governing Medicinal Products in the European Union, Volume 4, "EU Guidelines to Good Manufacturing Practice, Medicinal Products for Human and Veterinary Use Part 1, Annex 11 - Computerized Systems," June 2011.

6. International Society for Pharmaceutical Engineering (ISPE)/ Parenteral Drug Association (PDA), "Good Electronic Records Management (GERM)," Figure 4.1, July 2002.
7. European Compliance Academy (ECA), "GMP Data Governance and Data Integrity Guidance," Version 2, January 2018.
8. Scientific Archivists Group (SAG), "A Guide to Archiving of Electronic Records," February 2014.
9. Ingestion – The process that accepts e-records for archiving (8).
10. ECA, "Deletion of Data: Does it have to be regulated in an SOP?" June 2019. https://www.gmp-compliance.org/gmp-news/deletion-of-data-does-it-have-to-be-regulated-in-a-sop.
11. MHRA, "Good Manufacturing Practice (GMP) data integrity: a new look at an old topic, part 1," June 2015. https://mhrainspectorate.blog.gov.uk/2015/06/25/good-manufacturing-practice-gmp-data-integrity-a-new-look-at-an-old-topic-part-1/.

Additional Reading

ISPE/PDA, "Electronic Records," In: *Good Practice and Compliance for Electronic Records and Signatures. Part 1 Good Electronic Records Management (GERM)*, July 2002.

Chapter 3

Data and E-records Lifecycles – A Comparison

Introduction

The words "data" and "record" are used interchangeably by regulated users and regulatory authorities. However, the characterization of each one denotes a significant difference.

Data is defined as the contents of a record. It is the basic unit of information that has a unique meaning and can be transmitted (1).

Records are defined as a collection of related data treated as a unit (2).

This chapter delineates the difference between data and records. Based on the data/record state, the controls to data and records are dissimilar.

Typically, e-records are handled (3) in the electronic storage devices environment and while in transit.

Data is handled typically during the creation, while in transit, in the electronic storage devices environment, and during processing.

Data Lifecycle

Data, transformed data, and metadata follow the same lifecycle, where data are the textual, numerical, pictorial, video, or audio objects about something and metadata are the attributes about data that give it meaning. Data is collected for reference or analysis (4).

Figure 3.1 (5) depicts the life span of data. It includes the following events: Commit to Collect, Commit to Transform, Commit to Use, Commit to Archive, and Commit to Discard.

Besides, it includes the following periods: Capture, Transformation, Use, and Final Disposition.

- Capture – Actions that involve the data collection from instruments/equipment/computers, the verification of recording, and the steps that confirm what was collected was planned to be collected.

Data collected directly from equipment and control signals between computers and equipment is considered "Work in Progress," like draft documents.

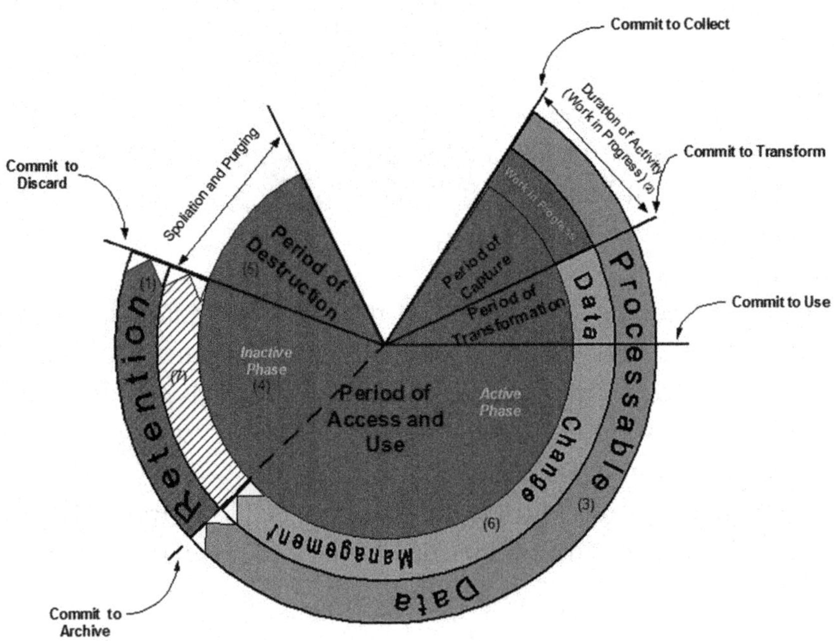

Figure 3.1 Data lifecycle.

This is identified in Figure 3.1 as item #2. Before the data is recorded in durable media, the data is time-stamped and transformed.

- Transformation – After the data is captured, it may need to be verified and transformed to make it suitable for use in e-records. During the transformation, activities such as verifying the input data (e.g., built-in checks (EU Annex 11 p5)), scaling, conversion, and normalization are performed by the data acquisition system. The transformation may include user-designated data manipulation, including arithmetic operations and logic operations.

Before the data is recorded in durable media, the data is time-stamped and transformed, as applicable.

- Use – Time in which data is committed, accessed, and used.

Committed data takes place after recording the transient data (Chapter 13) to the relevant database for e-records (6) in the respective database field (7). At the table level in a database, this data is called field-level data.

When a system, sensor, or instrument automatically populates a field-level data in a database, a data element identifier should be created that automatically identifies the system, sensor, or instrument (e.g., name and type) as the originator of the data element.

- Active Phase – Data in current use.

Data is typically processable and capable of being edited from the time it is collected through to retention. During processing, data is generally retained by computer storage. If edited, an audit trail is created. This is identified in Figure 3.1 as item #3.0

Change management represents governance that controls editing or modification of data. This is identified in Figure 3.1 as item #6.

- Inactive Phase – Data is off-line and not readily available. This is identified in Figure 3.1 as item #4.

During the Inactive Phase, the data is archived. In most cases, data is not in a form for analytical processing. There are, however, exceptions to this rule, where processability is extended for the full life of the data through to discard. This is identified in Figure 3.1 as item #1.

During the Inactive Phase and if there is no extended processability, the data is "write protected," maintaining a read/view attribute.

In situations where data processability is extended into the retention period, access and administration will also need to be extended to ensure controlled management of change. This is identified in Figure 3.1 as item #7.

The data may be superseded, replaced, and/or withdrawn. The data needs to be kept meeting retention schedule requirements.

- Field-level data quality.
  - Each field must be used consistently, as designed and per global and local procedures. This will ensure the data are usable and that ad hoc queries and reports will be accurate and complete.
  - In selection fields, "N/A" or "other" must not be selected unless all other selections have been deemed inappropriate.
  - Attachments must not be used as a substitute for entering data in the system fields as designed. Attachments generally cannot be queried. They must only be used for supporting information.
- Final disposition or destruction – The records holding the data are discarded as a final disposition. This is identified in Figure 3.1 as item #5.

  The final disposition is an event of very short duration and includes metadata and audit trail. It is performed following the corresponding procedural control(s).

Record Lifecycle

As information objects, e-records have a lifecycle. The lifecycle is needed to understand the essential controls to properly manage the e-records and ensure their integrity.

Figure 2.1 depicts the life span of e-records. This lifecycle includes the following periods: Creation, Access and use, and Final Disposition.

Besides, it includes the following events: Start Boundary, Committed Record, Archival, and End of Retention.

After the physical design phase of the database, the database is ready to receive data to be assigned to each specific database field (7). Refer to Figure 3.2.

- Creation and Transformation

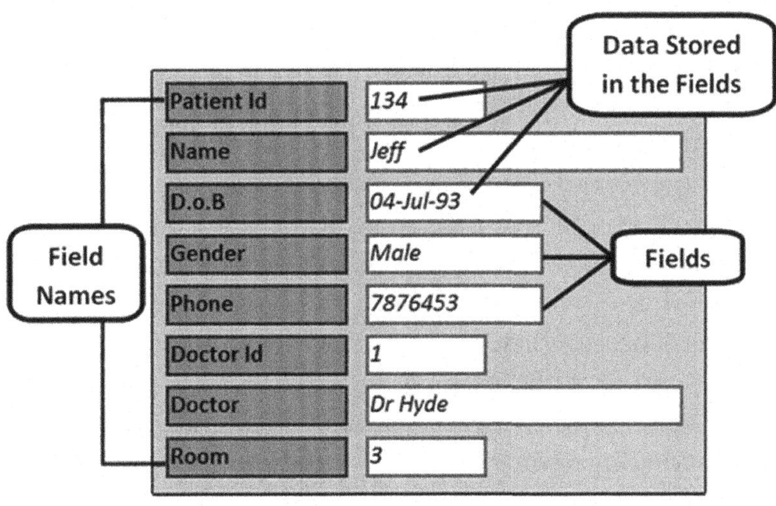

Figure 3.2 Example database fields.

Captured and transformed data is placed in the corresponding database field. This action creates an e-record. This is identified in Figure 2.1 as item #1. This action must follow the ordinary contemporaneous feature (21 CFR Parts 211.100 and 211.160, and EU Annex 11 p12.4 and 11 p14). If the database collects data related to a CGMP activity, then the data is to be inserted as part of an e-record in compliance with CGMP requirements (8). This is identified in Figure 2.1 as item #2.

The retention of e-records starts with the creation of each e-record.

- Access (9)

Physical and/or logical controls should be in place to restrict access to computer systems and data servers to authorized regulated users (EU Annex 11 p12.1 and p7.1).

These controls include physical protections, stamped audit trail, e-records handling (10), and archival and retrieval of records.

Refer to Chapter 11.

- Use

E-records are used for their intended purpose. The use of an e-record includes access, migration, transformation (e.g., business intelligence environments), archiving, processing, and so on.

These e-records can be edited from the time it is collected through to the final disposition. During the Use Period, e-records are largely retained in computer storage. If edited, the time-stamped audit trail is created. This is identified in Figure 3.1 as item #3.

The use of the e-records happens usually in the e-record active phase.

During the e-record inactive phase and if there is no extended processability, the data is "write protected" maintaining a read/view attribute. During this period, the e-record needs to be kept meeting retention schedule requirements. The complete or portion of the e-record may be superseded, replaced, and/or withdrawn.

In situations where e-record processability is extended into the retention period, access and administration will also need to be extended to ensure controlled handling of e-records use and change. Usage of the e-records rarely happens in the e-record inactive phase.

The record level quality consists of:

- Data in the record must be consistent with other data throughout the record.
- It is the responsibility of users to use the fields correctly and to ensure the data are complete and consistent with other parts of the record.
- For records with approvals, it is the responsibility of the approvers to ensure the record is complete and the data are in the appropriate fields and consistent throughout the entire record.

■ Final disposition

The final disposition of e-records is an event of very short duration and includes content, attributes, audit trail(s), and documentation. This is identified in Figure 2.1 as item #6. These e-records are discarded and purged according to an approved procedure.

E-records disposition should be an element to verify during the periodic review.

This is identified in Figure 2.1 as item #5.

Detailed information on e-records lifecycle can be found in Chapter 2.

Correlation of Data and E-records Lifecycles

Figures 3.1 and 2.1 are used in the following analysis.

Since a record is a set of data relating to a single individual or item (11), the connection between data and records starts once the data is captured and transformed, and the transient data written to the corresponding database field. This is the instant in which the transient data is converted to data and the data placed in the corresponding database field.

After the data is written to the data field, there is a commitment to use the data and the associated e-record. The e-records handling function takes over, including that all modification to a data field must be recorded contemporaneously through a time-stamped audit trail. The audit trail becomes another e-record linked with the original e-record.

Besides, after the commitment to the data, the data is an element of the associated e-record. Subsequently, the data and the e-record share the following lifecycle phases: active phase, inactive phase, and final disposition.

Chapter 12, "Defining and Managing Manufacturing Data," is a typical example of the correlation between data and records in an automated environment.

References

1. ISO/IEC 17025, "General Requirements for the Competence of Testing and Calibration Laboratories," November 2017.
2. ISPE/PDA, "Technical Report: Good Electronic Records Management (GERM)," July 2002.
3. Data Handling – The process of ensuring that data is stored, archived or disposed of safely and securely during and after the decommissioning of the computer system.
4. PIC/S Pharmaceutical Inspection Convention. "Good Practices for Data Management and Integrity," (PI 041-1 Draft 3), November 2018.
5. ISPE/PDA, "Good Electronic Records Management (GERM)," Figure 4.3, July 2002.
6. Database for e-records – A direct access device on which the e-records and metadata are stored.
7. Database field – It is a place for a piece of information in a record or file.
8. US FDA, "Data Integrity and Compliance with Drug CGMP – Questions & Answers - Guidance for industry," December 2018.

9. Access – The ability or opportunity to gain knowledge of stored information (DoD 50152).
10. E-records Handling – The process of ensuring that e-records are stored, archived or disposed of safely and securely during and after the decommissioning of the computer system.
11. wikidiff.com/data/record.

Chapter 4

MHRA Guidance – Revisited

Brexit

The MHRA had communicated their approach and the impact on the withdrawal of the United Kingdom from the European Union (Brexit). Refer to www.gov.uk/government/news/medicines-and-healthcare-products-regulatory-agency-statement-on-the-outcome-of-the-eu-referendum. At the moment of writing this book, in the interests of public health and safety, the approach is to retain a close working partnership with respect to the regulation of medicines after the UK leaves the EU.

Introduction

This chapter is an update of my analysis of the same subject in my first book related to MHRA DI guidance document (1). This updated chapter covers the most recent revision of March 2018.

The MHRA DI document guides the DI expectations that should be considered by organizations involved in any aspect of the pharmaceutical lifecycle or GLP studies regulated by MHRA.

The Heads of Medicines Agencies (HMA) and the European Medicines Agency (EMA) had determined in late 2015 that there

> is the need to ensure the integrity of the data on which regulatory decisions about medicines are based. Concerns about DI may arise for many reasons e.g. poor training, inadequate implementation or occasionally due to suspicions of falsification. The integrity of the data in the studies used to support market authorisation is fundamental to trust and confidence in the products themselves. (2)

The HMS and EMA "will ensure that all suspicions of problems with DI are thoroughly investigated working closely with other international partners where these data may have been generated or used" (2).

As part of the strategy by the HMA and EMA, the MHRA is setting emphasis on the integrity of the critical data (3) during inspections at regulated manufacturing sites. Also, the MHRA is stressing on self-inspection programs to address the effectiveness of the CGMP controls to ensure data reliability (4) and traceability (5).

In preparation for these inspections, the MHRA introduced their guidance document (6). This guidance outlines a data reliability governance system and supplementary principles for defining quality and data reliability in processes and systems. The guidance provides notes and examples about the definitions and the controls associated with e-records integrity.

The Data Integrity Definition and Guidance supplements the EU Annex 11 (7) GMP guidelines to the UK pharmaceutical industry on how to implement CGMP DI controls. It is an excellent reference to other regulated users and inspectors, ensuring a common understanding of terms and concepts.

Based on the National Institute of Standards and Technology (NIST) definition on DI (8), this chapter discusses the technical and procedural controls–related guidance provided by the MHRA on data reliability and the relationship with those relevant elements in the EU Annex 11. The attention of the controls to be discussed in this chapter will be automated manufacturing systems.

In this chapter, organizational controls are out of the scope.

Data Governance

People's views on data quality can often disagree, even when discussing the same set of data used for the same purpose. When this is the case, data governance is used to form agreed-upon definitions and standards for data quality. In such cases, data cleansing, including standardization, may be required to ensure data quality.

The MHRA guidance provides critical points to consider when implementing Annex 11 elements related to data reliability (9). The approach is based on the typical Annex 11 SLC phases: Project, Operations, and Retirement.

The MHRA guidance document endorses a strong data governance approach to GxP systems. Most of the cases related to the lack of data reliability have to do with bad practices, poor organizational controls, and/or a lack of technical controls which open possibilities for data manipulations. These elements should be covered in data governance and consist of all the arrangements to ensure that data, irrespective of the format in which it is generated, are recorded, processed, retained, and used to ensure a complete, consistent, and accurate record throughout the data lifecycle (10).

These deficiencies are corrected by applying good e-records integrity practices within all the components in the regulated user's organization.

E-records governance is met by:

- making accountable the senior management to support the controls associated with e-records integrity;
- offering training about e-records integrity to all computer systems users;
- addressing e-records ownership and the responsibilities associated with such a role (EU Annex 11 definition: System Owner); and
- periodic review of data governance.

The MHRA requires CGMP-regulated users to complete a CGMP Pre Inspection Compliance Report before an inspection (11), unless it is a triggered inspection which is notified only at short notice. One area covered in this compliance report is data reliability. In this DI section, the questionnaire includes if the regulated user has a policy on DI governance.

Figure 4.1 suggests an approach for the integration of good e-records integrity practices to the typical EU Annex 11 SLC. This approach is combined with the subject of this chapter.

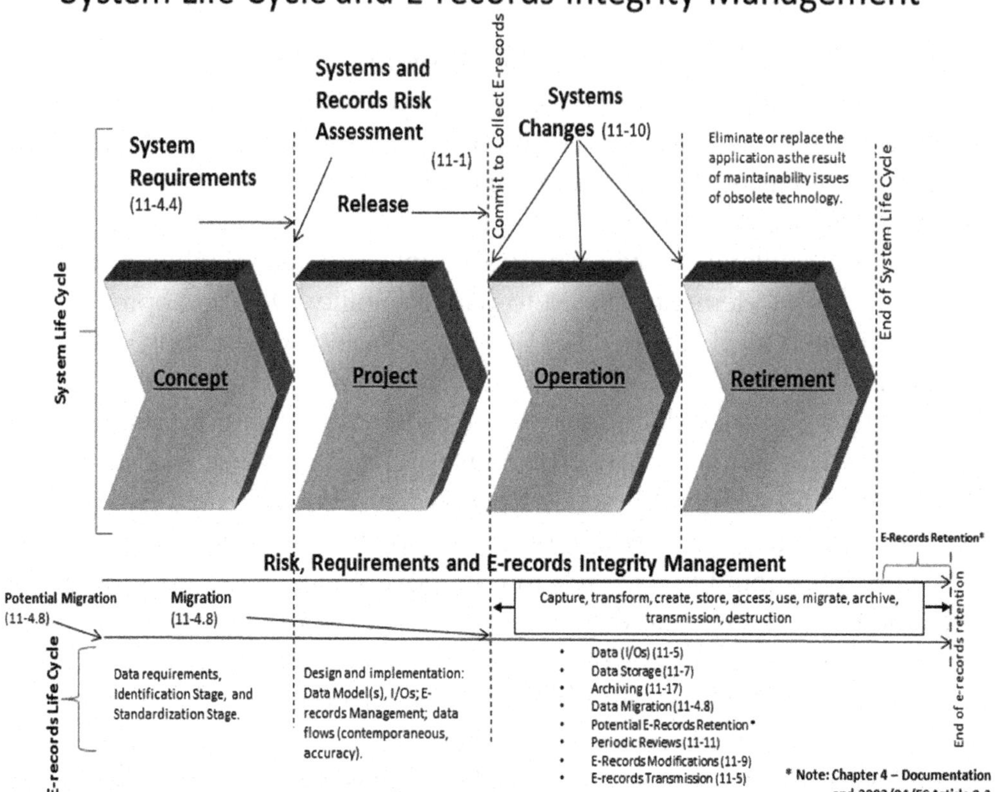

Figure 4.1 SLC and e-records integrity handling.

Computer Systems Validation

An element of governance is the computer systems validation process. If data reliability requirements are in the scope of the system, the computer systems validation process provides the initial assurance of the successful implementation of the data reliability controls. These controls are to be maintained through the operation, maintenance, and retirement of the computer system.

Computer systems validation is the formal assessment and reporting of quality and performance measures for all the lifecycle stages of software and system development; its implementation, qualification, and acceptance; and operation, modification, re-qualification, maintenance, and retirement. This should enable both the regulated user and the competent authority to have a high level of confidence in the integrity of both the processes executed within the controlling computer system(s) and those processes controlled by and/or linked to the computer system(s), within the prescribed operating environment(s) (12).

The MHRA guideline establishes the validation of computer systems based on the intended use and following the EU Annex 11 guidelines.

Requirements

The term "requirement" defines a bounded characterization of the system scope that can be generated by different relevant stakeholders. It includes the information essential to communicate an understanding of the problem and to support relevant stakeholders in its resolution. Various types of requirements include product, functionality, performance, regulatory, legal, reliability, supportability, usability, security, and non-functional requirements.

Business requirements (13) are gathered as part of the concept stage of the automated project (refer to Figure 4.1). The business requirements include the e-records reliability-related requirements. The e-records reliability-related requirements are traced throughout the lifecycle (EU Annex 11 p 4.4).

Related to e-records reliability, the following requirements are critical:

- Critical data must be identified.
- A data lifecycle methodology (Chapter 2) and associated data governance across the whole e-records lifecycle must be implemented to assure data reliability (MHRA DI Guidance, Section 6.6).
- Based on the intended use of the e-records, a risk assessment must be performed to determine the critical controls to be implemented.

Based on the NIST definitions on DI (8), the applicable controls for e-records reliability must be identified. The identified risk must be managed through the SLC (EU Annex 11 p1).

The controls of each risk will be presented based on the e-record location: creation, while in transit, in storage, and during processing. The controls applicable to transient data are discussed in Chapter 13.

- Data

  Data is considered the basic unit of information that has a unique meaning and can be transmitted (ISO/IEC 17025). The DI controls associated with data within the system are related to:

- transient data (Chapter 13); and
- the mapping to load the data to the correct field in the repository.

- Raw data

  Raw data is also known as source data. In manufacturing systems, as an example, the raw data is:
  - the first capture of information; and
  - written to an electronic storage device.

This data is extracted, as an example, from manufacturing equipment, sensors, and controllers. As applicable, it is transformed (digitized data, validated, normalized, scaled, and so on) and then loaded to the Supervisory Control and Data Acquisition (SCADA) or a historian. These are the typical e-record electronic storage devices (Figure 4.2).

The DI controls (8) associated with raw data are addressed during:

- the creation of e-records;
- the storage of e-records;
- the transit of e-records; and
- the processing of e-records.

A description of the controls associated with raw data can be found in Chapter 22.

- Metadata

It is data that describe the attributes of other data and provide context and meaning. Typically, these are data that describe the structure, data elements,

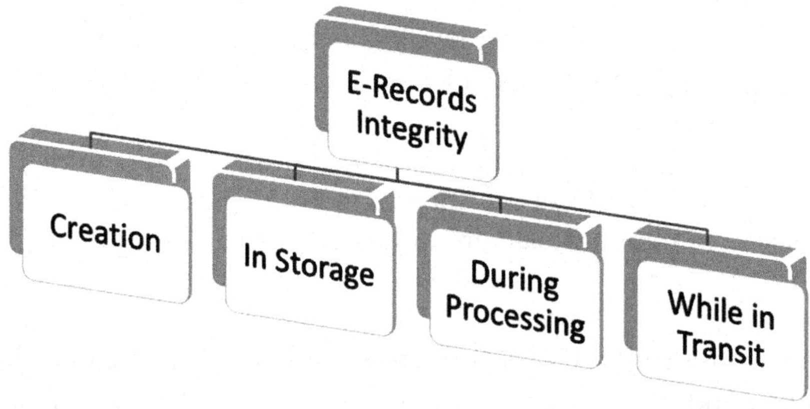

Figure 4.2 Data integrity NIST.

interrelationships, and other characteristics of data. Metadata also permits data to be attributable to an individual.

All the integrity controls implemented to e-records are also controls applicable to metadata. These controls include the logical link between the record and the associated metadata.

- Recording and collection of data

Data can be transcribed into a system from paper or electronic source systems. After the data is transcribed, the data is transferred for processing and/or loaded to the associated electronic storage device(s).

If the collection of data is entered manually (e.g., paper records), then there should be an additional check on the accuracy of the transcribed data. This check may be done by a second operator or by validated electronic means (EU Annex 11 p6).

The paper-based record(s) from which the data elements are transcribed are the source. These record(s) must be maintained and available to the inspector, if requested.

The other three types of "recording and collection of data" controls are:

- extracting;
- transferring; and
- data in a repository.

A brief description and the controls to transferring data can be found immediately below. A description of the other two controls listed above associated with raw data can be found in Chapter 22.

- Transferring/migrating data

The MHRA makes a distinction between e-records migration and e-records transfer.

- E-records migration is the process of moving stored data from one electronic storage device location to another. This may include changing the format of data but not the content or meaning.
- An e-records transfer is a process of transferring e-records between different electronic storage device types, formats, or automated systems.

An example of the migration of e-records is once a data server is replaced or when inactive e-records are archived. In this case, a sample plan is established to compare sample source system e-records with the corresponding transferred e-records. The e-records must not be altered in value and/or meaning during the migration process (EU Annex 11 p4.8).

If needed, e-records migration can change the e-records format to make it usable or visible in the alternative automated system.

E-records migration is highly dependent on the specific technology and file structure of portable e-records. E-records migration-related activities should include the use of software tools to automate some or all extraction operations, conversion, loading, and verification of the e-record (14).

The "checksum" can be utilized to demonstrate that the format and/or content of the files was not modified while transferring them between computers.

A checksum or hash sum is a fixed-size piece of information computed from an arbitrary block of digital data to detect errors that may have been introduced during a file's transmission or storage. The integrity of the data can be checked at any later time by re-computing the checksum for the file and comparing it with the stored checksum value. If the checksum values do not match, the data was almost certainly altered (either intentionally or unintentionally).

E-records migration procedural control must contain the basis to perform the migration process. This document must be carefully designed, and the executed procedure should ensure e-records integrity.

The definition of data transfer is related to exchanging e-records electronically between two computers. In this case, the logic of the system receiving the e-records may contain corroboration (e.g., built-in checks) that the e-records are not altered in value and/or meaning during the exchange of data (EU Annex 11 p5).

The correct I/Os ensure the secure exchange of data between automated systems and correct inputs on the processing of data. These built-in checks maximize the mitigation associated with I/Os errors.

The built-in check is the mechanism that can ensure the reliability of transmissions and the mutual trust between communicating parties. It provides:

- shared node authentication to assure each node of the others' identity (US FDA 21 CFR Part 11.10(h));

- transmission integrity to guard against improper information modification or destruction while in transit (refer to Chapter 22); and
- transmission confidentiality to ensure that information in transit is not disclosed to unauthorized individuals, entities, or processes (refer to Chapter 22).

This built-in check mechanism can support both application and machine credentials and user machines (user nodes).

- E-records processing

The validation/qualification process executed to the application's functionality, components, and/or interfaces demonstrate that the data integrity controls embedded into the software logic of the system achieve the intended purpose of designed controls during the processing of e-records. After deployment, these applications, components, and/or interfaces are maintained by following all CGMP-related controls applicable to automated systems during the operational and maintenance phases of the SLC.

Archiving – as applicable, e-records are moved from the processing environment to a retention environment.

Audit trails – in the context of e-records, audit trails are an electronic-based journal that can trace the modifications to the records.

Areas to verify periodically are if the audit trail functionality is activated, the source of the timestamp, and if the online clock adjustments are protected. These items and the periodic audit trial reviews will provide additional e-records controls.

Built-in checks – to maintain the reliability of the data while in transit, built-in checks are implemented between the computers that are interchanging data (EU Annex 11 p5). The objective of the built-in checks is to ensure the secure exchange of the data I/Os between systems. It also mitigates the I/Os errors that may appear downstream. Built-in checks enforce better control over the data interfaces. Complementing the built-in checks are the device checks, as defined in US FDA 21 CFR Part 11.10(h). The device checks verify the validity of the source system(s) of computer interfaces or manual input devices.

E-signatures – an e-signature is "a signature in digital form (bio-metric or non-biometric) that represents the signatory. This should be equivalent in legal terms to the handwritten signature of the signatory" (MHRA, GxP Data Integrity Guidance and Definitions, March 2018). The application of an electronic signature refers to the act of affixing, by electronic means, a signature to an e-record.

E-records integrity elements important to e-signatures are the electronic association between the e-signature and the e-record.

- how the signature is attributable to an individual;
- how the act of "signing" is recorded within the system so that it cannot be altered or manipulated without invalidating the signature or status of the entry;
- how secure the electronic signature is so that it can be applied only by the "owner" of that signature; and
- how the record of the signature will be associated with the entry made, and how this can be verified.

Regarding the last point, this association must be permanent until the record is modified. As part of the periodic review to e-records, there must be a process in place to review the state of these links between e-records/e-documents and the e-signature.

Operational checks – during the development of the automated system, operational checks are embedded in the software logic of the system. The objectives of these checks are to enforce the sequencing of steps and events applicable to the process that is managed by the automated system. This software, containing the operational checks, acts as procedural control. Instead of a manual execution following the procedural control, the process is being executed automated.

Printouts/reports – it is very common to see regulated users rely on printouts as a hardcopy to be attached to the batch record and/or rely on printouts to perform regulated activities.

If these printouts are used as quality records, then the design, qualification, and controls of these printouts are critical, including the audit trails and other metadata printouts. The reports are validated as per applicable procedural control.

Security – as a function related to security, e-records integrity service maintains information exactly as it was entered, and it is auditable to affirm its reliability.

The integrity controls associated with e-records processing are listed in Chapter 22.

- Original e-records and true copies

This is one of the most important topics in e-records integrity. The worldwide CGMP requirements establish that records must be "original."

It is defined that an original CGMP e-record is created when generated to satisfy a CGMP requirement and saved contemporaneously to an electronic storage device (15). In some instances, the data cannot be written contemporaneously. In the specific cases in which data cannot be written contemporaneously, the CGMP controls to transient data must be followed. Refer to Chapter 13.

EMA defined original records as records "in the same format as it was initially generated" (16).

EU Annex 11 established that paragraphs 8.2 and 9 are related to original records (17).

- EU Annex 11 p8.2, Printouts – For records supporting batch release it should be possible to generate printouts indicating if any of the data has been changed since the original entry.
- EU Annex 11 p9, Audit Trails – Consideration should be given, based on a risk assessment, to building into the system the creation of a record of all GMP-relevant changes and deletions (a system-generated "audit trail"). For change or deletion of GMP-relevant data, the reason should be documented. Audit trails need to be available and convertible to a generally intelligible form and regularly reviewed.

As a result of the EMA definitions, the MHRA considers an original record the "first or source capture of data or information e.g. an original paper record of manual observation or electronic raw data file from a computerized system, and all subsequent data required to fully reconstruct the conduct of the GXP activity."

To assure e-records integrity, the automated system and associated automated process must be properly designed. Refer to Section 5 in the MHRA DI guideline document.

The regulatory requirements for original e-records include (18):

- be periodically reviewed;
- be retained containing the original data content and meaning of the original raw data itself and/or a true copy, as well as a copy of a validated;
- be complete, enduring, and readily retrievable and readable throughout the records retention period.

There are simple electronic systems that do not provide e-records storage capability. The data is permanently located in transient memory. These simple systems may provide printouts of data. These printouts are considered the original record. Because the memory size is limited, there is the possibility that data is erased to provide space for new data and the data lost. A possible solution is to develop a time-based sample plan to collect the data.

The original paper-based record must be signed and dated manually by the person creating a record.

In other simple electronic systems, there is neither e-records storage capability nor printouts. In these cases, the data is recorded manually using forms designed appropriately for the process. The completed forms become the original record.

EU defines true copy as a "'verified copy,' which retains content and meaning."

A true copy of the source information must be an exact copy having all the same attributes and information of the original entry. A true copy must save integrity, accuracy, full content, date formats, electronic signature, permissions, and full audit trail. The process of creating a true copy (printed or electronic) must be certified and fully described; a copy must be certified by applying the date and signing on the paper or by using a confirmed electronic signature. A true copy may be stored in another electronic format by comparing with the original entry, if necessary, but must keep equivalent of the original entry (19).

One alternative to verify true records as a copy is utilizing digital notarization services. These services can notarize anything in digital form, including e-commerce transactions, database records, word processing documents, spreadsheets, images, audio samples, and video clips, providing indisputable proof of the existence of any type of digital data at a fixed point in time. Once notarized, any tampering of the data or its timestamp is easily detected.

The basic functions of digital notary services are to notarize and timestamp digital data and to validate that data anytime in the future to prove that it is genuine.

Electronic copies can be used as true copies of paper or e-records, provided the copies preserve the content and meaning of the original record, which includes all metadata required to reconstruct the CGMP activity and the nature of the original records.

E-records integrity elements important to original e-records and true copies are related to e-records in storage.

- Automated system transactions
  This is defined by the MHRA as a single operation or sequence of operations performed as a single logical "unit of work." The other rules that make these as an automated system transaction are:
  - The operation that makes a transaction may not be saved as a record until the user commits the transaction through a deliberate act or the system forces the saving of data.
  - The metadata is not captured in the system until the user saves the transaction to durable storage.
  - The e-signature may be required to be saved and to become permanent.

  Built-in checks (EU Annex 11 p5) may also be considered automated system transactions for checks that are related to the critical step (20) parameters. The automated systems managing critical step parameters must record these contemporaneously.

  21 CFR Part 11.10(f) describes a sequence of operation checks to enforce permitted sequencing of steps and events, as appropriate. This type of check is appropriate to create, delete, or modify records in a particular sequence.

  The e-records integrity controls associated with automated system transactions are e-records processing. Refer to Chapter 22.
- Data review and approval
  E-records must be periodically reviewed for accessibility, readability, and integrity. If changes are implemented (EU Annex 11 p10) to the computer infrastructure and/or application, then it is required to ensure and test the ability to retrieve e-records (EU Annex 11 p7.1).

  Automated controls system, as an example, is likely to be the primary source of batch records for batch record review of continuous processes. Data reporting and review considerations generated by the automated controls systems should include (but are not limited to):
  - manufacturing batch record: initial set-points and ranges and model versions;
  - actions performed: audit trail (including sub-systems) reports, process parameter and in-process material attribute control charts, and material collection report (documenting the conditions achieved when the material was collected, diverted, or when collection. commenced), and any reports from any other process-specific performance metrics;
  - deviations: alarm reports, periods of material diversion, and corrective actions reports; and

  - materials: reconciliation and material collected, segregated and diverted report, and actual and theoretical percentage yield.

- Automated system user access/system administrator roles
  Access to the computer systems and associated repositories must be restricted to authorized users only. The level of access must be based on the user assigned task(s).

  It is very critical to segregate duties between data entries, reviewers, and system administrators. Data must only be entered or amended by regulated users authorized to do so. Reviewers and system administrator must not have access to enter and/or amend data to the data storage areas. If the application software security service does not allow the implementation of configurable segregation of duties, it will be required to establish these controls in a procedure.

  There must be records documenting the individuals who have any access to the computer systems handling e-records. This includes users, reviewers, system administrators, analysts, programmers, and so on.

  The e-records integrity controls associated with automated system user access/system administrator roles are EU Annex 11 p7.

- E-records retention
  The requirements of e-records and documents retention period do not differ from paper documents. It should be ensured that e-signatures applied to e-records are valid for the entire retention period for documents or until the e-record are modified.

  Where e-records retention is contracted to a third party, attention is expected to be given to the ownership and retrieval of e-records held under this arrangement. The physical location in which the e-records are held, including the impact of any laws applicable to that geographic location, should also be considered.

  After completing the specified record retention requirement, the records can be physically deleted.

  In the EU, the e-records retention requirements can be found in Volume 4 "Good Manufacturing Practice Medicinal Products for Human and Veterinary," Chapter 4 Documentation (Retention of Documents).

  E-records may be stored or archived during the retention period. The storage for stored records is for short-term retention. The storage for archived records is for long-term retention.

  The e-records integrity controls associated with storage and archiving of e-records can be found in EU Annex 11 p7 and EU Annex 11 p17, respectively.

Technological and procedural requirements to the backup utility/process must be established to assure the availability of the stored e-records; backup copies should be made of such e-records that are required to reconstruct all CGMP-relevant documentation. This also applies to the system programs required to save and restore the e-records. The backup procedure must guarantee e-records integrity, including metadata, e-signatures, and system configuration. Each backup set should be checked to ensure that it is error-free (EU Annex 11 p7.2 and MHRA DI Guidance Section 6.17.2).

- File structure
  The e-records lifecycle should incorporate two stages defining the planning, requirements, and designing of the data model and the functionality to manage the data model. Refer section "Consideration to Identification and Standardization Stages" in Chapter 2.

References

1. López, O., "MHRA Guidance," In: *Data Integrity in Pharmaceutical and Medical Devices Regulation Operations.* (CRC Press, Boca Raton, FL, 1st ed., 2017), pp 121–132.
2. HMA and EMA, "EU Medicines Agencies Network Strategy to 2020," December 2015.
3. "Critical Data – Data with High Risk to Product Quality or Patient Safety," (ISPE GAMP COP Annex 11 – Interpretation, July/August 2011.
4. Record reliability – A reliable record is one whose content can be trusted as a full and accurate representation of the transaction, activities, or facts to which they attest and can be depended upon in the course of subsequent transaction or activities (NARA).
5. MHRA, "MHRA Expectation Regarding Self-inspection and Data Integrity," September 2014.
6. MHRA, "MHRA GxP Data Integrity Definitions and Guidance for Industry," March 2018. https://mhrainspectorate.blog.gov.uk/2018/03/09/mhras-gxp-data-integrity-guide-published/.
7. "EC (2011) Volume 4 – EU Guidelines to Good Manufacturing Practice: Medicinal Products for Human and Veterinary Use – Annex 11: Computerized Systems," European Commission, Brussels, June, pp 1–4.
8. Definition – Data integrity is the property that data has not been altered in an unauthorized manner. Data integrity covers data during creation, in storage, during processing, and while in transit (NIST SP 800-27rA and NIST SP 800-57P1).
9. López, O., "EU Annex 11 and the Integrity of Erecs," *Journal of GxP Compliance*, 18(2), May 2014. https://www.ivtnetwork.com/article/eu-annex-11-and-integrity-erecs

10. Churchward, D., "Good Manufacturing Practice (GMP) Data Integrity: A New Look at an Old Topic, Part 2 of 3," July 2015.
11. MHRA, "Comply with Good Manufacturing Practice (GMP) and Good Distribution Practice (GDP), and Prepare for an Inspection," December 2014.
12. PI 011–3, "Good Practices for Computerised Systems in Regulated 'GXP' Environments," *Pharmaceutical Inspection Cooperation Scheme (PIC/S)*, September 2007.
13. Business requirements are the critical activities of an enterprise that must be performed to meet the organizational objective(s) while remaining solution independent.
14. Russian SIDGP, "Data Integrity and Validation of Computerized Systems," August 2018.
15. US FDA, "Data Integrity and Compliance with Drug CGMP – Questions & Answers – Guidance for Industry," December 2018.
16. EMA, EudraLex - Volume 4 - *Good Manufacturing Practice (GMP) Guidelines*, Basic Requirements for Medicinal Products (Part I): Chapter 4 – Documentation (January 2011); Chapter 6 – Quality Control (October 2011).
17. EU, "Questions and Answers: Good Manufacturing Practice and Good Distribution Practice, Data Integrity." https://www.ema.europa.eu/en/human-regulatory/research-development/compliance/good-manufacturing-practice/guidance-good-manufacturing-practice-good-distribution-practice-questions-answers#data-integrity-(new-august-2016)-section.
18. WHO, "Guideline on Data Integrity," QAS/19.819, October 2019 (Draft).
19. Russian SIDGP, "Data Integrity and Validation of Computerized Systems," August 2018.
20. Critical step – It is a parameter that must be within an appropriate limit, range, or distribution to ensure the safety of the subject or quality of the product of data.

Chapter 5

E-records Integrity Expectations of EU GMP Inspectors (1)

Introduction

E-record comprises raw e-records, transformed e-records, e-signatures, and associated metadata.

An expectation pertinent to the computer systems performing CGMPs-regulations-related functions and the electronic storage devices storing CGMP records is that e-records must be protected to prevent undesired manipulation of CGMP records.

This expectation takes the highest priority in all worldwide health agency GMPs, including the EMA and its European Union (EU) member states.

E-records integrity is the foundation of CGMPs. Electronic information, properly recorded and managed, is the basis for manufacturers assuring the competent authority of their products' identity, strengths, purity, and safety. Reliable e-records also demonstrate that the production process of the regulated entity and the computer systems adhere to the CGMPs, including manufacturing instructions.

Any unintended changes to e-records as a result of a storage, inputs and outputs (I/Os) (2), or processing operation, including malicious intent, unexpected hardware failure, and human error, will compromise the integrity of e-records.

This chapter provides the key expectations of EU CGMP inspectors in the area of e-records integrity. These expectations are based on the following sources.

- European Community (EC) Commission Directives 2003/94/EC (3) and 91/412/EEC (4)
- EU Annex 11 Computerized Systems (5)
- Chapter 4 of the EC GMP guide concerning documentation (6)
- EMA Questions and Answers: Good Manufacturing Practices – Data Integrity (7)
- EudraGMDP Database (8)
- Medicines & Healthcare Products Regulatory Agency (MHRA) GxP Data Integrity and Definitions (9)

EMA E-records Integrity Technical Requirements

EMA has the overall responsibility of regulating human and veterinary products within the European Commission. In terms of what all EU countries must achieve related to the manufacturing of medicinal products, all EC member states are bound by a single set of directives. Computer systems and e-records associated with GMP-related activities are delineated in the Commission Directive 2003/94/EC.

> When electronic, photographic, or other data processing systems are used instead of written documents, the manufacturer shall first validate the systems by showing that the data will be appropriately stored during the anticipated period of storage. Data stored by those systems shall be made readily available in legible form and shall be provided to the competent authorities at their request. The electronically stored data shall be protected, by methods such as duplication or back-up and transfer on to another storage system, against loss or damage of data, and audit trails shall be maintained. (3)

The veterinary medicinal products' GMP requirements can be found in 91/412/EEC (4).

As noted, the EU's e-records integrity objectives are:

- E-records will be appropriately stored during the anticipated period of storage.

- E-records stored by computer systems shall be made readily available in legible form.
- E-records shall be provided to the competent authorities at their request.
- E-records shall be protected against loss or damage of data, by methods such as duplication or backup and transfer on to another storage system.
- There must be a record of all changes made to e-records, the previous entry, who made the change, and when the change was made. These audit trails shall be maintained.

It is up to the individual countries to decide how the applicable directive is integrated into national law.

EU GMP inspections comprise an on-site compliance assessment. These EU GMP assessments are performed by the official(s) of the EU competent authorities, or authorities find an equivalent under a mutual recognition agreement. The method used to verify e-records integrity may not be the same contingent of technology used by the regulated facility.

EU E-records Integrity Guidelines

There are two key guidelines associated with e-records integrity resulting from Commission Directive 2003/94/EC (3) and 91/412/EEC (4), one being EU Annex 11 Computerized Systems (5) and the other, EU GMP Chapter 4: Documentation (6).

EU GMP Chapter 4 relates to good documentation practices. It provides key definitions of records (see Table 5.1).

Complementing the definitions in Table 5.1, the author recommends the following:

- Records must be written (10) evidence of what has happened and are recorded contemporaneously either by personnel or automated equipment. As an example, automated equipment may measure process parameters.
- In automated environments, the events recorded contemporaneously and retained in the format in which they were originally generated are considered raw data.

Explicitly, the EU GMP Chapter 4 (6) establishes that suitable controls to ensure the integrity of documents must be established.

Table 5.1 Key Definitions of Records Based on EudraLex (4)

	Definition
Certificates of analysis	Records that provide a summary of testing results on samples of products or materials together with the evaluation of compliance with a stated specification
Records	Records that provide evidence of various actions taken to demonstrate compliance with instructions (e.g., activities, events, investigations, and in the case of manufactured batches, a history of each batch of product, including its distribution)
Raw data	Records that are used to generate other records. For e-records, regulated users should define which data are to be used as raw data. At least, all data on which quality decisions are based should be defined as raw data
Reports	Records that document the conduct of exercises, projects, or investigations, together with results, conclusions, and recommendations

The key EU Annex 11 e-records integrity-related clauses are depicted in Table 5.2. The e-records integrity controls listed are the most observed as part of the associated non-compliance report located at the EudraGMDP database (8).

There are many other e-records integrity-related paragraphs in EU Annex 11 (11, 12). These paragraphs are also implemented during the design phase or the operational and retirement phases as part of procedural controls.

Expectations of EU GMP Inspectors

Table 5.3 reviews deviations to data integrity in the EU Non-Compliance Reports. The complete list can be found in Appendix VI.

Comments such as "integrity and security of analytical data," as part of the non-compliance reports, do not provide relevant information to assign the deviation to a cause. The tabulation of these comments is not part of Table 5.3.

Delete, manipulated, or falsified data. Records retained in an electronic storage device must be secured by both physical and logical means against loss, damage, and/or alteration. Refer to paragraphs 7.1 and 12.4 in the EU Annex 11 (5). It excludes the issue related to unauthorized entry to the electronic storage device. These issues can be found in paragraph 12 of EU Annex 11.

Table 5.2 E-records Data-Integrity-Related Clauses, based on the EU Annex 11 (5)

Annex 11 clause	*Paragraph*
4	The validation of computer systems must be performed following the relevant GMP guidelines and based on risk assessment. It must be considered the integrity of the data. When determining data vulnerability and risk, it is important to consider the intended use of the computer system and associated data. (**Note:** As a result of computer systems validation not properly performed or not performed, the EU inspectors affirm that the integrity, reliability, up-to-date, originality, and authenticity of the e-records cannot be assured.)
7.1	Data should be secured by both physical and logical means against damage.
12.4	Management systems for data and documents should be designed to record the identity of operators entering, changing, confirming, or deleting data including date and time.
12.1	Physical and/or logical controls should be in place to restrict access to the computerized system to authorized persons. Suitable methods of preventing unauthorized entry to the system may include personal codes with passwords, restricted access to computer equipment and data storage areas.

Table 5.3 Data-Integrity-Related Issues Identified from a Collection of Non-compliance Reports by EU Inspectors (July 2013–February 2020)

Causes of non-compliance	*Occurrences*
Deleted data	13
Manipulated data	9
No logical access control to computer systems	8
Falsified data	8
Computer systems not properly validated	5
Entries not made contemporaneously	2

The design of the security of e-records warehouses must make provisions to protect original or true copy e-records and the associated metadata. These e-records cannot be deleted or changed without recording the modification. As an element of the e-records integrity in storage, there must be a record of any modification made that includes the previous entry, who made the change, and when the change was made (10, 13).

The modification of an e-record can be documented by an electronic- or paper-generated audit trail. The paper-based audit trail may be acceptable until electronic audit trailed functionality becomes available. To reduce the risk of losing e-records in the storage and guarantee e-records readiness to the users, periodic backups must be performed. The backup must be stored separate from the primary storage location, and at a frequency based on an analysis of risk to GMP e-records and the capacity of the storage device. Periodic reviews must be increased on those systems using paper-based audit trails.

Any rights to alter files must be assigned to personnel, independent of those responsible for the record content. Segregation of duties and frequent audit trails reviews provide safeguards against data integrity failure by reducing the opportunity for an individual to alter, misrepresent, or falsify data without detection (10).

No logical access controlled to computer systems. The main EU Annex 11 clause applicable to this item is EU Annex 11 p12.1 (5). All personnel must be provided with appropriate levels of access and defined responsibilities to carry out their assigned duties. This requirement must be backed up by an authorization policy specifying logical access rights to domains, computers, applications, and e-records. As a function related to security, e-records integrity service maintains information exactly as it was recorded and is auditable to affirm its reliability. For this reason, controlled access to the short- and long-term storage must be implemented.

Security must be instituted at several levels. Procedural controls must govern physical access to computer systems (*physical security*). The security of devices used to store programs, such as disks, should be considered a part of physical security.

Access to individual computer system platforms is controlled by network-specific security procedures (*network security and database server*). Access to these devices should be controlled (*logical security*). User access controls shall be configured and enforced to prohibit unauthorized access and the attributes of the e-records.

Computer systems not properly validated. The main EU Annex 11 paragraph applicable to this deviation is 4. As part of the inspection, the validation of the computer system is evaluated. The validation scope includes the interfaces between the originated system, data acquisition, and recording system(s). The validation process must include periodic verification to the accuracy of the data. I/Os errors can result in severe production errors and the distribution of adulterated or misbranded products. The extent and frequency of I/Os checking will be assessed on an individual basis and should be determined based upon the risk and built-in controls. These built-in checks provide the accurate exchange of electronic data to decrease issues of data integrity while the electronic data are in transit.

The computer system must incorporate validated checks to ensure the completeness of data acquired (6). For systems using automated data capture, the EU inspector reviews validation records to ensure correct I/Os and processing of data are implemented and are effective.

Audit trails and the validation records of the associated functionality for computer systems is to be verified as well.

Entries not made contemporaneously. Contemporaneous e-records should be recorded at the time they were generated. The main paragraph in the EU Annex 11 applicable to this item is 12.4 of EU Annex 11 (6).

Records of events provide written evidence of what had occurred and are recorded contemporaneously either by personnel or automated equipment. Automated equipment may measure process parameters. In automated environments, events recorded contemporaneously and retained in the format in which they were originally generated are considered raw data.

The following observation relates to a contemporaneous type of deviation: "Analysts routinely use the PC administrator privileges to set the controlling time and date settings back to over-write previously collected failing and/or undesirable sample results" (Appendix VI).

Conclusion

Manufacturers who want to market their medicinal products in the EU are required to meet EU's expectations around the integrity of the e-records for those computer systems performing CGMP-regulations-related functions. The occurrences of non-compliance to recent reports have driven EU inspectors to conduct a comprehensive initial evaluation on the integrity of the e-records, including computer systems validation, the accuracy of the e-records, physical and logical security, and the traceability of the modification to e-records. Ensuring the integrity of e-records as part of a system implementation will ensure a positive inspection outcome and, more importantly, reliable e-records.

References

1. López, O., "Data Integrity Expectations of EU GMP Inspectors," *Pharmaceutical Technology Europe*, 29(7), 2017.
2. Input/Output: Each microprocessor and each computer need a way to communicate with the outside world to get the data needed for its programs and to communicate the results of its data processing. This is accomplished through I/O ports and devices.
3. Commission Directive 2003/94/EC laying down the principles and guidelines of good manufacturing practice in respect of medicinal products for human use and investigational medicinal products for human use (October 2003).
4. Commission Directive 91/412/EEC laying down the principles and guidelines of good *manufacturing* practice for veterinary medicinal products (July 1991).
5. "EC Guide to Good Manufacturing Practice: Medicinal Products for Human and Veterinary Use—Annex 11: Computerized Systems, The Rules Governing Medicinal Products in the European Union Volume IV, Office for Publications of the European Communities," pp 139–142 (Luxemburg, January 2011).
6. EudraLex, "The Rules Governing Medicinal Products in the European Union Volume 4, Good Manufacturing Practice, Medicinal Products for Human and Veterinary Use, Chapter 4: Documentation," (January 2011).
7. EU, "Questions and Answers: Good Manufacturing Practice and Good Distribution Practice, Data Integrity," https://www.ema.europa.eu/en/human-regulatory/research-development/compliance/good-manufacturing-practice/guidance-good-manufacturing-practice-good-distribution-practice-questions-answers#data-integrity-(new-august-2016)-section.
8. EudraGMDP Database, http://eudragmdp.ema.europa.eu/inspections/gmpc/searchGMPNonCompliance.do.
9. MHRA, "GxP Data Integrity and Definitions," March 2018, https://mhrainspectorate.blog.gov.uk/2018/03/09/mhras-gxp-data-integrity-guide-published/.
10. The term "written" means recorded or documented on media from which data may be rendered in a human-readable form. (EU GMP Chapter 4, 2011).
11. López, O., "Annex 11 and Electronic Records Integrity," In: *EU Annex 11 Guide to Computer Validation Compliance for Worldwide Health Agency GMP*. (CRC Press, Taylor & Francis Group, Boca Raton, FL, 1st ed., 2015), pp 229–251.
12. López, O., "Electronic Records Handling: EMA Annex 11," In: *Best Practices Guide to Electronic Records Compliance*. (CRC Press, Taylor & Francis Group, Boca Raton, FL, 1st ed., 2016), pp 63–75.
13. Health Canada, "Good Manufacturing Practices (GMP) Guidelines for Active Pharmaceutical Ingredients (APIs)", GUI-0104, C.02.05, Interpretation #15, December 2013.

Chapter 6

Comparison of Health Authorities E-records Integrity Expectations (1)

Introduction

Since 2015, major regulatory authorities has been drafting regulations/guidance specifically addressing data management and data integrity. Besides, other related organizations have developed further guidance.

Some of these documents are listed below:

- EU OMLC Quality Management Guideline on Management of Documents and Records, January 2016
- ISPE, Considerations for a Corporate Data Integrity Program, March 2016
- OECD Application of GLP of the Working Group on GLP, April 2016
- EMA Q&A GMP Data integrity, August 2016
- ICH, Integrated Addendum to ICH E6 (R1): Guideline for Good Clinical Practice, E6 (R2), November 2016
- ISPE/GAMP, Records & Data Integrity, March 2017

- TGA, Data Management and Data Integrity, April 2017
- National Medical Products Association (NMPA (former CFDA)), "Drug Data Management Practices Guidance," December 2020
- ECA, GMP Data Governance and Data Integrity Guidance, January 2018
- Health Canada, GMP guide for drug products (GUI-0001-ENG), February 2018
- MHRA, "GxP" Data Integrity Guidance and Definitions, March 2018
- SIDGP (Russia), Data Integrity Guidance, August 2018
- ISPE/GAMP, Data Integrity – Key Concepts, October 2018
- PIC/S Good Practices for Data Management and Integrity in Regulated GMP/GDP Environments (PI041 Draft 3), November 2018
- US FDA, Data Integrity and Compliance with Drug CGMP – Questions & Answers – Guidance for industry, December 2018
- CEFIC, Practical Risk-based Guide for Managing Data Integrity, March 2019
- ISPE/GAMP, Data Integrity – Manufacturing Records, May 2019
- WHO, Guideline on Data Integrity (Draft), October 2019

One of the first published guidance describing the e-records integrity-related controls was the supplementary guidances to the EC-GMP Guide with specific requirements for computerized systems, EU Annex 11 (2). Annex 11 to the EC-GMP Guide titled "Computerised Systems" dates to the early 1980s. Revision 0 of the EU Annex 11 dates to January 1992.

Probably the first two regulations covering the data integrity controls were the European Union (EU) Commission Directives 91/412/EEC (1991) and 003/94/EC (1994) in Article 9 item 2.

This chapter highlights the e-records integrity-related guidance documents published by Health Authorities only.

It provides a practical look at the evaluation of and correlation to the e-records integrity guidance, such as:

- Key elements of each guidance document
- Consistencies between guidance documents
- Differences between guidance documents

Elements to Compare Guidance Documents

The following section establishes the basic elements that were used in the evaluation of e-records integrity guidance.

In each Health Authorities document, data integrity is defined as the extent to which all data are complete, consistent, and accurate, throughout the data lifecycle. This definition can be found in MHRA, USFDA, PIC/S, WHO, NMPA, and SIDGP (Russia) guidance documents.

This definition doesn't address data quality since the controls required for the integrity of the data do not necessarily guarantee the quality of the data generated. Refer to section 2.7 in the MHRA (March 2018) guidance.

Table 6.1 depicts the basic definitions referenced in this chapter to make a comparison of the Health Authorities guidance documents.

As the reader may note, the terms "complete, consistent, and accurate" in the definition by the Health Authorities are related to data reliability and not with data integrity. Data integrity is more related to features associated with avoiding alterations of e-records in an unauthorized manner.

Based on the above paragraph, the definition of data integrity in the guidance documents is incorrect. The definition in the guidances relates to reliable records, not to the integrity of the records.

Finally, according to MHRA (3), data quality is "the assurance that data produced is exactly what was intended to be produced and fit for its intended purpose."

Table 6.1 Data-Related Definitions

Data integrity (NIST SP 800-57P1, ISO 17025, INFOSEC, 44 USC 3542 or ANSI/IEEE)	*Data reliability (NARA)*	*Data quality (ISO 9000:2015)*
The property that data has not been altered in an unauthorized manner. Data integrity covers data entry or collection, data storage, data transmission, and data processing.	A reliable record is one whose content can be trusted as a full and accurate representation of the transactions, activities, or facts to which they attest and can be depended upon in the course of subsequent transactions or activities.	The degree to which a set of characteristics of data fulfils requirements. Examples of some critical characteristics are accurate, auditable, in conformance to requirement, complete, consistent, with integrity, provenance, and valid making data both correct and useful.

Based on the information in this section:

- Data integrity is related to security-related controls to maintain information exactly as it was inputted, and it mandates that modification(s) to the data are traceable to the author of each modification.
- Data reliability is related to the data integrity controls (above), and data completeness, data consistency, and data accurately.
- Data quality is related to reliability-related controls (above), and is auditable, in conformance to requirement, provenance, and validity. Other characteristics to be accounted are adherence of the data to a standard format (conformity-related controls), lack of conflict with other data values (consistency), and lack of repeated records (duplicate).

Note that without reliability, there is no data quality. Without integrity, there is no data reliability.

Key Elements of Each Guidance Document

Based on the definitions contained in Table 6.1, the scope of each guidance document can be classified accordingly. The following table depicts the scope of each guidance.

As the reader can note from Table 6.2, each guide provides a distinct principle of how to manage data. As an example, if the regulated user wants to achieve data quality, the PIC/S guidance is the correct guidance to review.

Differences between Guidance Documents

In addition to the scope of each guidance presented in Table 6.2, Table 6.3 depicts the applicable regulation per guidance.

As an example, if the regulated user wants to achieve data quality specifically of CGMP e-records, the PIC/S guidance is the correct guidance to read.

ALCOA and ALCOA+ are a set of principles applicable to the e-records lifecycle. The use of ALCOA ensures that data is properly documented and can be used to support informed decisions.

These principles are referenced in each guidance. Table 6.4 provides the relevant principles for each guidance.

Table 6.2 Quality Area in Scope

DI guidance	*Scope*
EMA	Data integrity
NMPA	Data reliability
EU OMLC	
ICH E6 (2)	
MHRA	
SIDGP (Russia)	
US FDA	
WHO	
Health Canada	
PIC/S and TGA	Data quality

Table 6.3 Quality Area in Scope

DI guidance	*Applicable regulation*
EMA	GMP
SIDGP (Russia)	
US FDA	
Health Canada	
EU OMLC/OECD	GLP
NMPA	GXP
MHRA	
WHO	
ICH E6_R2__Step_4	GCP
PIC/S & TGA	GMP and GDP

The information contained in Tables 6.2 and 6.4 can be correlated. Guidances associated with data integrity and data reliability can be typically related to the ALCOA principles. Except for the SIDGP and Health Canada guidance documents, the PIC/S guidance is linked with the data quality and ALCOA+ principles.

Table 6.4 ALCOA or ALCOA+ Impact

DI guidance	*ALCOA*	*ALCOA+*
NMPA	√	
EMA	√	
OMLC		
ICH		
MHRA		√ (section 3.10)
PIC/S		√
SIDGP (Russia)		√
Health Canada		√
US FDA	√	
WHO	√	

Consistencies between Guidance Documents

The main consistency between all data integrity guidance documents is the data risk analysis. Refer to Chapters 9 and 10. In particular, the CEFIC* is a risk-based guide to data integrity.

Each guidance document requires that regulated companies perform "complete data integrity criticality and risk assessments to ensure that the organizational and technical controls that are put in place are commensurate with the level of risk to quality attributes" (4).

Figure 6.1 depicts how the initial risk assessment is performed after concluding the Concept Phase, and the data risk assessments results are managed throughout the system and e-records lifecycles (EU Annex 11 p4.3).

All guidance documents cover ALCOA or ALCOA+ features of handling records properly.

The author of this book prefers to implement data handling based on the principles of data quality (Chapter 23). The handling of data is performed in a structural manner during the creation of the raw data, in storage, during processing, and while in transit (NIST SP 800-57P1). These function-based e-records integrity controls provide a consistent way to implement these data integrity controls (5).

* CEFIC, "*Practical Risk-based Guide for Managing Data Integrity*," March 2019.

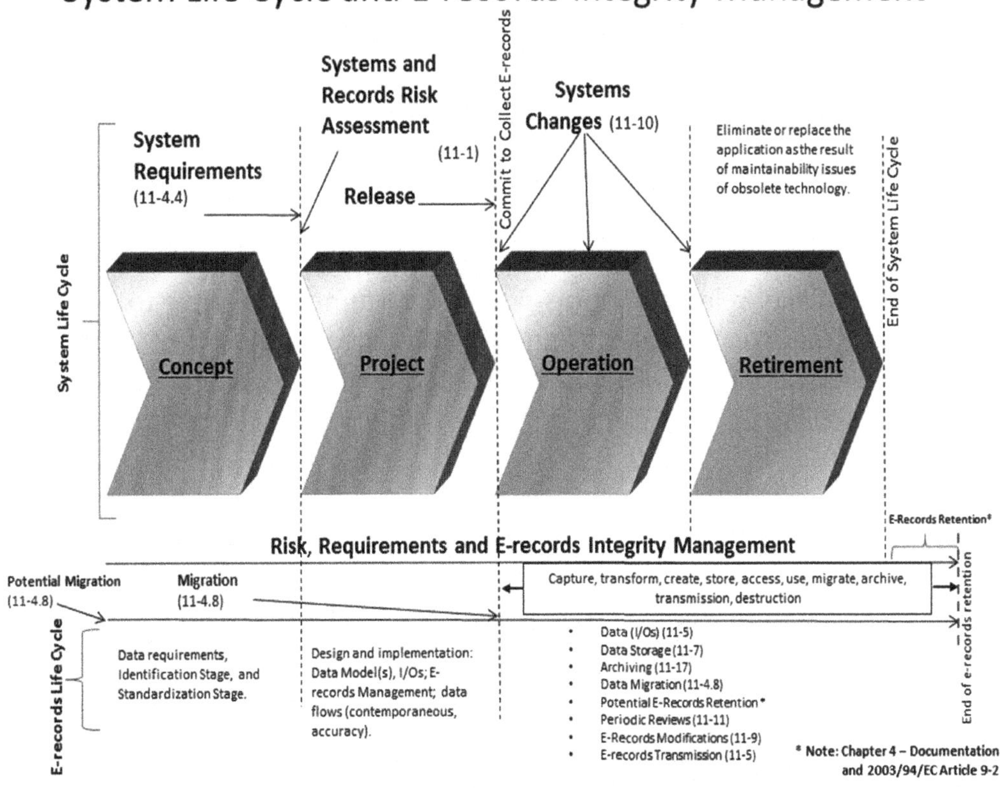

Figure 6.1 System lifecycle and e-records integrity management.

Those guidances associated with data integrity (Table 6.2) are consistent on risk assessment, data lifecycle, and security-related controls.

The consistency with those guidance documents associated with data reliability (Table 6.2) is on data lifecycle, accuracy checks, data storage, printouts, audit trails and periodic reviews, physical and logical security, archiving, business continuity, disaster recovery, data migration, and exchange of data or built-in checks.

The only guidance document associated with data quality (Table 6.2) covers ALCOA+, risk management, good data management, management governance, outsource organizations, and periodic review management.

Summary

The comparison of the guidance documents was based on the three (6) definitions presented in Table 6.1: data integrity, data reliability, and data quality.

Based on the definitions above, all guidance documents discuss elements of data reliability or data quality. Besides, the regulations in scope cover GMP, GCP, GLP, and GDP.

The consistencies between all guidances include risk assessment, data lifecycle, and security-related controls.

The focus of the data-reliability-related guidances is data-integrity-related controls and record completeness – consistence and accuracy.

The focus of the data-quality-related guidances is data-reliability-related controls, conformity-related controls which determine adherence to a standard format, consistency-related controls which determine lack of conflicts with other data values, and duplication-related controls which control the repeated records.

References

1. López, O., "Comparison of Health Authorities Data Integrity Expectations," In: *Paper Presented at the IVT 4th Annual Data Integrity Validation*, Cambridge, MA, 15–16 August 2018.
2. "Computerised Systems. In the Rules Governing Medicinal Products in the European Union. Volume 4: Good Manufacturing Practice (GMP) Guidance's: Annex 11," European Commission, Brussels.
3. MHRA, "MHRA GxP Data Integrity Definitions and Guidance for Industry," March 2018. https://mhrainspectorate.blog.gov.uk/2018/03/09/mhras-gxp-data-integrity-guide-published/.
4. CEFIC, "Practical Risk-based Guide for Managing Data Integrity," March 2019 (Rev.1).
5. López, O., "A Computer Data Integrity Compliance Model," *Pharmaceutical Engineering*, March/April 2015, pp 79–87.
6. US FDA, 21 CFR Part 11, "Electronic Records; Electronic Signatures; Final Rule," Federal Register Vol. 62, No. 54, 13429, 20 March 1997.

Chapter 7

Maxims of E-records Integrity

Introduction

E-records integrity is the validity of data and their relationships. For e-records to be trustworthy and reliable, the links between transient data, data, raw data, metadata, and e-records must not be compromised or broken. Without e-records integrity, it is difficult to regenerate a previous result reliably.

This chapter covers the e-records integrity maxims applicable to the medicine manufacturing operations. The lifecycle, the validity and fidelity, and the reliability of e-records integrity are governed by maxims or fundamental rules in an effective e-records integrity program.

These maxims are always elements to consider as part of the integrity of CGMP e-records.

Lifecycle

Maxim 1: E-records, as information objects, have a lifecycle.

E-records lifecycle refers to how e-records are identified, standardized, created, and used (active life), their inactive life, and how they are discarded (final disposition). In each of these phases, records are generated, recorded, processed (including analyzed, integrated, or migrated), reported, verified, used for decision-making, retained, archived, or finally discarded at the end of the retention period (1).

The precise management of the e-records must be completed through its lifecycle (2).

One element in quality management is the e-records integrity. This integrity can be affected at any phase in the e-records lifecycle. It is consequently important to understand the lifecycle components for e-records and ensure controls based on the criticality and risk at all phases (1).

During the operation stage of the system handing the e-records, e-records are generated, recorded, transformed, accessed, used, logically deleted, migrated, and retired (physically deleted). During this stage, the integrity of the e-records can be compromised. The objective of the implementation and enforcement of the e-records integrity requirements is to preserve e-records integrity. These requirements include:

- The data acquisition function must be validated to demonstrate accurate data conversion, integration, and/or transformation. The infrastructure associated with the data acquisition function must be installed according to the infrastructure manufacturer instructions, and the computer I/Os must be periodically verified for accuracy.
- Only authorized people can modify the e-records stored on e-records repositories (e.g., data servers or any other media).
- There are records of changes made to the e-records.
- Manually entered records considered critical are verified by a designated person other than the one who made the records or checked by the system itself.
- Procedural controls are implemented for the cancellation, changes to the level of approval, and for entering or editing e-records, including changing of a personal password.

The effectiveness of the controls associated with e-records integrity must be monitored.

To keep the focus on the e-records integrity (Figure 7.1), technical controls are used during the operation stage. These controls can be categorized into four spaces: e-records created, e-records storage, e-records during processing, and e-records while in transit.

US FDA (3) guidance discloses that data integrity is critical throughout the CGMP data lifecycle, including in the creation, modification, processing, maintenance, archival, retrieval, transmission, and the final disposition stages (4).

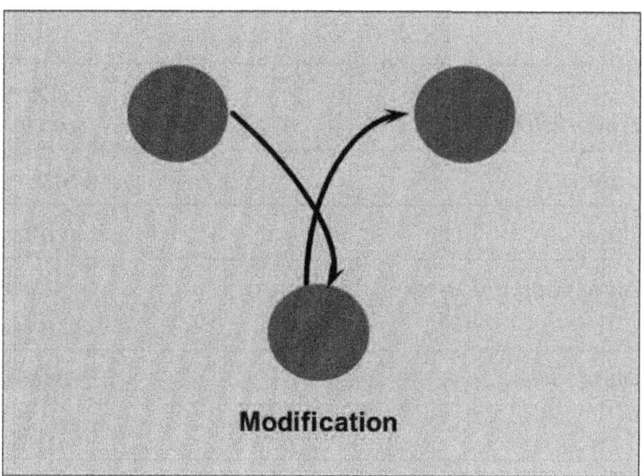

Figure 7.1 Records integrity.

Refer to Chapter 2 for additional information about the lifecycle of e-records.

A Measure of Validity

> ***Maxim 2***: As a state or condition, e-records integrity is a measure of the validity and fidelity of a data object (4).

E-records integrity is a requirement that information, programs, and configurations are changed only in a specified and authorized manner. E-records must be protected against alteration without appropriate permission. The vulnerabilities of e-records that may impact the validity and fidelity of a data object can be found in Chapter 8.

E-records integrity is the foundation of CGMPs. The information properly recorded is the basis for manufacturers to assure product identity, strengths, purity, and safety (5). The stored e-records also demonstrate that the manufacturing process adheres to the CGMPs, including instructions.

All workflows associated with e-records that need to be protected against alteration without appropriate permission are carefully designed and tested (3).

As applicable, the data and e-records handling workflows that must be carefully designed (1) and tested are:

Data and e-records workflows	*Categories of data integrity controls (6)*
Generation of the data	Creation
Recording of the data	Creation
Security of data and associated e-records electronic storage device	In storage
Processing of the data	Processing
Integration of data	Processing
Generation of audit trails, as applicable	Processing
Management of the metadata	Processing
Disposal of e-records during the retirement of the associated system(s) and the end of the e-records final disposition	Processing
Completeness of the data	Processing and while in transit
Correctness and completeness of printouts	Processing and while in transit
Data error checking	While in transit
Data mappings to e-records repositories	While in transit

For ease of organization of the above workflows, these can be grouped into one of the following: records creation, records retained by computer storage, during processing, and while in transit (6).

The regulatory expectations regarding the validity and fidelity of e-records are summarized in the EU guideline, "The electronically stored data shall be protected, by methods such as duplication or back-up and transfer on to another storage system, against loss or damage of data, and audit trails shall be maintained" (7).

Security

Maxim 3: As a function related to security, e-records integrity service maintains information exactly as it was recorded and is auditable to affirm its reliability (8).

Because maintaining e-records integrity is a primary objective of the CGMP principles, everyone associated with a computer system in a regulated entity must be aware of the necessity for security considerations. The regulated entity must ensure that personnel are aware of the importance of e-records security, the procedures and system features that are available to provide appropriate security, and the consequences of security gaps. Such system features could include routine surveillance of system access, the implementation of file verification routines, and exception and/or trend reporting.

Security controls must be established for all computer systems as a means of ensuring e-records protection. Computer security is the principal enabler of e-records integrity.

Several unrelated regulated entities have had problems linked to the proper control of computer systems to prevent unauthorized changes in e-records. Usually, these regulated entity sites alter or delete critical e-records.

The system owner is the person responsible for providing the e-records protection suitable controls over the application, infrastructure (e.g., network, database server), and database components. These record protection controls ensure that only authorized personnel can make changes to any component of the computer system and the security of the e-records residing on the system.

Finally, application-level security and associated authority checks control the access to the computer system applications (i.e., applications security).

US FDA states that "appropriate controls shall be exercised over computer or related systems to assure that changes in master production and control records or other records are instituted only by authorized personnel" (9).

References

1. EMA, "Guidance on Good Manufacturing Practice and Good Distribution Practice: Questions and Answers: Good Manufacturing Practices – Data Integrity," August 2016. https://www.ema.europa.eu/en/human-regulatory/research-development/compliance/good-manufacturing-practice/guidance-good-manufacturing-practice-good-distribution-practice-questions-answers#data-integrity-(new-august-2016)-section.
2. National Medical Products Association (NMPA (former CFDA)), "Drug Data Management Practices Guidance," (Beijing, China, December 2020).
3. US FDA, "Data Integrity and Compliance with Drug CGMP - Questions & Answers - Guidance for industry," December 2018.
4. López, O., "Control of Records," In: *Pharmaceutical and Medical Devices Manufacturing Computer Systems Validation*. (Routledge/Productivity Press, New York, NY, 1st ed., 2018), pp 138–140.

5. Wechsler, J., "Data Integrity Key to GMP Compliance," *Pharmaceutical Technology*, 38(9), September 2014.
6. NIST, *Recommendation for Key Management, Part 1: General*. (Special Publication 800–57 Part 1 Rev 4, National Institute of Standards and Technology, January 2016).
7. EU, "2003/94/EC Laying Down the Principles and Guidelines of Good Manufacturing Practice in Respect of Medicinal Products for Human Use and Investigational Medicinal Products for Human Use," (Brussels, October 2003).
8. López, O., "Security," In: *Data Integrity in Pharmaceutical and Medical Devices Regulation Operations*. (CRC Press, Boca Raton, FL, 1st ed., 2017), pp 162–166.
9. US FDA, 21 CFR 211.68(b), "Automatic, Mechanical, and Electronic Equipment," December 2007.

Chapter 8

Vulnerabilities of E-records

What Is Record Vulnerability?

> Poor data integrity practices and vulnerabilities undermine the quality of records and may ultimately undermine the quality of medicinal products.
>
> **SIDGP (Russia), Data Integrity & Computer System Validation Guideline, August 2018 (Draft)**

Vulnerability is defined as a weakness in system security procedures, design, implementation, internal controls, and so on that could be accidentally triggered or intentionally exploited and results in a violation of the systems' security policy (1).

The regulated user must recognize the vulnerabilities to DI issues. The inability of the regulated user to detect poor DI practices is equivalent to a lack of quality system effectiveness (2). A method to detect DI issues on data and e-records is performing risk assessments to the vulnerability of data to involuntary or deliberate amendments, deletions, or recreations (3).

Chapters 9 and 10 discuss the risk assessment and the handling, respectively, of the e-records vulnerabilities.

This chapter examines the typical vulnerabilities of e-records.

Protection and Security of Electronic Records

Any issues identified related to the protection of e-records must be addressed rapidly, and corrective and preventive actions and interim controls should be implemented to manage any identified risks (4).

The regulated user must identify, via risk assessment, the control factors that affect the integrity of the e-records during their records retention periods.

Through a risk assessment, threats to resources are identified, vulnerability to and the likelihood of occurrence is evaluated, and potential impact is estimated (5).

A few factors affecting the integrity of the e-records include:*

- Limitations of current software/hardware to protect and secure e-records
- Data encoded within an electronic record (e.g., computer readable representations of information)
- Metadata for an electronic record (e.g., information that gives the data meaning and context, such as data dictionaries for databases)
- Media (e.g., disk, tape, or flash memory devices) that record data and metadata
- Hardware used to retrieve and display the electronic record
- Software (both application programs and operating systems) used to read, process, and display electronic records
- The processes of extracting and presenting information in human-readable form.

The increase of e-record vulnerability, increases the e-records integrity controls. All controls are specified, giving evidence of what was decided against each hazard. For the highest priority risks, a demanding process for designing controls must be used, covering residual risk evaluation and risk/benefits analysis. All selected technical controls must be integrated into the system and validated/qualified. Procedural controls are established for those vulnerabilities in which there no technical controls.

If these factors affecting the integrity of e-records are not controlled properly, the information that the electronic records should convey might not be reliable.

---

* Former guidance FDA maintenance of e-records.

Threats that Can Impact E-records (6)

When looking at potential threats (7) to e-records in a manufacturing environment, consider the following.

Regulated Users (8)

User access controls, both physical and logical, ensure that regulated users have access only to the functionalities that are appropriate for their job role, and that actions, such as modifications to e-records, are attributable to a specific regulated user.

The potential threats associated with the regulated users are: sharing login credentials; a system without functional access controls; ineffective/inappropriate security training; failure to immediately record when an event occurs; improperly defined user access levels; undocumented user access levels; uncontrolled access; archived data access and readability of the data lost due to software application updates or superseded equipment; and so on.

Each of the above is a potential threat to the protection of programs and data against unauthorized access, misuse, and/or manipulation.

Malware and Phishing Attempts

Sophisticated malware and phishing schemes that plant malicious scripts on a computer or steal login credentials can compromise an entire system. As an example, the cost to the data breach underwent by Merck in late 2018 was 135 million dollars.

One of the most challenging issues dealing with malware is that it only takes one seemingly authentic link to introduce a nefarious cyber presence into your network. It's essential to train staff to recognize common phishing attempts.

Different types of viruses will mine records-related data and automatically send it back to the original host or leave a backdoor entrance open for later.

Service Providers

The role of service providers and suppliers has been put in the spotlight due to the trend of regulated companies' availing of computer systems services (e.g., business process as a service (BPaaS), hardware products, hardware services (e.g., infrastructure as a service (IaaS)), software products and/or software services (e.g., software as a service (SaaS)).

The choice of a contractor/supplier management by regulated companies must be documented. The contractor's/supplier's suitability is demonstrated through compliance with the prerequisites in the vendor requirements document and/or performance measurement contained in a system-level agreement (SLA).

SLA with the system supplier and/or integrator must be defined to assure the understanding of the roles and responsibilities and assure an adequate and timely maintenance/incident support.

Based on a vendor/supplier assessment, the potential e-records integrity threats associated with the service provider are:

- Absence of a comprehensive data governance system
- Poor periodic verification of the adequacy of an e-records integrity system by the contract giver to the contract acceptor
- Loss of information or e-record corruption at the boundaries during the transfer process (EU Annex 11 p5).

Unrestricted Access to Computers

Physical and/or logical controls should be in place to restrict access to the computer system to authorized persons (EU Annex 11 p12.1 and 21 CFR Part 211.68(b) as examples).

Computers that aren't in physically restricted areas can easily be accessed by unauthorized personnel, or others in the area could quickly make changes to or delete data. In other cases, successful phishing attempts on general-access computers provide a gateway for hackers into more sensitive areas of the network.

The potential e-records integrity threats associated with unrestricted access to a computer are:

- Unreasonable steps to ensure that the computer system is secure and protected from deliberate or inadvertent change
- Absence of procedures that manage system security and validation of security functionality
- Absence of physical security and paper-based security method to those systems without the security functionality
- Ineffective data review and backups to those systems without security functionality

System integrity (9) is one of the key factors in support of e-records integrity.

Logical security is discussed in Chapter 11.

Inadequate Disposal of Old Hardware

It's easy to believe that once you've deleted e-records from the electronic storage device, you no longer must worry about people accessing it. But when the regulated entity improperly disposes of the e-records on archiving repositories, information may be available to unauthorized regulated users. Well after drives have been deleted – or even reformatted – it is possible to recover the information on the drive, meaning anything that the regulated user saved is still vulnerable.

E-records Transfers

E-records reliability must be considered when the e-records are shared between many computing environments during the e-records lifecycle.

The potential e-records integrity threats associated with e-records transfers is the loss of information or e-record corruption at the boundaries during the transfer process (EU Annex 11 p5).

E-records Storage

E-records storage is accomplished through an electronic storage device for e-records that records (stores) or retrieves (reads) information (e-records) from any medium, including the medium itself. This is considered the processing environment.

As the e-records owner (10) changes from one area to another, it is relevant to consider e-records vulnerabilities in each of the computing environments. To avoid inconsistencies between the e-records owner (e.g., human error, interpretation of applicable policies and SOPs, and so on), the controls to avoid e-records integrity threats must be technologically controlled.

The potential e-records integrity threats associated with e-records storage are:

- E-records exposed to the tools and mechanisms that created the e-records
- Deficiency enforcement to the production of change documentation (e.g., audit trails of changes, replacement history, and e-records removal)

- No preservation of the integrity of the e-records content, structure, and context throughout the e-records lifecycle
- Access to data throughout the complete retention period (EU Annex 11 p7.1)
- No security access levels in computer storage
- Deletion of records before the end of the retention period
- Periodic backups are not performed
- No recovery plan

Assessment of E-record Vulnerability, Risks, and Implementation of Control Measures

Although a system may be validated, record vulnerabilities may exist which have to be managed.

Once the e-records vulnerabilities and risks are determined, it is important to consider the context of the intended use of the computer system within the business process (11). One axiom to consider is that the e-records managed by critical computer systems should be, at least, critical as well. The other way around is applicable as well.

The e-records risk assessment evaluates the vulnerability of e-records throughout the e-records lifecycle, to involuntary or deliberate amendment, deletion, or recreation. Procedural and technological control measures, which prevent unauthorized activity and increase visibility/detectability, are to be used as risk-mitigating actions.

Like Figure 2.1, Figure 8.1 is another representation of the e-records lifecycle. Refer to Chapter 2 on e-records lifecycle.

Table 8.1 provides sample control measures to elude e-records integrity issues. Applicable sections of fundamental regulatory guidelines are referenced. Note that the Identification and Standardization stages are elements of the definition and design of the e-records. These two are not addressed in Table 8.1.

One critical area in process automation systems is the data captured by the system from equipment but stored in transient memory (1). Refer to Figure 13.1. The analogue data is extracted from the controller(s) and transformed. After the transformation, this data saved in a server (e.g., Historian, SCADA). After the data is captured, until it is written on durable media, the data is vulnerable to manipulation, loss, or change. This transient data

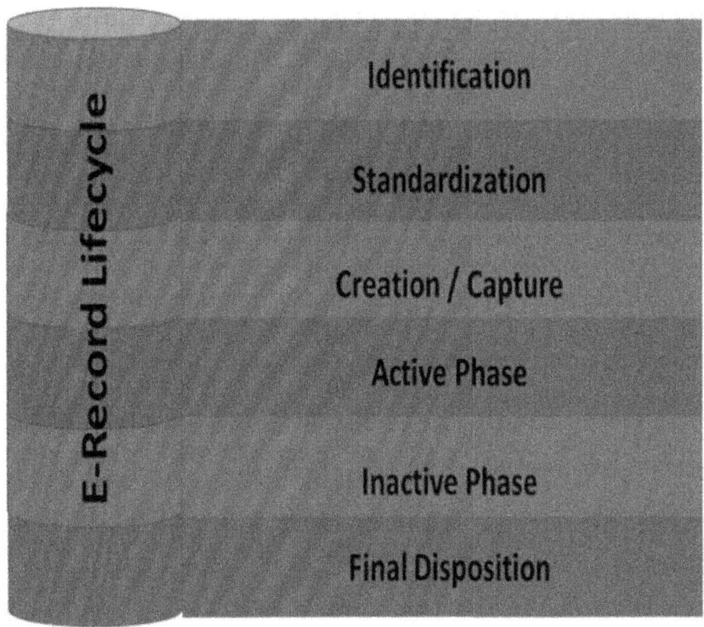

Figure 8.1 E-records lifecycle.

should be checked by verification circuits/software to confirm accuracy and reliability to ensure the e-records integrity. Refer to Chapter 13 for the CGMP controls applicable to the data stored in transient memory.

Chapter 22 provides a categorization to DI controls based on the stage in which the e-record is placed: data creation, data storage, data during processing, and data while in transit. Table 8.1 and Chapter 22 both provide a better understanding of what needs to be done during the implementation of a new or remediation of a legacy computer system.

Case Study

The vulnerabilities of the e-records in the business intelligence (BI) (14) environments are an excellent example of the applicability of Table 8.1.

BI applications comprise the entire range of e-records access methods such as ad hoc queries, real-time analytics, dashboards, scorecards, standard reports, ad hoc reports, operational reporting, process monitoring, data mining, and other BI applications. By using BI applications, the data consumers leverage the organization's internal and external information assets to support improved business decision-making. A data mart (DM) (15) as part of

Table 8.1 E-records Lifecycle and Associated Control Measures

E-records lifecycle	*Sample control measures*
Data capture and e-records creation • Inaccurate analog to digital conversion for data captured from instruments/sensors/equipment • Inaccurate manual entering of data • Inaccurate importing of data from other data source (e.g., big data) • Transient data up to writing e-records to the electronic storage device)	• The infrastructure must be qualified (12). • Data acquisition and recording functionality must include built-in controls. The embedded verification workflow must be qualified to ensure the accuracy of the data. • Inputs and outputs (I/Os) between equipment, I/O card/controller, and SCADA/Historian must be periodically verified (21 CFR Part 211.68(b), CPG 7132a.07 (13) and EU Annex 11 p5). • Critical data entered manually is provided by an authorized person and accurately. (EU Annex 11 p6 and ICH Q7 5.45). The accuracy checks include assessing the entry against specification values, formats, and the right sequence of the processing (21 CFR Part 11.10(f)). • The accuracy checks assessment is to be performed by a second operator, or by a validated computer means. • The system should enforce saving immediately after critical GxP data entry. • Transient data must be secure for access. No users can manipulate transient data. • The length of time that GxP data is held in temporary memory should be minimized.
Active Phase (access and use) in a processing environment. • Media failure • Accidental editing or deletion • Unauthorized use, editing, or deletion • Software faults manipulating data/e-records	Access • Data migration and archiving outputs must not alter the value and/or meaning of data during these processes. (EU Annex 11 p4.8 and p17). • Physical security and logical security must restrict access to unauthorized regulated users (EU Annex 11 p12.1 and 7.1), 21 CFR 211.68(b), ICH Q7 5.43). • Role-based security and segregation of duties must be implemented (21 CFR Part 11.10(g)). • A tracking mechanism must be implemented in case of data and e-records modification (EU Annex 11 p9; 21 CFR Part 11.10(e) and paragraph 186, 1978 revision US FDA CGMP preamble). • Periodic backups must be performed periodically (21 CFR 211.68(b); EU Annex 11 p7.2). • Significant modifications to the computer infrastructure must be verified against the e-records on storage (EU Annex 11 p4.8, ICH Q7 5.43).

(*Continued*)

Table 8.1 (Continued) E-records Lifecycle and Associated Control Measures

E-records lifecycle	*Sample control measures*
	• Periodic verification of the e-records must be performed. This verification must include: accessibility, readability, audit trails, accuracy, and storage capacity. Periodical reviews of audit trails and e-records for readability, accessibility, and accuracy (EU Annex 11 p11, EU Annex 11 p7.1and EU GMP Guidelines – Chapter 9, Self-Inspections). Transformation Integration • Refer to Capture and Creation. Incidents • Incidents related to computer systems that could affect the reliability of records must be recorded and investigated (ICH Q7 5.46 and EU Annex 11 p13). Disaster Recovery • Ensure a comprehensive plan to data recovery in the event of a disaster (Section 5.5, PI 041-1 (Draft 3)).
Inactive Phase in a retention environment.	Archiving • It should contain similar controls as the Active Phase.
Final Disposition Phase	• The records must be purged.

a data warehouse (DW) environment, Figure 8.2, is the backend component for achieving BI.

The infrastructure related to the data mart(s) and associated interfaces (I/Os) are qualified. Except for ad hoc reports and queries, all access methods must be qualified (e.g., standard reports).

E-records to be read by an access method are extracted from the DW into the DM. The access to these DM e-records, also called as persisted e-records (16), is read-only and based on the role associated with the user. As required on user's need, the integration of e-records in the related DM is the main task performed by the BI applications.

The e-records in the DM should never be modified directly by the users. In the case of an e-record modification in any warehouse database system, the modification must be performed on similar operational application source e-records device set and the updated data loaded to the staging area using the same automated tool initially used to load e-records from the

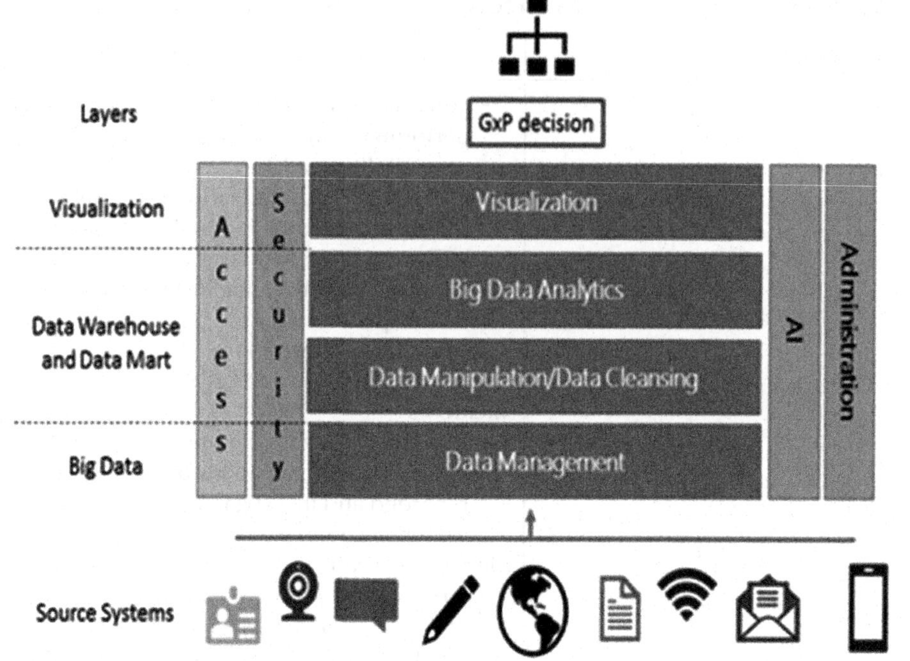

Figure 8.2 Sample big data environment.

source to the staging area. From the staging area, the e-record will be integrated, as applicable, and moved to the warehouse area, and the DM.

If technical limitations require the e-records to be modified in the DM or intermediate database as part of the DW systems, the modification must have traceability to the same modification in the source system. Consequently, for the typical DMs, the tracking of changes (e.g., electronic audit trail) to e-records is not applicable.

Based on the above description of a typical BI environment, the following are the vulnerabilities related to the e-records residing in DMs.

- Qualified access to records located in the BI environment
- Verification of inputs and outputs (I/Os) between the DW and the DMs and, DMs and users
- As applicable, data migration to populate the DMs, upgrading of data servers or databases
- Security associated with the e-records by the users (read-only access). The system administrator role, including the rights to alter databases, files, and settings must be assigned to personnel independent from those users accessing the record content

- Periodic backups and verification of the restoration process
- Periodic verification of the e-records accessibility, readability, and storage capacity
- Verification of the e-records accessibility and readability after significant modification to the computer infrastructure
- Moving the e-records to the retention environment to the e-records that are not active

Regulatory Agencies Expectations (17)

Controls are needed to ensure the integrity of e-records built upon information databases to ensure that representations of database information have been generated in a manner that does not distort data or hide noncompliant or otherwise bad information, and that database elements themselves have not been altered to distort the truth or falsify a record.

Such controls include:

- Using time-stamped audit trails of information written to the database, where such audit trails are executed objectively and automatically rather than by the person entering the information
- Using business continuity plans to ensure the integrity of e-records in case system failure or trouble
- Limiting access to the database search software

Absent of the above controls, it is very easy to modify e-records to render them indistinguishable from original, true records.

Summary

Typical vulnerabilities and associated controls were discussed in this chapter.

It is essential to understand the vulnerabilities of the e-records and the applicable controls to mitigate the vulnerability of such e-records. Based on a risk assessment, the e-records vulnerabilities and the controls to mitigate such vulnerabilities are identified. The identified risk and respective mitigation are to be managed through the SLC (EU Annex 11 p1) (18).

Lastly, the implementation of each mitigation is quantified.

References

1. NIST SP 800–33, *Underlying Technical Models for Information Technology Security.* (Special Publication 800-33, withdrawn: August 2018, National Institute of Standards and Technology, December 2001).
2. Hart, S., "Data Integrity: TGA Expectations," In: *Paper Presented at the PDA Conference*, Tel Aviv, Israel, July 2015.
3. EU, "Questions and Answers: Good Manufacturing Practice and Good Distribution Practice, Data Integrity," https://www.ema.europa.eu/en/human-regulatory/research-development/compliance/good-manufacturing-practice/guidance-good-manufacturing-practice-good-distribution-practice-questions-answers#data-integrity-(new-august-2016)-section.
4. PI 041–1, "Good Practices for Data Management and Integrity in Regulated GMP/GDP Environment," *Pharmaceutical Inspection Co-operation Scheme (PIC/S)*, November 2018 (Draft 3).
5. ISO 11799: 2003(E) Information and Documentation – Document Storage Requirements for Archive and Library Materials.
6. ISPE/PDA, "Good Practice and Compliance for Electronic Records and Signatures. Part 1 Good Electronic Records Management (GERM)," July 2002.
7. "Threat – The Potential for a "Threat Source" to Exploit (Intentional) or Trigger (Accidental) a Specific Vulnerability," (NIST SP 800–33, Withdrawn: August 2018).
8. In this chapter, the regulated user is also de "acquirer" or the organization that acquires or procures a system, software product or software service from a supplier.
9. "System Integrity – The Quality That a System Performs its Intended Function in an Unimpaired Manner, Free from Unauthorized Manipulation," (NIST SP 800–33, Withdrawn: August 2018).
10. E-records Owner – The person ultimately responsible for the integrity and compliance e-records at various stages of the e-records lifecycle following applicable policies and SOPs.
11. SIDGP (Russia), "Data Integrity & Computer System Validation Guideline," September 2018 (Draft).
12. López, O., *Computer Infrastructure Qualification for FDA Regulated Industries.* (PDA and DHI Publishing, LLC, River Grove, IL, 2006).
13. US FDA CPG 7132a.07, "Computerized Drug Processing; Input/Output Checking," September 1987.
14. López, O., "Electronic Records Integrity in a Data Warehouse and Business Intelligence," *Journal of Validation Technology*, 22(2), April 2016.
15. A data mart is a structure/access pattern specific to data warehouse environments, used to retrieve client-facing data.

16. Persisted E-records – E-records residing in the diverse data warehouses (DW) acquired from a source system(s).
17. US FDA, "Section D in the 21 CFR Part 11 Preamble," March 1997.
18. López, O., "Integration Between Computer System and E-records Life Cycles," In: *Pharmaceutical and Medical Devices Manufacturing Computer Systems Validation.* (CRC Press, Boca Raton, FL, 1st ed., 2018), pp 189–200.

Chapter 9

CGMP E-records Risk Management

Introduction

Risk management is the systematic application of quality management policies, procedures, and practices to the tasks of assessing, controlling, communicating, and reviewing risk (1).

The e-records risk management looks for possible mitigations and the associated solutions to prevents e-records from being lost, obscured, or modifying without a trace, and ensures that activities are recorded at the time of performance (see 211.68, 211.100, 211.160(a), 211.188, and 211.194).

The basis for e-records risk management is the CGMP e-records requirement, including good documentation practices.

In the context of this book, e-records integrity is the property that the e-records have not been altered in an unauthorized manner (2). E-records security protects from unauthorized modification (accidental or intentional), destruction, or disclosure (3).

NIST SP 800-39 (4) identifies four distinct steps for risk management. Risk management requires organizations to frame risk, assess risk, respond to risk, and monitor risk.

- Framing risk – It describes how the regulated entities establish a risk context for e-records integrity. The purpose of the risk framing component is to produce a risk management strategy that addresses how the regulated entities intend to assess, respond to, and monitor risk – while making explicit and transparent the risk perceptions that regulated entities routinely use in making operational decisions. The framing is established typically as part of the governance document. This document ensures controls are in place to prevent and detect data integrity issues throughout the SLC and e-records lifecycle (4).
- Assessing risk – It describes how the regulated entity analyzes risk within the context of the regulated entity risk frame. The purpose of the data integrity risk assessment component is to identify key high-level risks to patient safety, product quality and data integrity, and identifying the required controls to manage those risks. Typically, at this stage, no assumptions are made about the nature or exact functionality and design of the computerized system(s) that will support the process. Chapter 10 provides additional information about assessing the risk.
- Responding to risk – It addresses how the regulated user responds to risk once that risk is determined based on the results of risk assessments. The purpose of the risk response component is to provide a consistent, organization-wide response to risk following the organizational risk frame by (i) developing alternative courses of action for responding to risk; (ii) evaluating the alternative courses of action; (iii) determining appropriate courses of action consistent with organizational risk tolerance; and (iv) implementing risk responses based on selected courses of action.
- Monitoring risk – Risk monitoring provides organizations with the means to (i) verify compliance; (ii) determine the ongoing effectiveness of risk response measures, and (iii) identify risk-impacting changes to organizational information systems and environments of operation. Analyzing monitoring results gives organizations the capability to maintain awareness of the risk being incurred, highlight the need to revisit other steps in the risk management process, and initiate process improvement activities as needed.

The general principles of good documentation practices apply to the handling of records regardless of media (e.g., paper records or electronic records), throughout its lifecycle from the time data is first generated and any modifications made thereafter (5).

Risk Management (6, 7)

Risk management is integral to the e-records handling process and the drive process on the digital transformation.

Risk management is about identifying the risks to compliance area and understanding the impact of the risk.

Annex 20 (8) summarizes an approach to quality risk management pertinent to computer systems and computer-controlled equipment.

- Determine the CGMP criticality of the system and its impact on patient safety, product quality, or e-records integrity; identify the critical performance parameters; and determine the extent of validation.
- Develop requirement specification considering the basis of the criticality and perform a detailed risk assessment to determine critical functions.
- Select the design of computer hardware and software (e.g., modular, structured, fault tolerance) and implement appropriate controls via design as much as possible;
- Perform code review and data flows, as applicable.
- Determine the extent of testing and test methods of the controls implemented during the design.
- Evaluate the reliability of e-records and signatures, as applicable.
- Manage the risks uncovered during this activity through the SLC (EU Annex 11 p1).

The risk management process supports the assessment against the computer requirements and within its operational environment. Decisions regarding risks identified must be made before starting the design of the computer system.

According to the MHRA guidance (9), "the effort and resource assigned to data governance should be commensurate with the risk to product quality."

Below is an example of the controls based on the impact of e-records to patient safety, product safety, and compliance.

Control	*No impact*	*Indirect impact*	*Direct impact*
Access Control	• controlled access	• authorization process • access management • password management • documentation	• rigorous authorization control • strict and proactive access management • user profiles • unique accounts • stringent PW management • physical security • full documentation
Backup and Restore	• checking of outcome • multiple copies (redundancy)	• checking of outcome • multiple copies (redundancy) • formal periodic testing • documentation	• checking of outcome • multiple copies (redundancy) • formal periodic testing • full documentation • remote storage locations • automated processes

Risk mitigation strategies, like the above, need the understanding of many factors, including (10):

- The degree to which e-records can be configured
- System complexity
- User access permissions and system configuration
- Transaction windows
- E-records structure
  - Dynamic vs. static e-records
  - Access, security, and hosting of e-records
  - File structure
- Validation for intended purpose vs. functional verification
- Audit trails and metadata

The selected mitigation strategy(ies) will determine the associated controls. The integration of the SLC and the risk management must exist to effectively implement and maintain the e-records integrity controls.

As part of the assessment of the risks associated with the possible issue about e-records integrity, failure analysis is performed to find out where the loss of e-records integrity would have the greatest impact, including the regulated entity reputation.

It is centered on the failure analysis results, the combination of techniques to be used, and the effort to be applied to implement and maintain an e-records integrity program.

It is important that the risks are reviewed periodically and if appropriate mitigation systems revised. The effectiveness of a risk management process is dependent on the quality of information fed into the risk assessment process which in turn is reliant on the robustness of the quality system in place.

Failure to manage e-records integrity risks can have the following impact:

- Authorization, completeness, and accuracy of transactions may be incorrect as they are entered, processed, summarized, and reported.
- There may be inadequate handling controls concerning the integrity of processed e-records or databases, which ultimately may affect the quality of a product.

E-records integrity risks should be communicated throughout the e-records lifecycle

Regulatory Agencies Expectations

Two primary principles of quality risk management are (1):

- The evaluation of the risk to quality should be based on scientific knowledge and ultimately link to the protection of the patient.
- The level of effort, formality, and documentation of the quality risk management process should be commensurate with the level of risk.

References

1. ICH Harmonized Tripartite Guideline, "Quality Risk Management, Q9," November 2005.
2. NIST, *Systems Security Engineering: Considerations for a Multidisciplinary Approach in the Engineering of Trustworthy Secure Systems* (Special Publication 800-160 Vol. 1, National Institute of Standards and Technology, June 2004).

3. Committee on National Security Systems Instruction (CNSSI), "Glossary," CNSSI 4009, April 2015.
4. NIST, *Managing Information Security Risk* (Special Publication 800–39, National Institute of Standards and Technology, March 2011).
5. Health Canada, "GMP Guide for Drug Products (GUI-0001-ENG)," February 2018.
6. NIST, *An Introduction to Computer Security: The NIST Handbook*, Chapter 6, Computer Security Risk Management (Special Publication 800-12 Rev. 1, National Institute of Standards and Technology, June 2017).
7. Graham, L., "Compliance Matters, Good Laboratory Practice," *Blog MHRA Inspectorate*, September 2015.
8. EudraLex, The Rule Governing Medicinal Products in the European Union, "Volume 4, EU Guidelines for Good Manufacturing Practices for Medicinal Products for Human and Veterinary Use, Annex 20, Quality Risk Management," February 2008.
9. MHRA, "'GxP' Data Integrity Guidance and Definitions," March 2018.
10. Churchward, D., "GMP Compliance and Data Integrity," In: *Paper Presented at the PDA/PIC's Quality and Regulations Conference*, Brussels, Belgium, June 2015.
11. ICH Harmonized Tripartite Guideline, "Quality Risk Management, Q9," November 2005.

Additional Reading

CEFIC, "Practical Risk-based Guide for Managing Data Integrity," March 2019 (Rev 1).

Chapter 10

CGMP E-records Risk Assessments

Introduction

The need to identify both the criticality of the e-records and the e-records integrity risks has become a focal point to the appropriate implementation of the control(s) and improving the data quality.

As an example, Health Canada developed a Risk Classification of GMP Observations (GUI-0023) (1). In relationship falsification of data, Health Canada recognized that

> the evaluation of the conformity to the Good Manufacturing Practices (GMP) should be commensurate with the risk involved considering the nature and extent of the deviation concerning the category of products evaluated. Nonetheless, most of the situations involving fraud, misrepresentation or falsification of products or data will generate a Non-Compliant rating, irrespective of the category of products involved.

A Risk 1 observation is catalogued a Non-Compliant rating, the highest observation noted during an inspection. Poor e-records integrity by regulated entities is a serious CGMP deficiency.

The effort and resources assigned to the e-records handling function (2) should be commensurate with the risk to product quality (3).

All CGMP-critical e-records (4) must be identified and standardized, and the risk in the access of these critical e-records in an unauthorized manner assessed, mitigated, and reviewed throughout the e-records lifecycle (EU Annex 11 p1).

How Can E-records Risk Be Assessed? (5)

Data and e-records risk assessments should consider the vulnerability of data to involuntary or deliberate amendment, deletion, or recreation. Chapter 8 discusses the vulnerability of e-records. Control measures, which prevent unauthorized activity and increase visibility/detectability, can be used as risk-mitigating actions.

Examples of factors, which can increase the risk of e-records integrity failure, include complex, inconsistent processes with open-ended and subjective outcomes. Simple tasks, which are consistent, well defined and objective, lead to reduced risk.

Risk assessment should include a business process focus (e.g., production, QC) and not just consider automation system functionality or complexity. Factors to consider include:

- Process complexity
- Process consistency and degree of automation/human interface
- Subjectivity of outcome/result
- Open-ended and well-defined process

The inherent risk to data integrity associated with equipment and computer systems may vary depending on how and to what degree the system (generating or using e-records) can be configured, as well as on the ability to manipulate e-records during transfers between computer systems throughout the lifecycle e-records. The use of available technologies should be encouraged, as appropriately configured to reduce the risk of e-records integrity (6).

As applicable, manual interfaces with automated systems must be considered in the risk assessment process. Automated system validation in isolation may not result in low e-records integrity risk when the user can influence the reporting of e-records from the validated system.

Risk Assessment

The initial risk assessment associated with the e-records integrity determines the necessary controls that must be considered based on the environment and utilization context of those e-records. Controls should be appropriate to ensure the security, integrity, and confidentiality of records (7). Refer to Figure 10.1 (8).

The type of the impact of the e-records can determine the controls based on the risk assessment to the patient safety, product safety and compliance. DI policy, DI governance, and procedural controls are to be developed to achieve the integrity of the e-records.

The MHRA guidance suggests the following mitigations to address the risk of e-records manipulations in an unauthorized manner.

- Access controls to ensure that only authorized individuals can access and use the system based on the job role (EU Annex 11 p12.1 and EU Annex 11 p12.2). The access controls apply to database servers or any server containing CGMP related e-records.
- The regulated entity must have documentation about users and access level (EU Annex 11 p12.3).

Controls Based on Risk and Impact
Effect on:
Patient safety
Product safety
Compliance
Direct Impact:
Use risk assessment to identify specific controls & rigor
Increasing rigor of control required
Consider:
Stricter controls
More controls
More frequent controls
Automatic controls
Increased internal audit
Indirect Impact:
Use Generic Checklist controls
Severity
No Impact:
Use "Good IT Practices"
Potential for:
Loss of record
Corruption of record
Wrong record
Risk

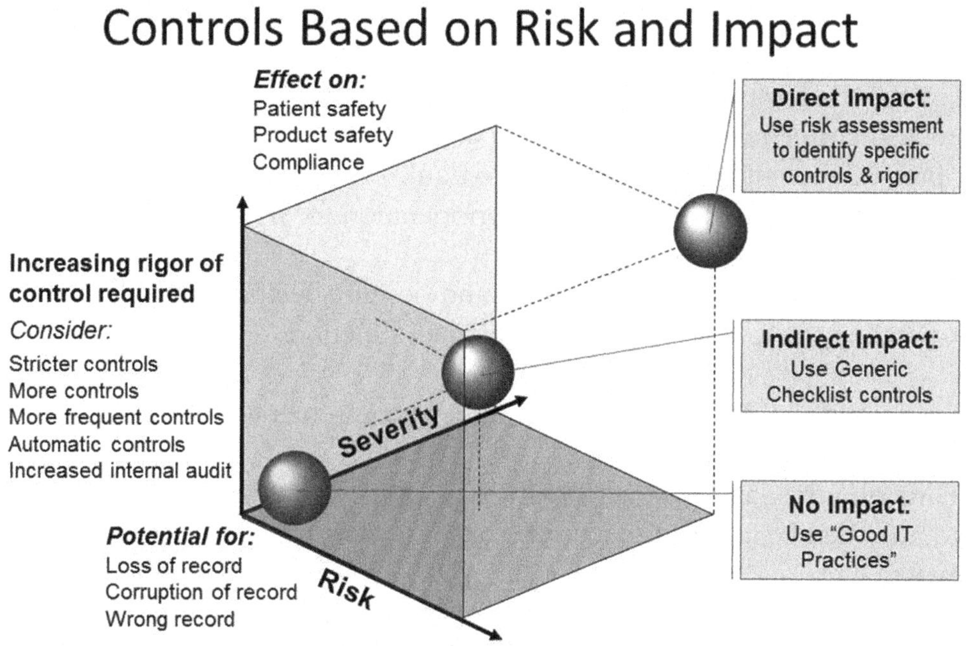

Figure 10.1 Control Based on Risk and Impact.

- In case that technological or design constraints do not allow unique access to the computer application and/or database server(s), a paper-based method must provide access traceability.
- The access to system administrators should be minimal, unique per administrator and traceable. The preferred traceability method for actions performed by a system administrator is audit trails (EU Annex 11 p9). It is not specified if the audit trails must be electronically recorded.
- Separation of roles must be enforced on e-records maintenance.
- E-records maintenance must be controlled (EU Annex 11 p12.4) and an approval method must be implemented (EU Annex 11 p10).

As part of the assessment of the risks associated with the possible issue about e-records integrity, failure analysis is performed to find out where the loss of e-records integrity would have the greatest impact, including the regulated entity reputation.

Another area to consider is the risk associated with e-records migration from an existing system(s) over to a new system. The risk of e-records migration may be mitigated by verifying "that data is not altered in value and/or meaning during this migration process" (EU Annex 11 p4.8).

Besides, the MHRA had communicated to the regulated user that must carry out a routine effectiveness review of their governance systems to ensure e-records integrity and traceability is maintained. The effectiveness review can be performed during the periodic review. Investigations and associated correction action preventive action (CAPA) related to e-records can provide the efficiency of the DI program.

The risk assessment is taken into consideration for the following activities:

- Creating the system requirements and design specifications
- Creating the test plans for the individual functions

The requirements document must include a requirement(s) related to the mitigation of the uncovered risks.

Through a risk assessment, threats to resources are identified, vulnerability to and the likelihood of occurrence is evaluated, and potential impact is estimated.

Considering the vulnerability of the e-records (Chapter8), the risk of such vulnerabilities can be quantified.

References

1. Health Canada, "Good Manufacturing Practices Guide for Drug Products, GUI-0001," February 2018. https://lnkd.in/dU8N7PB.
2. E-records Handling – The process of ensuring that data is stored, archived or disposed of safely and securely during and after the decommissioning of the computer system.
3. WHO, "Guideline on Data Integrity," QAS/19.819, October 2019 (Draft).
4. Critical e-records – Critical e-records is interpreted as meaning e-records with high risk to product quality or patient safety. (ISPE GAMP COP Annex 11 – Interpretation, July/August 2011).
5. EU, "Questions and Answers: Good Manufacturing Practice and Good Distribution Practice, Data Integrity," August 2016. https://www.ema.europa.eu/en/human-regulatory/research-development/compliance/good-manufacturing-practice/guidance-good-manufacturing-practice-good-distribution-practice-questions-answers#data-integrity-(new-august-2016)-section.
6. Russia Federal State Institute of Drugs and Good Practices (SIDGP), "Data Integrity & Computer System Validation Guideline," September 2018 (Draft).
7. ISPE GAMP Forum, "Risk Assessment for Use of Automated Systems Supporting Manufacturing Processes – Part 2 – Risk to Records," *Pharmaceutical Engineering*, 23(6), November/December 2003.
8. Figure 10-1, "Control Based on Risk and Impact (from Perez, A.D., New GAMP Good Practice Guide for Electronic Record and Signature Compliance," In: *Paper Presented at the FDA Part 11 Public Meeting*, Washington, DC, June 2004).

Additional Reading

CEFIC, "Practical Risk-based Guide for Managing Data Integrity," March 2019 (Rev 1).

Chapter 11

Security Service

Introduction

Regardless of the tools and technologies used, managing access is critical when it comes to data integrity.

As a function related to security, e-records integrity service maintains information exactly as it was inputted and is auditable to affirm its reliability (see Figure 11.1).

The regulated entity must ensure that personnel are aware of the importance of data security, the procedures and system features that are available to provide appropriate security, and the consequences of security gaps. Such system features could include routine surveillance of system access.

This chapter addresses the security (1) controls expected by worldwide regulatory agencies and competent authority. Items that need to be covered as elements of the security controls include access control, password policy, and audit trails.

Computer Access

> Computer systems should have enough controls to prevent unauthorized access or changes to e-records.
>
> **US FDA 21 CFR 211.68(b)**

The system owner is the person responsible for providing protection to the e-records by enabling suitable controls over the application, infrastructure (e.g., network, database server), and database components (2). These e-record protection controls ensure that only authorized personnel can make changes to any

Figure 11.1 Security.

component of the computer system and the security of the e-records residing on the associated electronic storage device(s).

Physical and/or logical controls should be in place to restrict access to computer systems and electronic storage devices to authorized regulated users (EU Annex 11 p12.1 and p7.1).Computer systems and/or electronic storage devices must have the appropriate level of access to carry out their assigned duties (EU Annex 11 p2).

The access to computer systems should be authorized by the system owner or representative and, after the approval, access must be provided by the system administrator.

Changes to the regulated user's level of access and resetting of passwords can be performed by the system administration as well. A defined procedure(s), at all levels, should be established for the issue, cancellation, and alteration of authorization to enter and amend, including resetting personal passwords.

Personnel with system administrator access should log in with unique credentials that allow actions in the audit trail(s) to be attributed to a specific individual. The intent of this is to prevent giving access to users with potentially a conflict of interest so that they can make unauthorized changes that would not be traceable to that person (3). The system administrator access should not be used for routine operations.

Access to individual computer system platforms is controlled by network-specific security procedures (network security and database server). Access to these devices should be controlled (logical security).

The objectives of the network and database server security are the integrity, authenticity, availability, and confidentiality of e-records (4).

The application-level security and associated authority checks bring about access to the computer system applications (*applications security*).

Attempts by unauthorized persons to access network and application levels should be recorded (5). The time and the system which an unauthorized person attempted to access but failed should be recorded. These data should be checked as part of the periodic review.

Legacy computer systems support only a single user login or a limited number of user logins. Where no suitable alternative computer system is available, equivalent control may be provided by third-party software or a paper-based method of providing traceability. The suitability of alternative systems should be justified and documented.

Any modifications or changes to the systems are restricted and subject to change control management.

Finally, upon placing the e-records in retention environments, the same level of e-records security imposed throughout their earlier lifecycle still needs to be maintained.

Password Policy

A password policy is a set of rules intended to improve computer security by encouraging users to employ strong passwords and use them accurately. A password policy is often part of an organization's official regulations and may be taught as part of security awareness training. Either the password policy is merely advisory or the computer systems force users to comply with it. Some governments have national authentication frameworks that define requirements for user authentication to government services, including requirements for passwords.

Audit Trails (6)

As part of the reliability of e-records, audit trails refer to a journal, paper-based or computer-based, that records modifications to the records.

Regulatory agencies worldwide expect that there is a record of all data change made, the previous entry, who made the change, and when the change was made (ICH Q7).

The audit trails mechanism provides the capability to reconstruct modified e-records and consequently does not obscure previously recorded e-records. The use of audit trails or alternative methods that fulfill the audit trail requirements helps to confirm that only authorized additions, deletions, or alterations of CGMP-relevant e-records have occurred and allows a means to reconstruct significant details about manufacturing activities and data collection. This is necessary to verify the quality and data integrity relevant to CGMP-relevant e-records.

The need for audit trails should be determined based on a justified and documented risk assessment that takes into consideration circumstances surrounding system use, the likelihood that information might be compromised, and any system vulnerabilities. Should it be decided that audit trails or other appropriate methods are needed to ensure e-records integrity, personnel who create, modify, or delete e-records should not be able to modify the documents or security measures used to track e-record changes. Computer-generated, time-stamped electronic audits trails are the preferred method for tracking changes to electronic source records.

Audit trails or other appropriate methods used to capture e-record activities:

- As any CGMP-relevant e-records, are subject to all requirements regarding e-records integrity
- Should describe when, by whom, and the reason for which changes were made to the e-record. Original information should not be hidden using audit trails or other security measures used to capture e-record activities
- Must be available and, if necessary, convertible to a readable form
- Must be regularly reviewed
- Should be retained if the associated e-records need to be readable
- Must prevent changes to audit trail data

The audit trail tracking mechanism includes a timestamp that indicates the time of the entry. The date and time of an audit trail should be synchronized to a trusted date-time service. Computer-generated, time-stamped audit trails or other appropriate methods can also capture information related to the creation, modification, or deletion of CGMP-relevant e-records and may be useful to ensure compliance with the appropriate regulation.

"*What shall be done in the case of legacy systems without an audit trail?* (7) First of all, it must be clarified whether the data can be changed at all (e.g.: electronic recorders or SPS). If not, this should be the reasoning within the risk assessment for the audit trail not being necessary. Define in an SOP that each change has to be documented e.g. in a logbook and verified by a second person."

Regulatory Agencies' Expectations

1. Computer systems should have enough controls to prevent unauthorized access or changes to data (ICH Q7).
2. Computer systems and electronic storage devices for e-records should support different user authorization levels (8).
3. There should be continuously updated lists of approved users and their authorization levels (9).
4. Incidents related to computer systems that could affect the reliability of records must be recorded and investigated (ICH Q7).

References

1. Security – The protection of computer hardware and software from accidental or malicious access, use, modification, destruction, or disclosure. Security also pertains to personnel, data, communications, and the physical protection of computer installations. (IEEE)
2. EU Annex 11, "Glossary – System Owner."
3. MHRA, "MHRA GxP Data Integrity Guidance and Definitions," March 2018.
4. ISPE/PDA, "Good Practice and Compliance for Electronic Records and Signatures. Part 1 Good Electronic Records Management (GERM)," July 2002.
5. TGA, "Australian Code of Good Manufacturing Practice for Human Blood and Blood Components, Human Tissue and Human Cellular Therapy Products," Page 28 of 29, V1.0, April 2013.
6. US FDA, "Guidance for Industry Computerized Systems Used in Clinical Investigations," Section IV.D.2, May 2007.
7. Mangel, A., "Q&A on Annex 11," *GMP Journal*, (8), April/May 2012.
8. PI 041-1, "Good Practices for Data Management and Integrity in Regulated GMP/GDP Environment," *Pharmaceutical Inspection Co-operation Scheme (PIC/S)*, November 2018 (Draft 3).
9. CEFIC, "Computer Validation Guide," API Committee of CEFIC, January 2003.

Chapter 12

Defining and Managing Manufacturing Data (1)

Introduction

E-records integrity is the validity of data and their relationships. For e-records to be trustworthy and reliable, the links between transient data, raw data (2), metadata, and records must not be compromised or broken. Without e-records integrity, it is difficult to regenerate a previous result reliably.

> Good data management practices influence the quality of all data generated and recorded by a manufacturer and these practices should ensure that data is accurate, auditable, in conformance to requirements, complete, consistent, with integrity, provenance, and valid.

The raw data related to the manufacturing operation is the essential data in which the integrity-related technological controls must be established, providing the evidence to operational and quality system activities.

This chapter discusses the needed controls on computer-generated raw data in the medicine manufacturing operations. These controls are carried out to facilitate the identification, creation, storage, use, retention time, and final disposition of CGMP records (3).

Data Lifecycle (4)

Refer to Chapter 3.

Medicine Manufacturing Operations

In this type of operations, the data loaded from the field sensors contain a measurable attribute of a physical entity, process, or event (5). The loaded data is recorded, becoming raw data. The raw data is considered original data or source capture of data (6). When multiple raw data are generated to satisfy a CGMP requirement, such raw data become a CGMP record (7).

Some examples of raw data in a typical medicine manufacturing environment include:

- Analog readings: temperature, pressure, flow rates, levels, weights, central processing unit (CPU) temperature, mixer speed, fan speed, and so on.
- Digital readings: valves, limit switches, motors on/off, discrete level s ensors, and so on.
- Product info: product id, batch id, material id, raw material lot id, and so on.
- Quality info: process and product limits, custom limits, and so on.
- Alarm info: out of limits signals, return to normal signals, etc.

Properly recorded and managed raw data are the foundation to demonstrate the product identity, strength, purity, and safety. The raw data holds the content of the e-record that will reproduce the full CGMP automated activities. The e-records associated with raw data demonstrate that the manufacturer's process adheres to the CGMPs, including process sequencing and instructions (8).

The accurate handling of data objects during the data entry or collection, storage, transmission, and processing (9) provides the controls during the "Processable Data" and "Retention" stages of loaded data, raw data, and e-records. Refer to Figure 3.1.

Specifically, to the medicine manufacturing operations, the integrity of the manufacturing raw data is a precondition for the Continued Process Verification (CPV). CPV is an essential element in the US FDA Process Validation activities (10). The objective of the CPV is the continual assurance that the process remains in a state of control during commercial manufacturing. The collection of information about the performance of the process will allow detection of undesired process variability so that the process remains in control.

Identification of CGMP Record (11)

Identification of the CGMP records to be acquired and the associated controls are crucial to the success of any medicine manufacturing operation. The characterization of these CGMP records begins during the Records Identification Phase and the Records Standardization Phase. Refer to Chapter 2. The outcome of these two phases is documented on a design document such as a process and instrumentation drawing (P&ID). A process flow diagram (PFD) or some other form of the schematic may be used.

As an example, Table 12.1 depicts the critical process parameters related to the solid dosage process. Equipment, related to the process, contains instrumentations to control and/or acquisition of the data about each critical process parameter.

The primary concern for cell controllers is to work accurately in the intended process. This is dynamically verified during the qualification of the cell controller. The qualifications of automated cell controllers are essential to ensure the proper functioning of the process and product quality.

The I/Os list refers to the information coming into and going out of the manufacturing system. Taken from Table 12.1, the air temperature, air volume dew point, and the product temperature are the I/Os associated with, for example, a fluid bed dryer. This information comes from field instruments by terminating wires in the digital system I/O processing section. After a certain transformation, the data is to be transmitted to the SCADA/Historian system over the communications link.

The first step in documenting the I/O requirements is to compile a list of all the applicable points that are referenced on the P&ID. This is necessary so that the specific signal and termination data can be associated with each point or each instrument.

Other areas to be considered during the design are alarms and reporting.

Exchange of Data

Computer systems exchanging data electronically with other systems fall into one of two categories: those that exchange data between computers

Table 12.1 Critical Process Parameters Solid Dosage (12)

Process	*Critical process parameters*
Blending	Blending time
	Number of revolutions of the blender
High shear wet granulation	Kneading time
	Impeller and chopper speed
	Binder addition time
Fluid bed drying	Inlet air temperature
	Fluidization air volume
	Dewpoint
	Product temperature
Roller compaction	Roll gap
	Roll width
	Roll pressure
	Screen size
Fluid bed granulation	Spray volume
	Spray rate
	Inlet air temperature
Milling	Screen size
Compression	Compression force
	Compression speed
	Dwell time
Coating	Spray rate
	Inlet air temperature
Encapsulation	Speed of encapsulation
	Tamping pressure

or those that exchange between computers and peripheral components. CGMP-applicable data may be transported automatically from one system to another system (e.g., from a remote data capturing system to an electronic storage area central (e.g., SCADA/Historian system)).

All communication links are potential sources of error and may result in the loss or corruption of data.

Appropriate controls of interfaces for security and system integrity must be adequately addressed during the interface lifecycle. The exchange between systems of electronic data should include appropriate built-in checks (EU Annex 11 p6) for the correct and secure processing of data. Network infrastructure must be qualified.

Storage of Records (14)

Raw data are original records generated through computer systems and become the contents of an e-record. The E-records storage device is a device that records (stores) or retrieves (reads) e-records from any medium, including the medium itself. This is considered a short retention environment.

Design specification or similar document must describe the file structure(s) in which the e-records are stored, the capacity requirements of the storage, and how the security scheme is implemented. File structures are verified during the design review(s) and file security is verified/tested during the qualification.

After the data is recorded and retained into the electronic storage device (e.g., Historian/SCADA storage), the designed physical and logical controls to the e-records must be in place. These controls include physical protections, stamped audit trail, records handling,* and archival and retrieval of records. Alarms and the associated actions to the alarms are managed by the PLC. The associated alarm records are saved in the corresponding repository system at the storage device level.

Physical protections to the e-records comprise the protection of e-records storage device from the environmental impacts influencing the respective e-records storage devices.

Media can be deteriorated as a result of the environment. Copying information without changing it offers a short-term solution for preserving access to digital material by ensuring that information is stored on newer media before the old media deteriorates beyond the point where the information can be retrieved.

As an element of the e-records integrity in electronic storage devices, there must be a record of any e-records change made that includes the previous entry, who made the change, and when the change was made (14).

---

* Data Handling – The process of ensuring that data is stored, archived, or disposed in a safe and secure manner during the data lifecycle.

To reduce the risk of losing the e-records in the storage and guarantee e-records readiness to the users, periodic backups must be performed. The backup must be stored separate from the primary storage location, and at a frequency based on an analysis of risk to GMP e-records and the capacity of the storage device.

The efficacy of the backup and restore processes must be verified using the related procedural control as part of the qualification process. Besides, the capacity level of the storage must be monitored.

As in archived e-records, the e-records in electronic storage devices need to be verified periodically for accessibility, readability, and integrity. If changes are implemented to the computer infrastructure and/or application handling the e-records, then it is necessary to ensure and test the ability to retrieve e-records.

One critical element to consider as part of the implementation of e-records retained by electronic storage devices is the legal holds to the e-records. These are records in which the regulated entity is involved in litigation. These records cannot be destroyed even after the retention period has expired. The regulated entity is under a legal obligation to retain all records involving or related to the legal matters. A mechanism must be implemented to tag the e-records impacted by a legal hold.

As applicable, web and database servers should be separated as an element of physical location. Database servers should be isolated from a website's demilitarized zone (DMZ) (15). These servers can locate them on a physically separate network segment from the web and other internet-accessible servers that support the business. Preferably, partition the database server off from the web servers by a dedicated firewall. This firewall should only allow database traffic between the web server and database server. The firewall should also deny and log all traffic from any other location, or other types of traffic from the webserver.

As appropriate, the regulatory authorities expect that the data written in the storage device must be saved at the time the data is generated (16).

Protection of Data and E-records

The protection of transient data, raw data, and e-records includes e-records created, in storage, during processing, and while in transit (9).

Based on Figure 12.1, the protection to transient data, raw data, and e-records may be set in two environments: transient data and raw data.

Data Integrity and E-records (ER) in Process Automation

Data collected directly from equipment and control signals between computers and equipment should be checked by verification circuits/ software to confirm accuracy and reliability.

TGA, Code of GMPs, 2013.

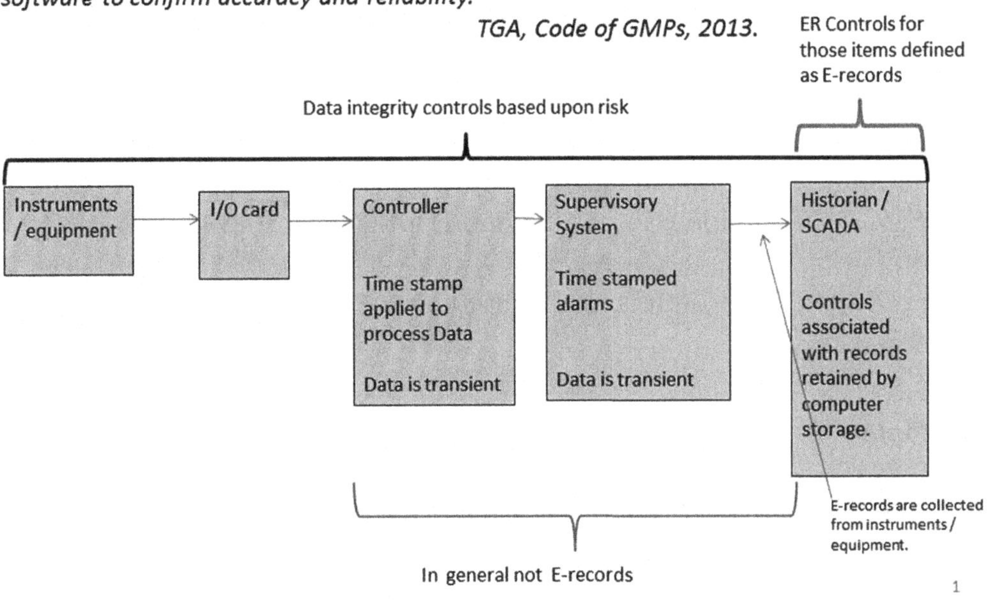

Figure 12.1 Data and e-records in process automation.

Transient Data

At the PLC level, the analogue data is extracted from the PLC memory, transformed (digitized data, validated, normalized, scaled, and so on), and sent to the SCADA system.

The data collected directly from manufacturing equipment and control signals between the equipment and a data server (e.g., SCADA) may be regarded as transient and should not be edited by reasonable means or reprocessed by the human user.

Like the controls associated with e-records in transit, the data integrity controls for transient data are:

- The infrastructure must be qualified (13). The outcome of this qualification provides documentary evidence that accounts for the correct implementation of the integrated hardware and associated devices.
- Built-in checks for the correct inputs and outputs (I/Os) must be available. These built-in checks are, at first, validated. During the operational

stage, the built-in checks must be periodically verified (US FDA 21 CFR Part 211.68(b) and EU Annex 11 p.5).

- Accuracy checks, usually performed at the Supervisory System level, are required to critical data entered manually by authorized personnel. This critical data requires input verification to prevent incorrect data entries.
- The data written in the electronic storage device must be saved at the time the data is created. The controls addressed above ensure the reliability of the transient data and mitigate, as applicable, the contemporaneous related requirements (21 CFR Part 211.160; EU Chapter 4 Section 4.8; ICH Q7 Section 6.14., EU Annex 11 p12.4 and 11 p14).

Refer to Chapter 13, "Controls on Transient Data," for additional information about this subject.

Raw Data

The data handling function must be designed such that original data cannot be deleted and for the retention of audit trails reflecting changes made to original data (18).

After the data is recorded and retained by an electronic storage device (e.g., Historian/SCADA storage), the physical and logical controls to the e-records must be implemented and deployed. These controls include security, access authorization, backups, periodic reviews, stamped audit trails, built-in checks (19), and other relevant data handling controls. The alarms and the associated actions to the alarms are managed by the PLC. These alarm records are saved in the corresponding repository system at the storage device level.

If the e-records and the associated raw data need to be transferred from the original processing environment, this transfer needs to be managed by the appropriate procedural control. After concluding the migration process, a verification must be performed to ensure that the information in the original e-records has not been altered. This successfully verified copy becomes a true or certified copy of the e-records on the processing environment.

Retrieval of E-records

The e-records are kept and used for their intended purpose. Access to e-records should be ensured throughout the retention period (EU Annex 11 p7.1). The access to these records must be controlled to ensure the integrity of the e-records in storage. The controls associated with e-records in storage allow those individuals who depend on the e-records to correctly fulfill their job function.

Manufacturing-related e-records, during the Active Phase, will be held in the environment in which the records were initially created. In this processing environment, the e-records are visible to the tools that create these e-records. The functionality changing and deleting these e-records must ensure audit trails to record the reason and other required information.

Periodic (or continuous) reviews must be performed after the initial validation (EU Annex 11 p11) of the processing environment. As part of a periodic review the stored, backup, and archived e-records are checked for accessibility, readability, and accuracy; the output of the backup, the accuracy of audit trails, correct final disposition of e-records, and so on are also verified. A reconciliation process must be performed periodically to the source e-records. As applicable, the accuracy and reliability of the transferred e-records are verified as well (20). The periodic review should include the accurate final disposition of e-records.

A procedural control for the periodic review should define the frequency, roles and responsibilities, and nature of these reviews.

In addition to the above controls, the processes to read and manage e-records must ensure the integrity of the records. The infrastructure between the records on storage and the processing environment must be a controlled environment. The controls associated with the infrastructure must include qualification of such infrastructure, built-in checks, and accuracy checks. During the Active Phase, change management represents governance that controls editing or modifying the data.

Resulting from the criticality of the raw data, periodically raw data may be cleansed to correct inconsistent values after the use of the data. This activity must be suitably managed using procedural control and documented (e.g., audit trail).

Retention Time (21)

The EU GMPs establishes that raw data which supports information in the marketing authorization (22), such as validation or stability, should be retained while the authorization remains in force. In some cases, up to 30 years of raw data must be retained. It may be considered acceptable to retire certain documentation where the data has been superseded by a full set of new data. In such cases, the justification for this should be documented and should consider the requirements for retention of batch documentation and the accompanying raw data should be retained for a period at least as long as the records for all batches whose release has been supported based on that validation exercise.

For a medicinal product, the batch documentation shall be retained for at least one year after the expiry date of the batches to which it relates or at least five years after the certification referred to in Article 51(3) of Directive 2001/83/EC, whichever is the longer period.

At least two years of data must be retrievable on time for regulatory inspection.

In the case of the US FDA, the applicable pharmaceutical CGMP regulations, 21 CFR 211.180(a), established on retention of data that are part of the drug product production and control specifies that records "shall be retained for at least one year after the expiration date of the batch or, in the case of certain over the counter (OTC) drug products lacking expiration dating because they meet the criteria for exemption under 211.137, 3 years after distribution of the batch." As the results of the traceability requirements from raw data to data, the raw data will be retained as specified in 21 CFR 211.180(a).

When computer systems are used instead of written documents, the manufacturer shall first validate the systems by showing that the e-records will be appropriately stored during the anticipated period of storage. E-records stored by those systems shall be made readily available in a legible form and shall be provided to the competent authorities at their request. The electronically stored e-records shall be protected, by methods such as duplication or backup and transfer to another storage system, against loss or damage of e-records, and audit trails shall be maintained.

Disposition of E-records

Active records may be transferred from the processing environment to retention environment. If active records are transferred to another data format or system, validation should include checks that data are not altered in value and/or meaning during this migration process (EU Annex 11 p4.8).

E-records that are placed in retention environments should preserve the integrity of the raw data, associated e-record and protection mechanisms used to prevent informational loss and/or corruption. Should records require modifications in retention environments, the mechanism must be planned to enforce change documentation to preserve an audit trail of change or replacement history that includes also record removal.

Once e-records have been transferred and placed in the retention environments, the e-records should never be directly modified. In the case of modifications to records in the retention environment, the same modifications must be performed first to the records in the processing environment. The processing environments' updated records are then loaded to the retention environment by using the same automated tool/interface used to load the original records from the processing environment to the retention environment. If technical limitations require the electronic records to be modified in the retention environment, the change must have traceability to the same change in the processing environment.

The Inactive Phase starts with records archival. Records in scope include inactive, superseded, replaced, and withdrawn. These records need to be kept meeting retention schedule requirements and traceability. These records usually maintain read/view attributes. However, there are exceptions where "processability" is extended for the full life of the records through to when they are discarded.

During the Final Disposition Phase, the e-records are discarded. This is a phase of short duration and includes metadata and audit trails.

Summary

This chapter introduced the differences between transient data, raw data, and e-records, and explained the typical medicine manufacturing environments.

These concepts are used to describe the controls necessary to manage transient data, raw data, metadata, and records in a typical medicine manufacturing environment. Through the identification, storage, protection, retrieval, retention time, and disposition of CGMP records, the illustration of these controls is presented to the reader.

References

1. López, O., "Defining and Managing Raw Manufacturing Data," *Pharmaceutical Technology Europe*, 31(6), June 2019, pp 19–25.
2. Raw data is defined as the original record (data) which can be described as the first capture of information, whether recorded on paper or electronically (MHRA).

3. ISO 9001:2015, "Quality Management Systems – Requirements," 4.2.4 Control of Records.
4. López, O., "Electronic Records Life Cycle," In: *Data Integrity in Pharmaceutical and Medical Devices Regulation Operations.* (CRC Press, Boca Raton, FL, 1st ed., 2017). pp. 39–45.
5. ISPE/PDA, "Technical Report: Good Electronic Records Management (GERM)," July 2002.
6. MHRA, "GxP Data Integrity Guidance and Definitions," March 2018.
7. US FDA, "Data Integrity and Compliance with CGMP, Q&A - Guidance for Industry," December 2018.
8. López, O., "Preface," In: *Data Integrity in Pharmaceutical and Medical Devices Regulation Operations.* (CRC Press, Boca Raton, FL, 1st ed., 2017). pp xv–xvii.
9. NIST, *Recommendation for Key Management, Part 1: General.* (Special Publication 800–57 Part 1 Rev 4, National Institute of Standards and Technology), July 2015.
10. US FDA, "Guidance for Industry - Process Validation: General Principles and Practices," January 2011.
11. Amy, L. T., "Automation Systems for Control and Data Acquisition," ISA, 1992.
12. Kane, A., the sidebar to "Designing Optimized Formulations," *Pharmaceutical Technology,* (4), 2017.
13. López, O., "Electronic Records Controls: Records Retained by Computer Storage," In: *Data Integrity in Pharmaceutical and Medical Devices* Regulation *Operations.* (CRC Press Boca Raton, FL, 1st ed., 2017). pp 169–177.
14. Health Canada, "Good Manufacturing Practices (GMP) Guidelines for Active Pharmaceutical Ingredients (APIs)," GUI-0104, C.02.05, Interpretation #15, December 2013.
15. A DMZ is a physical or logical subnetwork that contains and exposes an organization's external-facing services to a larger and untrusted network, usually the Internet. The purpose of a DMZ is to add a layer of security to an organization's local area network (LAN); an external network node only has direct access to equipment in the DMZ, rather than any other part of the network.
16. 21 CFR Part 211.160; EU Chapter 4 Section 4.8; ICH Q7 Section 6.14.
17. López, O., *Computer Infrastructure Qualification for FDA Regulated Industries.* (PDA and DHI Publishing, LLC, River Grove, IL, 2006).
18. EU, "Questions and Answers: Good Manufacturing Practice and Good Distribution Practice, Data Integrity," August 2016. https://www.ema.europa.eu/en/human-regulatory/research-development/compliance/good-manufacturing-practice/guidance-good-manufacturing-practice-good-distribution-practice-questions-answers#data-integrity-(new-august-2016)-section
19. US FDA, "CPG Section 425.400 – Computerized Drug Processing; Input/Output Checking," September 1987.
20. WHO, "Validation of Computerized Systems," Technical Report #937, Annex 4 Appendix 5, 2006. Note: There is an updated draft version dated 2016.

21. López, O., "Records Retention on Raw Data," In: *Data Integrity in Pharmaceutical and Medical Devices Regulation Operations.* (CRC Press, Boca Raton, FL, 1st ed., 2017). pp. 55–56.
22. EudraLex, "The Rules Governing Medicinal Products in the European Union Volume 4, Good Manufacturing Practice, Medicinal Products for Human and Veterinary Use, Chapter 4: Documentation," June 2011, Volume 4: Documentation, Section 4.12.

Chapter 13

Controls on Transient Data (1)

What Is Transient Data?

> The system should enforce saving immediately after critical data entry. Data entry before saving to permanent memory with audit trail (server, database) is considered to be temporary memory. The length of time that data is held in temporary memory should be minimized.
>
> **CEFIC, "Practical Risk-based Guide for Managing Data Integrity," March 2019 (Rev 1)**

It is recognized by regulatory authorities worldwide that CGMP records must be reliable. One element of reliability is the integrity of such records. A CGMP e-record is created when data is saved at the time of performing the creation of an e-record in compliance with CGMP requirements.

In manufacturing systems, as an example, data is collected directly from manufacturing equipment, sensors, and controllers. This data is not contemporaneously recorded because it may be stored as a temporary file or on random access memory (RAM) without power applied before transfer to an electronic storage device. When a device powers down, all the data that was in memory goes away.

In another example from a manufacturing environment, at the PLC level, the analogue data is extracted from the PLC memory, transformed (digitized data, validated, normalized, scaled, and so on), and then, sent to the SCADA. The SCADA is the e-records repository.

The control signals between equipment/sensors/controllers and an electronic storage device (e.g., SCADA or Historian) may be regarded as transient data. Refer to Figure 13.1.

The technologies supporting transient data have limited audit trail provision for amending, deleting, or recreating data. This is a vulnerability of transient data.

Even though transient data are not considered e-records, they must be reliable (2) as inputs to e-records. Transient data must still be secure from unauthorized access. The length of time that data is held in temporary memory should be minimized.

Protection of Transient Data

Transient data captured by the system should be saved on to memory in a format that is not vulnerable to manipulation, without creating a permanent record (3), loss or change (4).

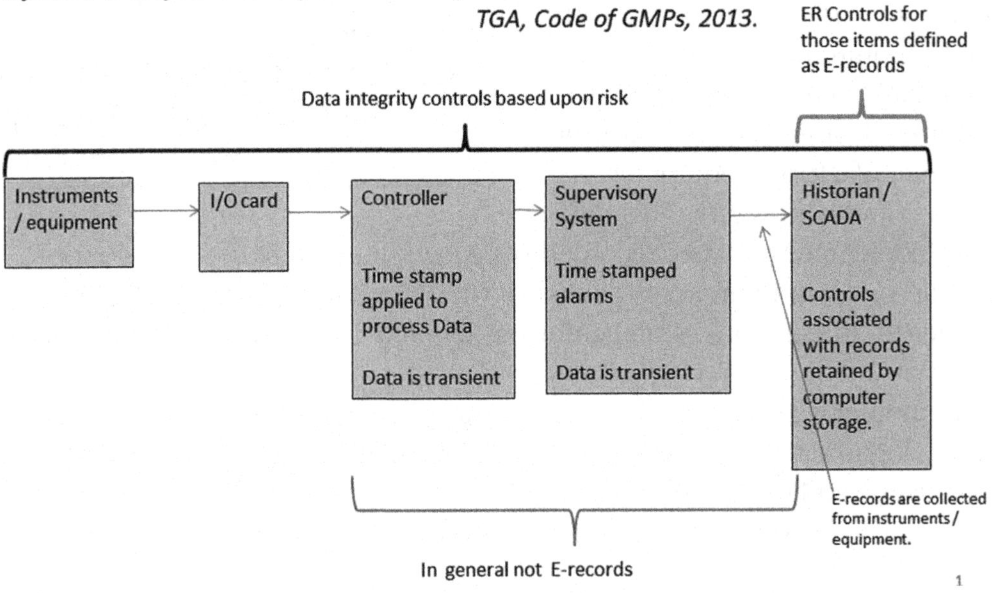

Figure 13.1 Transient data in process automation.

However, available technologies (e.g., controllers) may not be suitable to meet the regulatory authorities' expectations. Refer to Figure 13.1.

In this issue, the risk is a high threat and the mitigation features must be the technical controls applicable to meet the CGMPs.

Appropriate CGMP controls shall be established to ensure the integrity of the transient data up to the point of writing the data to an electronic storage device. These controls are like the controls associated with e-records in transit and include:

- Qualification of the infrastructure (5). The outcome of this qualification provides documentary evidence that accounts for the correct implementation of the integrated hardware and associated devices supporting transient records.

  Of special interest is the interface (6) between the data acquisition and the transport infrastructure, and the transport infrastructure and the recording repository system. These must be qualified to ensure the accuracy of the transient data (4).

  The qualification of the infrastructure demonstrates that appropriate controls are in place, ensuring the protection of the transient data.
- Built-in checks for the correct inputs and outputs (I/Os).

  If technically feasible, the system may be designed to ensure the completeness of transient data as well as any metadata associated with the transient data (4, 7) by automatically comparing data on input with predefined limits.

  These built-in checks are, at first, qualified. During the Operational Period, the built-in checks must be periodically verified (US FDA 21 CFR Part 211.68(b) and EU Annex 11 p5).
- Accuracy checks, usually performed at the Supervisory System level, are required to verify critical data entered manually by authorized personnel. This input verification is required to prevent incorrect data entries.
- The automated system must be designed to save the data to an electronic storage device before prompting users to make changes (8), creating raw data.
- A timestamp (9) by the controller is a data attached to the transient data containing the time of occurrence of an event. Time-stamping (10) refers to the use of an electronic timestamp to provide an order among a set of events. Time-stamping is covered in Chapter 14.

  The US FDA relies on the recording time as a critical component in documenting a sequence of events (21 CFR Part 11.10(f)). Within a given manufacturing batch, several events and operator actions may take place, and without the recording time, documentation of those events would be incomplete (11).

Also, timestamps are used during the creation of audit trails. These timestamps allow for reconstruction of the course of events relating to the creation, modification, and deletion of e-records.

Consequently, for a better understanding of good data integrity practices, time-stamping of transient data is a key service that supports, if properly controlled, non-repudiation of transactions, adding integrity to e-records.

- Transient data must still be secure from unauthorized access.

  Appropriate procedural controls should be followed if the transient data transfer does not occur properly (8).

Regulatory Agencies' Expectations

Transient data should be checked by verification circuits/software to confirm accuracy and reliability (12). The data integrity controls are equivalent to the controls associated with data while in transit.

- Qualification of computer infrastructure
- Built-in Checks
- Accuracy Checks

The transient data must be reliable by implementing the CGMP controls described above.

In addition, data captured by the system shall be saved into memory in a format that is not vulnerable to manipulation, loss, or change.

Summary

The data written in the electronic storage device must be saved at the time the data is created. The controls addressed above ensure the reliability of the transient data and mitigate the contemporaneous related requirements (21 CFR Part 211.160; EU Chapter 4 Section 4.8; ICH Q7 Section 6.14., EU Annex 11 p12.4 and 11 p14).

References

1. López, O., "Defining and Managing Raw Manufacturing Data," *Pharmaceutical Technology*, 43(6), July 2019.
2. Reliable data – A reliable data is one whose content can be trusted as a full and accurate representation of the transaction, activities, or facts to which they attest and can be depended upon during subsequent transaction or activities. (NARA).
3. US FDA, "Data Integrity and Compliance with Drug CGMP, Q&A," December 2018.
4. PI 041–1, "Good Practices for Data Management and Integrity in Regulated GMP/GDP Environment," *Pharmaceutical Inspection Co-operation Scheme (PIC/S)*, November 2018 (Draft 3).
5. López, O., *Computer Infrastructure Qualification for FDA Regulated Industries*. (PDA and DHI Publishing, LLC, River Grove, IL, 2006).
6. Interface – In this chapter interface means that data is received from a sending system and forwarded to a receiving system without permanent storage of data in this interfacing system. (CEFIC, "*Practical Risk-based Guide for Managing Data Integrity*," March 2019 (Rev 1)).
7. EU Annex 11 p5.
8. MHRA, "GxP Data Integrity and Definitions," March 2018.
9. López, O., "Digital Date and Time Stamps," In: *Pharmaceutical and Medical Devices Manufacturing Computer Systems Validation*. (CRC Press, Boca Raton, FL, 1st ed., 2018). pp 201–205.
10. López, O. "Overview of Technologies Supporting Security Requirements in 21 CFR Part 11 – Part II," Pharmaceutical Technology, March 2002.
11. US FDA. "21 CFR Part 11 - Electronic Records; Electronic Signatures; Final Rule – Preamble," Comment 74, March 1997.
12. TGA, "Australian Code of Good Manufacturing Practice for Human Blood and Blood Components, Human Tissues and Human Cellular Therapy Products," Version 1.0 April 2013.

Chapter 14

Digital Date and Timestamps (1)

Introduction

> Timestamp shall ensure that a computerized system time/date stamp security, not to be tampered with, and the establishment of procedures and maintenance procedures to ensure that the time GXP activities in the areas covered by / date synchronization.
>
> **NAPA (former CFDA) Data Integrity Guidance, December 2020**

In digital environments, a timestamp is an e-record enclosing the time of occurrence of an event. Time-stamping (2) refers to the use of an electronic timestamp to provide an order among a set of events.

The US FDA specifies that recording time is a critical component in documenting a sequence of events. Within a given manufacturing batch, several events and operator actions may take place, and without recording time, documentation of those events would be incomplete (3).

Besides, timestamps are used during the creation of audit trails. These timestamps allow for reconstruction of the course of events relating to the creation, modification, and deletion of e-records.

Time-stamping e-records is a key service that supports, if properly controlled, non-repudiation of transactions and adds integrity to e-records.

System Clock

As part of the controls to e-records integrity, the system clock or networked master clock provides the date and timestamps required for e-records and e-signatures. Typically, the networked master clock is placed in the time server.

An accurate system clock is a necessary condition for the reliability of manufacturing-related e-records; it is, therefore, necessary to guarantee the correct time sequence for all the e-records as the basis for all decisions that impact the quality of manufacturing products.

E-records to be time-stamped are those loaded in database structures during the insertion or immediately after an update.

Date and time stamps or timestamps create a notation that indicates, at least, the precise date and time of an action. It is recognized as a valuable service that supports the non-repudiation of transactions.

An accurate system clock is a necessary condition for the consistency of the related information; it is, therefore, an element to assure the reliability of all the e-records.

Timestamps add integrity and trust to messages and records sent through a network. Therefore, as part of the e-records controls, unauthorized modifications to the system clock and time drift (4) between servers must be prevented (2).

Refer to https://www.fda.gov/ICECI/EnforcementActions/WarningLetters/2017/ucm563067.htm. It accounts for a WL report containing an observation that includes unauthorized access and manipulation of the system clock.

When writing an application program, the programmer is usually provided with a time-stamping service that the operating system provides, if required, during the execution of the application.

Computer Clock Reliability

The reliability of the system's date and time can be achieved by synchronizing:

- The networked master clock with a reliable source
- All networked computer clocks using the master clock

In addition to the above synchronization practices, the reliability of the system clock is enhanced by maintaining programs to verify the correct functionality of the master and networked computer clocks.

A time server accomplishes the above two functions by reading the actual time from a reference clock and distributing this information to its clients using a computer network.

Supplementary controls to create reliable computer clocks can be found under "Computer Clock Controls."

Digital Time-Stamping Service (2)

Supporting time controls include an infrastructure that supports time-stamping from a trusted time, such as the coordinated universal. This technology, which in some cases is compliant with X.509 (Public Key Infrastructure Certificate and Certificate Revocation List (CRL) Profile), is linked with a time-calibration service. Applications or computer logs may require time-stamping services on the server.

One of many time-stamping services is the digital time-stamping service (DTS). DTS issues a secure timestamp, which includes the time, a hash of the digital information being time-stamped, and a time certification that can be used for digital signatures. A message digest is produced from the record and sent to the DTS. The DTS sends back the timestamp, as well as the date and time the timestamp was received, with a secure signature. The signature proves that the document existed on the stated date. The document contents remain unknown to the DTS – only the digest is known. The DTS must use lengthy keys because the timestamp may be required for many years.

DTS and digital certificates provide the mechanism to authenticate the source (device checks) of the timestamp in the audit trails and electronic signatures. Access-right lists and digital certificates can be used to control access to the DTS.

The certificate server and client clocks must remain synchronized as closely as possible. Kerberos (5) recommended maximum tolerance settings for computer clock synchronization is 5 minutes. Kerberos uses timestamps to determine the validity of entities' authentication requests and to help prevent replay attacks.

Periodic coordination between the service and the local computer clock is expected, as well as limiting access to the computer date and time local function. The local computer date and time function must not be accessed by users.

Time Zone

The timestamp should be expressed in a form that indicates its frame of reference so that timestamps are universally comparable, apart from different time zones and seasonal adjustments. It allows for the discerning of the timing of one activity in relation to another (e.g., time zone).

ISO 8601, *Data elements and interchange formats – Information interchange – Representation of dates and times*, can be implemented to avoid misinterpretation of the signing date and time representation, resulting in confusion and other consequential errors or losses of the time across national boundaries.

Computer Systems Not Networked

In case of systems not connected, a process for the manual updating of the clock for equipment that performs time-stamping of production e-records must be implemented. This process must cover the preventive maintenance and updates in case of recovery of the system.

Computer Clock Controls

Controls should be established to ensure that the system's date and time are reliable in all computers connected to the local network.

Some of the critical controls are:

- Maintenance procedural controls are established to ensure the accurate synchronization of time and date to regulated activities.
- Alteration of the time server used to synchronize all networked computer clocks to record timed events is controlled and limited for modifications to authorized personnel.
- All changes to the time server are recorded.
- The timing of one activity is discerned in relation to another (e.g., time zone controls).
- The unit of time must be meaningful in terms of documenting human actions. The unit of time must be specified in the requirements document.

- Timestamps should be implemented with a clear understanding of time zones in systems that extend across different time zones. The time zone references must be specified in the requirements document.

Regulatory Agencies' Expectations

1. The system clock should be synchronized with the clock of connected systems and access restricted to authorized personnel. (PI 041-1, "*Good Practices for Data Management and Integrity in Regulated GMP/GDP Environment*," Pharmaceutical Inspection Co-operation Scheme (PIC/S), November 2018 (Draft 3))
2. Operators shall be not allowed to change the time reference and/or the time zone. (Russia Federal State Institute of Drugs and Good Practices (SIDGP)), "Data Integrity & Computer System Validation Guideline," September 2018 (Draft)

References

1. López, O., "Digital Date and Time Stamps," In: *Pharmaceutical and Medical Devices Computer Systems Validation*. (Routledge/Productivity Press, New York, NY, 1st ed., 2018). pp 201–205.
2. López, O., "Overview of Technologies Supporting Security Requirements in 21 CFR Part 11 – Part II," Pharmaceutical Technology, March 2002.
3. US FDA, "21 CFR Part 11 - Electronic Records; Electronic Signatures; Final Rule – Preamble," Comment 74, March 1997.
4. Time drift is when two or more servers do not have identical times. The discrepancy can vary from seconds to minutes and can become extensive if left unchecked.
5. Kerberos (http://www.isi.edu/gost/info/Kerberos/) is an industry-standard authentication system suitable for distributed computing using a public network.

Additional Readings

Information Security Committee American Bar Association (ABA), "Digital Signature Guidelines," August 1996.

ISO 8601:2004, "Data Elements and Interchange Formats – Information Interchange – Representation of Dates and Times."

US FDA, "Guidance for Industry - Computerized Systems Used in Clinical Investigations," May 2007.
US FDA, "Guidance for Industry – 21 CFR Part 11; Electronic Records; Electronic Signatures, Time Stamps," February 2002 (obsoleted).

Chapter 15

E-records Migration and Its Integrity

Introduction

During their lifecycle, e-records and their metadata may be migrated from one electronic storage device or location to another, as their activity decreases and/or their use changes (1).

E-records migration is the process of transferring e-records and related metadata from one electronic storage device, format, or computer system to another (2). E-records migration is usually performed programmatically to accomplish a comprehensive migration.

The aging of the durable storage is not necessarily measured in years but in terms of storage capabilities and usefulness.

Changes in factors that affect how reliably an e-record can preserve and present information might not always be readily apparent. Examples of such changes include, but are not limited to, the following:

- Moving from one type of record storage media to a different one
- Installing a new version of an application or operating system software program
- Retirement of computer systems
- Website consolidation
- Server maintenance
- Data center relocation
- Media deterioration or obsolescence
- Moving from one electronic file format to another

The outcome of the migration process should be, as much as possible, the "true copy" attributes of the original e-records set.

Migration Process

Before any e-record can be migrated, it is important to identify differences between the current and the future environment, and how these environments might affect the reliability of the migrated e-record. Also, precautions should be taken for the end of lifecycle data migration.

> If data are transferred to another data format or system, validation should include checks that data are not altered in value and/or meaning during this migration process.
>
> **EU Annex 11 p4.8**

The migration of e-records to new media as technology advances would need to be considered by the regulated entity.

The objective of the verification of the migration is the completeness and integrity of the e-records. Where migration with full original data functionality is not technically possible, options should be assessed based on the risk and the importance of the data over time.

The e-records and associated metadata must not be altered during the migration. There should be an audit trail for this process. Appropriate quality procedures should be followed, including an investigation, if the operation has not occurred correctly.

E-records migration needs to be verified after concluding the migration process to ensure that migrated e-records have the same information as the original, including metadata. Metadata includes records that describe the context, content, and structure of the e-record migrated. The challenges of migrating data are often underestimated, particularly regarding maintaining the full meaning of the migrated records.

The verification should include corroboration that e-records are not altered in value, meaning, structure, context and links (e.g., audit trails and metadata), and/or meaning during this migration process.

As soon the verification is completed, a team of data subject manner experts (SME) must perform a more comprehensive set of tests between the data sets and the application interfacing with the data sets to assess and accept the new system before the regulated users start using the migrated e-records set.

The e-records quality assessment process should involve verification that the data complies with standards and is complete; that duplicate contents are detected and eliminated; that data quality checks to confirm expected data quality levels, completeness, and conformity are conducted; that files not relevant to current or future business processes are discarded; and, if applicable, that a master data file is created. Refer to Chapter 23, "Introduction to Data Quality."

The e-records migration process should be explained in a Data Migration Strategy document. This document provides an overview of the data migration process involved in the implementation. This document describes the migration activities necessary for the migration project. This document shall form the basis for all data migration activities.

It should be used as a statistically relevant sample to verify the migration process.

Automated Migration (2)

The data migration effort may involve the use of software tools to automate some or all the extraction, transformation, loading, and verification activities. The tools must be fit for the intended use.

When a software tool is used to make an identical copy of an e-record, the software typically has a built-in error checking mechanism to help ensure that the copy is, in fact, a true copy.

The rigor of tool specification and verification activities must be commensurate with associated risks. This automated migration verification provides objective evidence that the data migration software tools are fit for the intended use and provides a level of confidence in the overall migration process. A typical approach during this step is to work with a relatively small amount of data, which can later be completely verified to assure that no data errors occurred.

Checklist for Data Migration

The following checklist provides action items to verify that the migrated e-records do not loose accuracy, conformity, validity, consistency, reliability, and completeness.

- Are the migrated e-records accurate, conforming to standards, valid, consistent, reliable, and complete?

- Do the migrated e-records show a reliable representation of events, e-record, and actions as required?
- Do the migrated e-records show, as applicable, the identification of people and signatures as appropriate?
- Is it able to reconstruct from the migrated e-records who did what, when, and how; production values and conditions; and study observations and findings?
- Does the metadata associated with the e-record being migrated still provide the context, meaning, and security attributes to the migrated e-records?
- Does the new hardware, as applicable, that is being used in any way affect the reliability of information preserved and presented?
- Does the new software, as applicable, that is being used maintain the same level of reliability as the old system?
- Are the audit trails, links between signatures, and e-records associated with the record being preserved and transferred as appropriate?
- Are the associated audit trails of the migrated e-records incorporated in the migration process?
- Is the ability to search, sort, and process information in the migrated e-record available as in the old system?

Regulatory Agencies' Expectations

Data transfer should be verified. The data should not be altered during or after it is transferred to the worksheet or other application. There should be an audit trail for this process. Appropriate Quality procedures should be followed if the data transfer during the operation has not occurred correctly (3).

A tracking feature is needed to record the change of location both for ease of access and to meet regulatory requirements (1).

References

1. Interchange of Data between Administrations (IDA), "Model Requirements for the Management of Electronic Records", www.cornwell.co.uk/moreq.html, October 2002.
2. Russia Federal State Institute of Drugs and Good Practices (SIDGP), "Data Integrity & Computer System Validation Guideline," September 2018 (Draft).
3. MHRA, "GxP Data Integrity Guidance and Definitions", March 2018.

Chapter 16

Ensuring E-records Integrity of Cloud Service Providers (1)

Introduction

A cloud service provider (2) is a company that offers some component of cloud computing, typically Infrastructure as a Service (IaaS), Software as a Service (SaaS), Platform as a Service (PaaS), Backup as a Service (BaaS), or Data as a Service (DaaS), to other businesses or individuals. Oracle recently made 10 predictions of cloud and they said that "80% of all enterprise (and mission-critical) workloads will move to the cloud by 2025" (3).

The above sample services are been integrated in a single integrated infrastructure of computing, storage, and networking.

XaaS is an all-purpose term that refers to the delivery of anything as a service. It recognizes the vast number of products, tools, and technologies that vendors now deliver to users as a service over a network, typically the internet, rather than provide locally or on-site within an enterprise.

In a typical IT setting, the regulated entity buys IT equipment (hardware and/or software) and manages the equipment by itself. In this setting, e-records integrity includes prevention of loss, alterations, and erasure of e-records. These controls are extended to the creation, transmission, processing, and storage of data. It also controls who is authorized and/or able to write, change, or access e-records. Security procedural control provides the process and consistency to comply with the e-records integrity controls.

The same principles are applicable in SaaS, BaaS, and DaaS environments.

This chapter provides the activities which the regulated entity and the cloud service provider must implement to safeguard the integrity of e-records.

As any setting of a XaaS, the most important elements to ensure e-records integrity through the e-records lifecycle are the cloud service requirements, the selection of the provider matching the service requirements, the SLA to understand roles and responsibilities, and the periodic audits to verify the fulfillment of the SLA and other contractual agreements.

Cloud Service Requirements (4)

The intent of the cloud service requirements is establishing project criteria to identify the cloud regulated entity needs (5) and associated requirements, criteria to evaluate and accept of requirements, and ensure through an analysis or review process that the established criteria are met.

> Cloud computing services are to be treated as a contracted service, with risks identified and addressed, and responsibilities clearly outlined in a contract or service agreement.
>
> **Health Canada GMP Guideline (GUI-0001), February 2018.**

Some requirements to be taken into consideration are:

- Access control

To avoid intrusion into computer systems, physical and/or logical controls must be established, enabling access to authorized persons only (6). The level of access controls to a system includes infrastructure and applications levels.

For those users allowed to access a computer system, the precise access level to the applications and resources must be assigned based on an authorization level per his field of work.

In all moments, the creation, change, and cancellation of access authorizations and the level of authorization must be documented (7).

Procedures for granting these rights should be defined.

- Data management and regulatory compliance

Enterprise cloud service regulated users expect cloud service providers to indicate with which national and international policies and regulations they comply.

The cloud provider should ensure that the provided service complies with data protection and data privacy regulation, as applicable. Where data is transferred across international borders, especially in the case of non-anonymized personal data, the national, regional, and international regulation for data protection and privacy should be respected.

- Monitoring

All cloud services need to be monitored. This includes cloud infrastructure and network access but also deployed services and applications. This is, for instance, required for supervising the agreed level of service quality agreement as defined in SLA and to trigger corrective actions if required, but also for cost control, chargebacks, and provisioning.

- Network access

Networks allow the sharing of information and resources within, and between, the regulated entity and cloud service provider computing environments.

The interface between the regulated entity and the cloud service provider may be via the network of networks, the internet. This infrastructure must be monitored to ensure the trustworthiness of the information shared.

Mitigation of this threat can be performed using the Hash Message Authentication Code or Secure Sockets Layer (SSL) protocol for assurance of the integrity of transmitted data.

It must be guaranteed that unauthorized third parties cannot access company computer systems via data transmission lines and networks.

- Management and governance

Governance is a collection of written procedures that are directed by a strong management commitment with the power to implement and enforce these procedures. It ensures that strategy, policies, and procedures are consistently implemented, and that required processes are correctly followed.

Governance includes defining roles and responsibilities, measuring and reporting, and taking actions to resolve any issues identified.

The e-records governance refers to an organizational structure that includes written policies and procedures documenting processes to prevent and detect situations that may have an impact on e-records integrity.

The regulated entity and the cloud service provider must have an approved data governance document and must be, as much as possible, consistent.

- Security

Security covers, as applicable, confidentiality, integrity, availability, authenticity, accountability, and non-repudiation.

Security-related requirements include:

- Physical
- Network
- Hosting
- Web
- Cryptographic

For details, refer to http://kambing.ui.ac.id/onnopurbo/library/library-ref-eng/ref-eng-3/network/network-security/sans/template/asp_standards.pdf

Security can, for instance, map to and concern one or more of the following areas:

- Data protection (and information classification, data encryption, and so on)
- Data access
- Identity management

- Authorization
- Authentication
- Data privacy
- Data integrity
- Accessibility
- Operations

The cloud service provider should describe the levels of data security, confidentiality, integrity, and availability, including data backup, and the means the cloud service provider employs to deliver these levels of data security (e.g., through certifications to be listed). Relevant operational details are of interest, including any antivirus and anti-malware protection as well as network intrusion detection and prevention.

- Interoperability

Interoperability is closely related to portability. It involves software and data simultaneously active in more than one cloud infrastructure, interacting to serve a common purpose.

- Portability and deployment

Portability, in general, refers to the ability to migrate applications between different clouds. This is required to allow customers of cloud services to avoid the situation of being locked into a specific cloud infrastructure provider, and to run an application in the cloud.

Reducing the mismatch between different cloud infrastructure systems would not only enable a competitive market but also enable new business models where different cloud infrastructures can be traded according to price and demand.

- Reversibility

Once the regulated entity has engaged with a cloud solution provider, it is extremely difficult to change provider. Each cloud solution provider uses a proprietary set of interfaces and data formats. Opening this market requires standardization, at the level of architecture, building blocks, and system level. Therefore, there is a need for standardization.

The regulated entity should be able to retrieve all or part of their data on demand and without special action on the part of the cloud service provider. The regulated entity should be able to select data and filter specific items of interest.

If the regulated entity cannot retrieve data, as a minimum the provider should be contractually bound to give the data back in a defined period, with significant penalties (specified in the SLA).

- SLAs

Refer elsewhere in this chapter.

- Lifecycle Management

The cloud service provider must manage the lifecycle of applications and documents. This need includes versioning of applications and the retention and destruction of data. There are substantial legal liabilities if certain data is no longer available. Some of this material may be stored in cloud services, so there is a need for clear specification of how the lifecycle of information is managed.

This covers data retention, including resilience and availability. Besides, in some cases, the regulated entity will want to make sure data is destroyed at some point, consistent with applicable regulation and corporate policy.

Selection of the Cloud Service Provider

Where the regulated user chooses to outsource cloud computing, the regulated user shall ensure control and hold responsibility for the suitability and operability over such computer-related services. Control of such outsourced computer-related services shall be identified within the quality management system (8) and a clear statement of the responsibilities of the cloud service provider shall be devised. The statement of responsibilities is defined in a formal quality agreement (e.g., SLA).

Such regulated user control over the cloud service provider is established by defining clear requirements of the regulated entity, comprehensive selection of the cloud service provider, all-inclusive SLA between the regulated entity and the cloud service provider, and periodic evaluation of the cloud service providers. Refer to Figure 16.1.

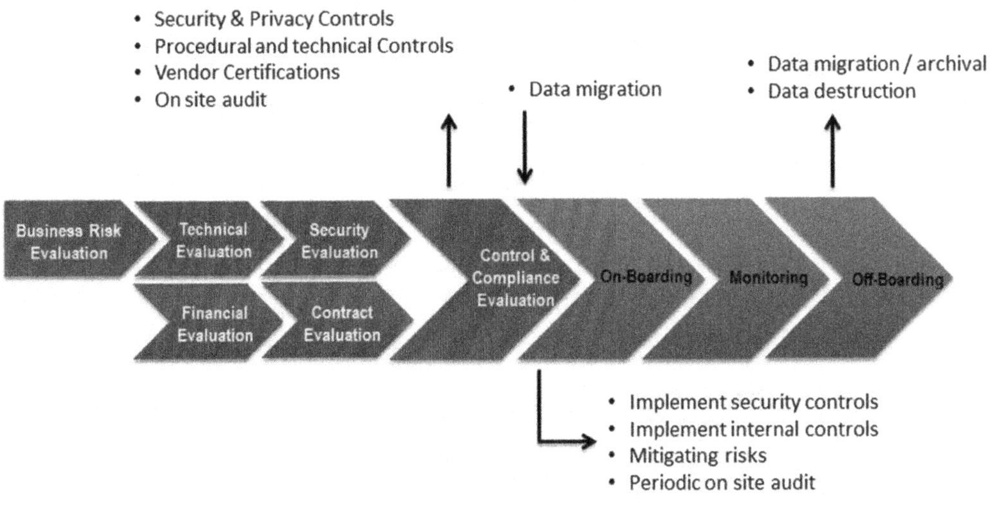

Figure 16.1 Cloud project implementation.

Implement a Cloud Governance Policy to establish a standard and effective cloud SLC. This SLC contains your approach to the selection, integration, ongoing management, and subsequent decommissioning of cloud-based services.

The Cloud Governance Policy points to procedures and records that indicate how and on what basis (e.g., risk assessment and requirements) the cloud service provider is evaluated and selected (PIC/S PI-011-3-11.2), the tools for assessing fitness for purpose against predetermined requirements, specifications, and anticipated risks, and periodic reviews to assess if the cloud service is maintained and operated following the specified requirements and quality agreement. How to add new services and how these services are developed, qualified/validated and deployed must be part of this evaluation.

The evaluation may consist of technical capabilities, security-related evaluation, and procedural and technical control evaluations. Other critical evaluations are financial and contract.

Service Level Agreement

Figure 16.2 (9) depicts the outsourced tasks to a cloud service provider based on the types of services.

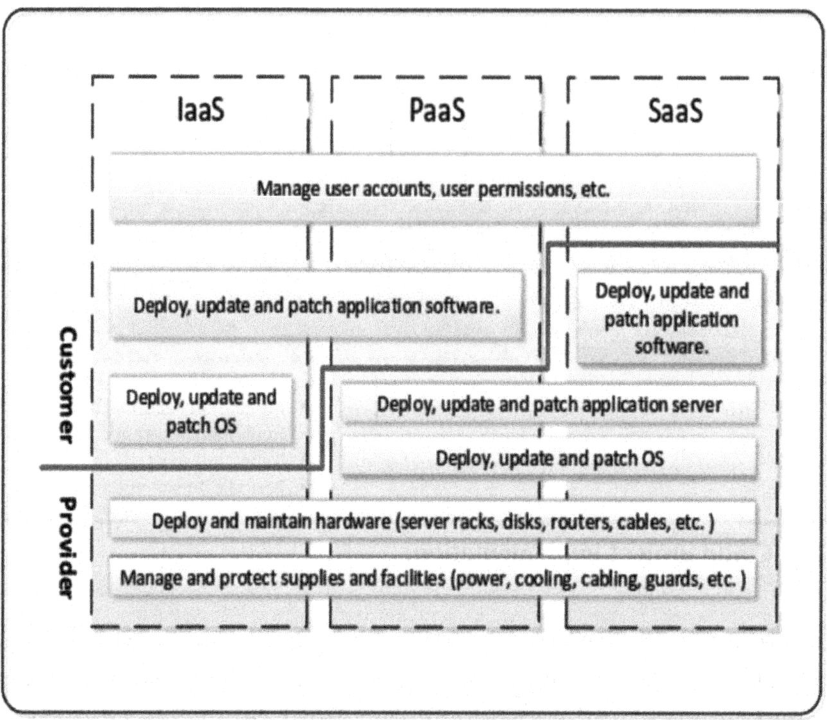

Figure 16.2 Outsourced tasks based on the type of service.

The expectation and responsibilities of both users and providers of cloud services of the outsourced task are described in an SLA.

It specifies the function performed by the service, the agreed-upon bounds of performance, the obligations on both parties to the contract, and how any deviations are to be handled. An SLA is made in a business context and therefore will include all aspects of the interaction between the provider and the regulated entity relevant to the service.

The obligations of the provider are described in the contract the two parties countersign; the contract should address SLA issues, jurisdiction, liability, indemnity, and so on. The contract needs to be negotiated carefully and fully understood especially by SMEs.

Customers should assess the risk of outages caused by administrative or legal issues and assess whether security measures need to be taken to mitigate this risk. Cloud customers should also check the SLA which should guarantee the availability of their service.

All critical elements important for the cloud customer must be part of the SLA and understood by the cloud service provider. The cloud service provider must commit to compliance with these requirements.

Periodic Audits

The regulated entity must perform periodic audits as part of their vendor assurance program. These audits must consider the management of e-records integrity as part of the overall cloud service provider's E-records Integrity Governance.

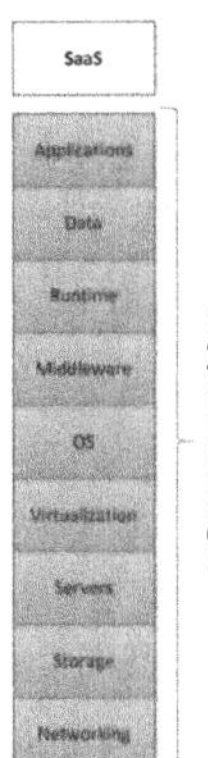

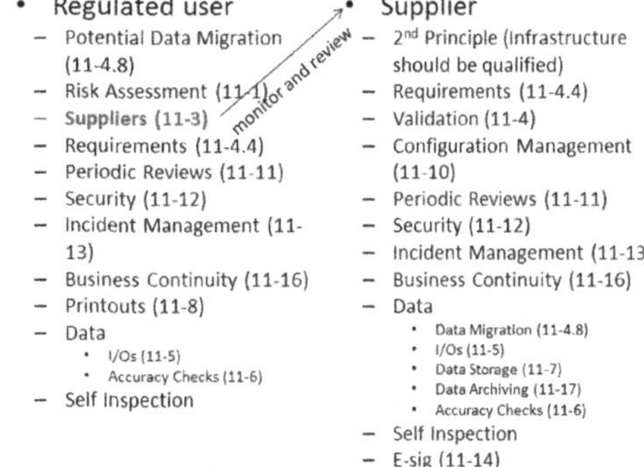

E-records Migration

E-records migration is the process of transferring e-records between storage types, formats, or computer systems. It is a key consideration for any system implementation, upgrade, or consolidation. E-records migration is usually performed programmatically to achieve an automated migration, freeing up human resources from tedious tasks. E-records migration occurs for a variety of reasons, including server or storage equipment replacements or upgrades; website consolidation; server maintenance; and data center relocation.

If e-records are transferred to another format or system, the verification of the e-records migration should include corroboration that e-records are not altered in value, meaning, structure, context and links (e.g., audit trails), and/or meaning

E-records Accessibility

Access to e-records should be ensured throughout the retention period (EU Annex 11 p7.1).

The integrity of e-records stored in the cloud server must be ensured by the following methods:

- Access permissions must be assigned properly by cloud customer and cloud service provider based on "need to have," "need to know," and "minimum possible access level" principles.

- The cloud service provider must run the technical infrastructure in line with good IT practices. The cloud environment must be properly secured and that includes professional patch management, malware protection, intrusion detection and prevention, and so on.

If these e-records need to be transferred, the integrity of the e-records is ensured by using strong data encryption. It will increase the regulated entity confidence in cloud services.

Regulatory Agencies' Expectation

Where external or third-party facilities are utilized for the archiving of data, these service providers should be subject to assessment, and all responsibilities recorded in a quality technical agreement (e.g., SLA). Due consideration has been given to ensuring the integrity of records in the electronic storage device.

Summary (10)

- Data integrity requirements should be incorporated into the company's contractor/vendor qualification/assurance program and associated procedures.
- In addition to having their data governance systems, regulated companies outsourcing activities should verify the adequacy of comparable systems at the contract acceptor. The contract acceptor should apply equivalent levels of control to those applied by the contract giver.
- Formal assessment of the contract acceptors competency and compliance in this regard should be conducted in the first instance before the approval of a contractor, and thereafter verified periodically at an appropriate frequency based on risk.

References

1. López, O., "Trustworthy Computer Systems," *Journal of GxP Compliance*, 19(2), July 2015.
2. Service provider – An organization supplying services to one or more internal or external customers. (ITIL Service Design, 2011 Edition).

3. Erickson, J., "Prediction: 80% Of Enterprise IT Will Move To The Cloud By 2025," *Forbes*, Chapter 5, February 2019. (https://www.forbes.com/sites/oracle/2019/02/07/prediction-80-of-enterprise-it-will-move-to-the-cloud-by-2025/#39f100b92a67).
4. ETSI, "CLOUD; Cloud Private-Sector User Recommendations," November 2011.
5. ETSI, "Identification of Cloud User Needs," ETSI SR 003 381 V2.1.1, February 2016.
6. "Section C.02.005 Item 15 in the Computer Systems GMP Guidelines for API in Canada's GUI-0104," December 2013.
7. "Article 579 Item 2 in the Resolution of the Executive Board No. 17, Brazilian GMPs," April 2010.
8. ISO 9001, Quality Management Systems – Requirements (Section 4.1).
9. European Union Agency for Network and Information Security (ENISA), "Cloud Security Guide for SMEs," April 2015.
10. Cuddy, B., "EMA's Guidance on Data Integrity," In: *Presented at the Indian Pharmaceutical Alliance Annual Congress*, Mumbai, India, 23–24 February 2017.

Additional Readings

Cloud Service Alliance, "Cloud Control Matrix, Rev 3.0.1," July 2014.

Cloud Service Alliance, "Security Guidance for Critical Areas of Focus in Cloud Computing Reviews 3.0," November 2011.

US FDA, "Guidance for Industry: Contract Manufacturing Arrangements for Drugs: Quality Agreements," November 2016.

ECA, "Ensuring the Data Integrity of Cloud Service Providers," https://www.it-compliance-group.org/icg_news_7259.html, August 2019.

ECA IT Compliance Working Group, "Shared Platform and Cloud Services Implications for Information Governance and Records Management," http://www.it-compliance-group.org/icg_downloads.html.

EU, "EudraLex The Rules Governing Medicinal Products in the European Union Volume 4 EU Guidelines for Good Manufacturing Practice for Medicinal Products for Human and Veterinary Use Chapter 7 Outsourced Activities," January 2013.

Chapter 17

E-records Integrity in Hybrid Systems

Introduction

E-records may exist in hybrid forms, some elements in electronic format and others paper-based. Hybrid systems include combinations of paper records (or other non-electronic media) and e-records, paper records and electronic signatures, or handwritten signatures executed to e-records.

Paper and e-records and signature components can co-exist (i.e., a hybrid situation) if predicate rule requirements are met and the content and meaning of those records are preserved.

In this chapter, only e-records signed with handwritten signatures will be discussed. This arrangement must be designed to ensure that the regulated requirements are met (1).

E-records Signed with Handwritten Signatures

A hybrid approach may be used to sign e-records when the system lacks features for electronic signatures.

To execute a handwritten signature to an e-record, a simple means to do so would be to create a single-page controlled form, associated with the written procedures for system use and data review, that would list the electronic dataset reviewed and any metadata subject to review, and that would provide fields for the author, reviewer, and/or approver of the dataset to apply a handwritten signature.

These paper printouts of original e-records from computer systems may be useful as summary reports if the requirements for original e-records are also met. To rely upon these printed summaries of results for future decision-making, a second person would review the original e-records and any relevant metadata, such as audit trails, to verify that the printed summary is representative of all results. This verification would then be documented, and the printout could be used for subsequent decision-making.

This paper record with the handwritten signatures should then be securely and traceably linked to the electronic dataset (e-dataset), either through procedural means, such as the use of detailed archives indexes, or through technical means, such as embedding a certified true copy scanned image of the signature page into the e-dataset. The hybrid approach is likely to be more difficult than a fully electronic approach.

Relationships and control measures for data and records handling need to be stated in a procedural control for both hybrid and homogenous systems. Specifically, the procedural control must contain detail around the interaction between the manual and the computer system. Accuracy checks are an important part of this interface (EU Annex 11 p6).

As an example (2):

- Manual input of manually generated data into computer systems
- Transcription (including manual) of data generated by the computer systems onto paper records
- Automated detection and transcription of printed data into computer systems

Applicable quality risk management principles should be followed when assessing, defining, and demonstrating the effectiveness of control measures applied to the hybrid system.

As part of the system description, it should be documented what constitutes the whole data set and all records that are defined by the data set should be reviewed and retained. As part of the system description, it shall be identified from where the raw data comes.

Where hybrid records are stored, references between physical and e-records must be maintained such that full verification of events is possible throughout the retention period.

Increased data review is expected to be required for hybrid systems because they are vulnerable to non-attributable data changes.

Regulatory Agencies' Expectations

Where hybrid systems are used, what constitutes the whole data set should be clearly documented and all records that are defined by the data set should be reviewed and retained (3).

Hybrid systems are accepted if they provide adequate level of control.

In the case of the example explained in this chapter, Section 21 CFR Part 11.70, Signature/record linking, defines the linkage between e-records signed by a handwritten signature. Handwritten signatures executed to e-records must be linked to their respective e-records to ensure that the signatures cannot be removed, copied, or otherwise transferred to change an e-record by conventional means.

References

1. EudraLex, "The Rules Governing Medicinal Products in the European Union Volume 4, Good Manufacturing Practice, Medicinal Products for Human and Veterinary Use, Chapter 4: Documentation," June 2011.
2. Pharmaceutical Inspection Convention (PIC/S), "Good Practices for Data Management and Integrity PI 041–1 DRAFT 3," November 2018.
3. MHRA, "GxP Data Integrity Guidance and Definitions," March 2018.

Chapter 18

Technologies Supporting E-records Integrity (1)

Introduction

An expectation pertinent to the computer systems performing regulated functions is the integrity (2) in e-records (3). This expectation takes the highest priority in the CGMPs of health agencies worldwide and the foundation of the CGMPs. The electronic information properly recorded and managed is the basis, for example, for manufacturers to assure competent authority in the product identity, strengths, purity, and safety (4). The e-records also demonstrate that the regulated entity computer systems adhere to the CGMPs, including instructions.

All operations with e-records should be performed in a secure environment. This requirement applies to e-records creation, while in transit, in storage, and during processing (5).

Any unauthorized modification to e-records during the creation, while in transit, in the repository, or processing operation, including modifications made with a malicious intent, unexpected hardware failure, and human error, is considered a failure of e-records integrity.

To assure the integrity of e-records, the computer systems managing e-records, the repositories holding such records, and the communication of related infrastructure must be, essentially, trustworthy (6). The computer system must execute the intended function free from unauthorized e-record manipulations.

E-records integrity is a critical aspect to be well thought out during the design, implementation, and usage of any system which stores, processes, or retrieves e-records. It should be adopted as a quality-by-design approach. Refer to Chapter 22. The system design must make provisions such that original e-records cannot be deleted and for the retention of audit trails reflecting changes to original e-records. Security must be built into the infrastructure and the applications (7) managing the creation, storage, archiving, modifying, and/or transmit e-records. Another example is the communication security through an open link, such as the internet, which can be reinforced by using controls such as encryption processes.

The quality-by-design approach supports e-records integrity. The idea of "data integrity/quality by design" (DIQbD) is something that aligns with the computer-related quality processes such as the EU Annex 11, ICH Q7, US FDA 21 CFR 211.68, and many more. To implement the applicable regulations appropriately, the regulated user must understand the:

- Required e-records
- Criticality of the e-records to the patient
- Collection method and processing
- Risk of the e-record integrity
- Technical and procedural controls required

Based on the intended use of the system, each of the requirements establishing management of e-records integrity must be documented and the associated risks assessed before implementing the e-records integrity technical and procedural controls. The validation process provides an ideal framework for documenting the e-records integrity lifecycle (8).

Centered on information security (9), this chapter provides a broad overview of the cryptographic (10) technologies that can keep e-records integrity for any CGMP-regulated activity (11).

The following sections describe cryptographic algorithms such as e-records encryption, digital signatures (12), and services family (e.g., Virtual Private Network (13)). These are the set of cryptographic tools and techniques ensuring the integrity and validity of the information throughout the e-records lifecycle (14).

In the context of e-records integrity, the statement that a cryptographic algorithm provides data integrity means that the algorithm is used to detect unauthorized alterations (5).

Cryptographic tools, access control, and authority checks to computer resources; audit trails controls; authentication; security of the electronic signatures; signature-e-records linkage; time controls; uniqueness of the electronic signatures; and integrity and privacy of e-records in transit are some of the technical controls in which the e-records can be protected. The applicable level of control may be a result of the criticality of the e-records and associated risks. Only within the control of business needs and risks can management define security (15). Risks to be considered are, for example, the degree to which e-records or the system generating or using the e-records can be configured, and therefore potentially manipulated (16).

Cryptographic Technologies

Cryptographic mechanisms are often used to protect the integrity and confidentiality of data that is sensitive, has a high value, or is vulnerable to unauthorized disclosure or undetected modification during transmission or while in storage (17).

The following paragraphs contain a simplified depiction of cryptographic technologies (18) supporting e-records integrity.

Hashing refers to the process of computing a condensed message or record of any length to a string of a fixed length with the use of a one-way mathematical function so that one cannot retrieve the message from the hash (Figure 18.1). The output of a hashing or hash value is called a message digest. The probability that two different e-records will generate the same hash value is 1 in 10^{87}. Consequently, a hash value is unique and has a low probability of collisions providing a digital identifier for each e-record. A minor change in a message will result in a change to the hash value.

Because hashing is a one-way function and the output of the function has a low probability of collisions, it can be used with a cryptographic product or services family for authentication, non-repudiation, and e-records integrity. Hashing also is a key element in the Digital Signature Algorithm (DSA).

An example of a hashing algorithm data integrity mechanism in cryptography is the use of Race Integrity Primitives Evaluation Message Digest

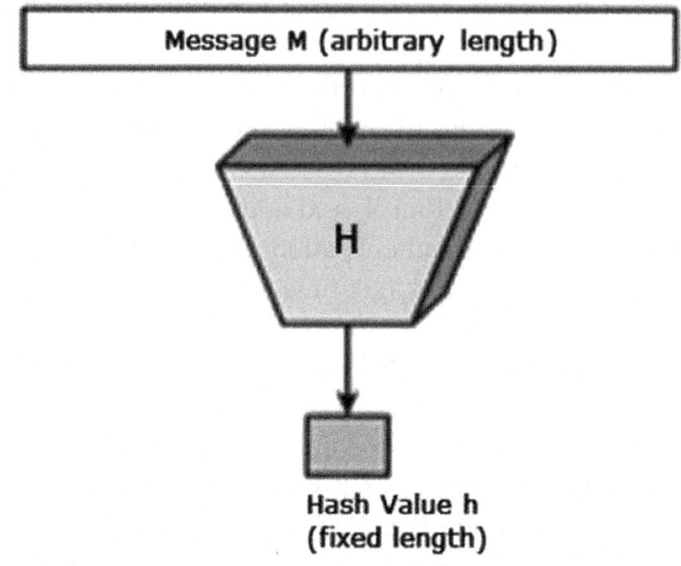

Figure 18.1 Hashing.

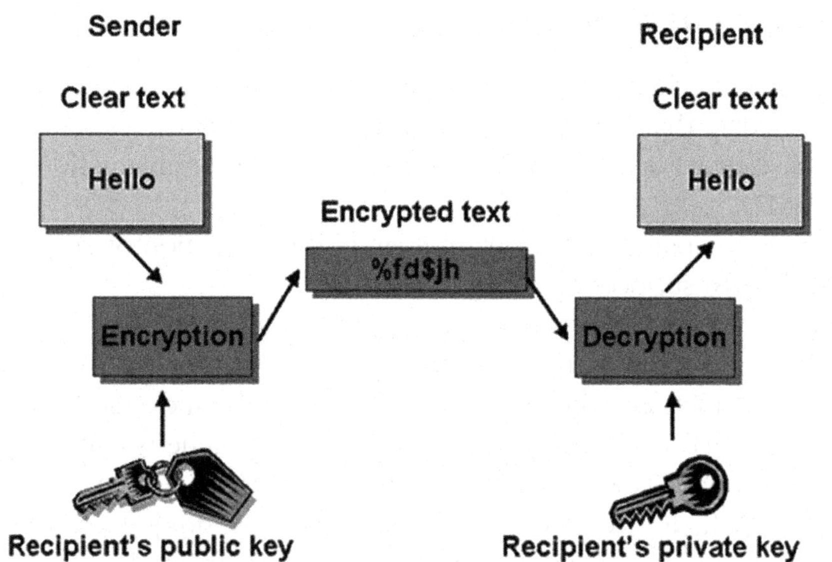

Figure 18.2 Encryption.

(RIPEMD), which is a family of cryptographic hash functions. RIPEMD-160 has not been broken. As the name implies, RIPEMD-160 produces a hash digest of 160 bits (20 bytes) (see Figure 18.2).

Encryption refers to the process of scrambling input clear text or records, called the plaintext, with a user-specified password (password-based encryption algorithm) or key (secret-key algorithm) to generate an encrypted text or output called a ciphertext. No one can recover the original plaintext from a ciphertext in a reasonable amount of time without the user-specified password or key. The algorithms that combine the user-specified password or key and plaintext are called *cyphers*. Encryption most often is used to protect the privacy of messages or e-records.

The data encryption standard (DES) was once a predominant symmetric-key algorithm (19) for the encryption of e-records. It was highly influential in the advancement of modern cryptography in the academic world.

DES is now considered to be uncertain for many applications primarily due to the 56-bit key size being too small. In January 1999, the DES key was broken in 22 hours. There are also results which demonstrate speculative weaknesses in the ciphertext, although they are undetectable to mount in practice. The algorithm is believed to be practically secure in the form of Triple DES, although there are theoretical attacks. In recent years, the ciphertext has been superseded by the Advanced Encryption Standard (AES).

AES is used by the US government to protect classified information and is implemented in software and hardware throughout the world to encrypt sensitive e-records. It was published by NIST as the US FIPS PUB 197. The AES became effective as a federal government standard in 2002. It is also part of the ISO/IEC 18033-3 standard which specifies block cyphers for e-records confidentiality.

The following table compares the encryption strength as determined by a key length in bits (20) of the above-referenced encryption algorithms.

Factor	*AES*	*Triple DES*	*DES*
Key length	128, 192, or 256 bits	(k1, k2, and k3) 168 bits (k1 and k2 is the same) 112 bits	56 bits
The time required to check all possible keys at 50 billion keys per second	For a 128-bite key: 5 × 10^{21} years	For a 112-bit key: 800 days	22 hours

Public-key infrastructure (PKI) is the combination of software, encryption technologies, server platforms, workstations, policies, and services used to administer public-key certificates (21) – credentials issued by a trusted authority – and public- or private-key sets.

PKI enables regulated entities to protect the security of their communications and business transactions on networks. PKI is used to secure e-mails, web browsers, virtual private networks (VPNs), and end applications.

In a traditional PKI design, a certification authority (CA) is a trusted party that guarantees the authenticity of the entity in question by confirming the integrity of the public-key value in a certificate. The CA issues and manages, from a certificate server, security credentials and public keys for message encryption and decryption. The CA notarizes public keys by digitally signing public-key certificates using the CA's private key and links to entities. An entity, which is a person, server, organization, account, or site, can present a public-key certificate to prove its identity or its right to access information. It links a public-key value to a set of information that identifies the entity associated with the use of the corresponding private key. This entity is known as the *subject* of the certificate. Certificates are authenticated, issued, managed, and digitally signed by a trusted third party, the CA.

A certificate server is a repository for public-key certificates. End applications that are PKI-enabled verify the validity and access privileges of a certificate by checking the certificate's profile status protected in the repository. The certificate server provides services for managing users, security policies, and trust relationships in a PKI-enabled environment.

Certificate servers must possess controls that provide tamper evidence such as logging and alerting, and tamper resistance such as deleting keys upon tamper detection. Each server may contain one or more secure cryptoprocessor chips to prevent tampering and bus probing. These may come in the form of a plug-in card or an external device that attaches directly to a computer or networked server.

The next critical concept in a PKI is the root certificate. It is an unsigned or a self-signed public-key digital certificate that identifies the root CA. A root certificate contains the private key of which is used to "sign" other certificates. The most common commercial variety is based on the X.509 standard. It uses the widely accepted international X.509 PKI standard to verify that a public key belongs to the user, computer, or service identity contained within the certificate. An X.509 certificate (22) binds a name to a public-key value. The role of the certificate is to associate a public key with the identity contained in the X.509 certificate.

Authentication of a secure application depends on the integrity of the public-key value in the application's certificate. If an impostor replaces the public key with their public key, they can impersonate the true application and gain access to secure e-records. To prevent this type of attack, all certificates must be digitally signed by a CA.

An X.509 certificate contains information about the certificate subject and the certificate issuer (the CA that issued the certificate). A certificate is encoded in Abstract Syntax Notation One (ASN.1), a standard syntax for describing messages that can be sent or received on a network.

As stated before, the role of a certificate is to associate an identity with a public-key value. In more detail, a certificate includes:

- A subject distinguished name (DN) that identifies the certificate owner
- The public key associated with the subject
- X.509 version information
- A serial number that uniquely identifies the certificate
- An issuer DN that identifies the CA that issued the certificate
- The digital signature of the issuer
- Information about the algorithm used to sign the certificate
- Some optional X.509 v.3 extensions, for example, an extension exists that distinguishes between CA certificates and end-entity certificates

A digital signature is an advanced form of electronic signature that encrypts documents with digital codes that are particularly difficult to duplicate. The use of digital signatures provides the mechanism to verify the integrity of a signature or e-record linkage and the identity of the signatory. Digital signatures can be implemented in software, firmware, hardware, or any combination.

Encoded with the CA, there is a digital signature with the CA's private key. The CA's public key is made available to applications by distributing a certificate for the CA. Applications verify that certificates are validly signed by decoding the CA's digital signature with the CA's public key.

The Public-Key Cryptography Standards (PKCS) describes how to sign a message or e-record in such a way that the recipient can verify who signed it and that the message or e-record hasn't been modified since it was signed. Figure 18.3 shows a typical digital signature process.

Summary

- The sender's digital signature is associated with a pair of keys: private key and public key.

Digital Signature

Original document/records

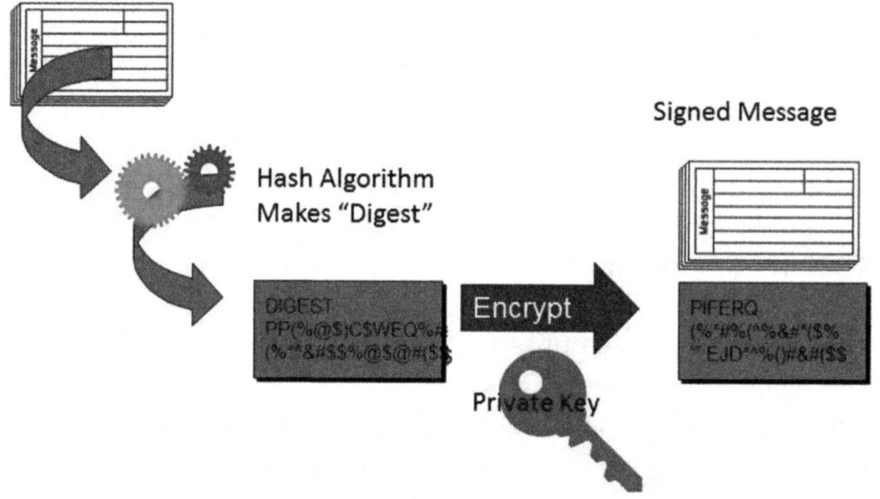

Figure 18.3 Digital signature.

- To sign an e-record, the e-record and the private key are the inputs to a hashing process.
- The output of the hashing process is a bit of string (message digests) appended to the e-record. The plaintext, the digital signature, and the sender's digital signing certificates are sent to the recipient. A signing certificate contains the public signing key assigned to an individual.
- At the recipient site, after the sender's certificate is received, the CA digital signature is checked to ensure that someone the recipient trusts issued it.
- The recipient of the transmitted e-record decrypts the message digest with the originator's public key, applies the same message hash function to the e-record, and then compares the resulting message digest with the transmitted version. Any modification to the e-record after it was signed will cause the signature verification to fail (integrity).
- If the signature was computed with a private key other than the one corresponding to the public key used for verification, then the verification will fail (authentication).
- In digital signatures, the private-key signs and the public key verify the authenticity of signatures. For confidentiality, the public key encrypts messages, and the private key decrypts messages (see Figure 18.4).

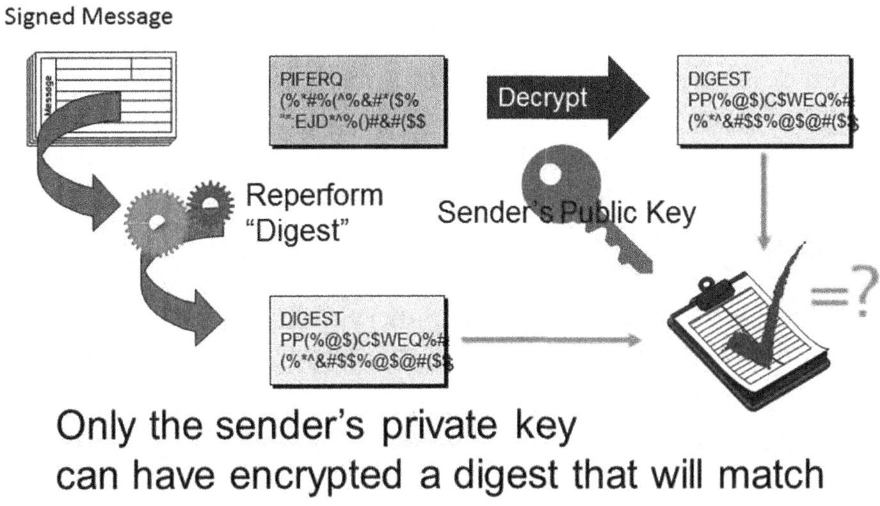

Figure 18.4 Digital signature verification.

The DSA, in which hashing is a key element, is a Federal Information Processing Standard (FIPS) for digital signatures. It was proposed by the National Institute of Standards and Technology (NIST) in August 1991 for use in their Digital Signature Standard (DSS). The most recent DSA revision is the FIPS 186-4 in 2013.

A digital signature is a technology that fully supports the reliability of signed e-records.

Cryptographic Technologies Apply to E-records Integrity

The following illustrates the combinations of the tools described above. These combinations mitigate threats and vulnerabilities related to e-records integrity.

The electronic environments, such as computer systems, pose challenges to establishing the integrity to e-records. This is due to the ease of technique with which e-records may be altered and copied, which can result in the possibility of a multiplicity of versions of an e-record and the associated document.

Trustworthy computer systems (23) provide confidence to the regulated users that the e-records are the same as those expected, based on a prior reference or understanding of what they purport to be. This expectation includes that the e-records have not been altered in an unauthorized manner (NIST 800-57 Part 1 Rev 4 and IEEE Glossary).

Methods used in storing, transmitting, or representing e-records may result in misrepresentations, must be investigated, and the investigation results documented.

A range of strategies for affirming the reliability and integrity of e-records have been developed, and the choice of a method will depend upon the criticality for which e-record integrity verification is required through a risk analysis process. Hashing and digital time-stamping are "public" methods, which confirm the integrity of an e-record which, in the case of the latter method, involves a specific time.

Another class of methods for establishing the authenticity of an e-record includes encapsulation techniques and encryption strategies. A digital watermark can only be detected by appropriate software and is primarily used for protection against unauthorized copying. Digital signatures are used to e-record authorship and identify the people who have played a role in a document.

The types of security services that are needed in support to e-records integrity vary depending upon the intended use of the application managing the e-records and the e-records by itself. As a rule of thumb, it is needed to deal with identity and access management, encryption of e-records retained at rest, and encryption of the e-records in transit (e-records moving from storage to storage).

The required security services must be designed in such a way to encourage compliance with the principles of e-records integrity (24).

Every so often ignored are the links of the e-records security solution at the e-records level, and the security solution for the entire enterprise. These must be integrated. If they aren't, they are working against each other.

E-records integrity is an essential element of any successful enterprise IT program. It is required to have a strong plan behind it and a strategy embracing all the major issues.

E-records in Storage

Computer storage is a device that records (stores) or retrieves (reads) e-records from any medium, including the medium itself.

E-records should be secured by both physical and electronic means against damage (25). This guideline is found in several worldwide regulatory and guidance documents and it applies to short- and long-term storage of e-records.

Critical e-records retained by computer storage can be protected via encryption or a comprehensive service such as PKI.

Access Controls and Authority Checks to Computer Resources

User access controls to computer resources are the basic security function since trustworthiness of the computer system may be compromised even if the e-records themselves are not directly accessed.

User access controls shall be configured and enforced to prohibit unauthorized access to, changes to, and deletion of e-records (EU Annex 11 p12.1 and US FDA 21 CFR 211.68(b)).

Access controls and authority checks "ensure that people have access only to functionality that is appropriate for their job role, and that actions are attributable to a specific individual" (26).

Access controls apply to the system administration functions as well. These functions can be in the applications or infrastructure levels. System administrator rights (permitting activities such as e-records deletion, database amendment, or system configuration changes) should not be assigned to individuals with a direct interest in the e-record (generation, review, or approval).

Public-key certificates can be used to authenticate the identity of a user, and this can be used as an input to access-control decision functions. Access-control decision functions are defined through access rights lists – for example, access-control lists (ACLs) with functions such as use, read, write, execute, delete, or create privileges.

In Windows, as an example, an ACL is a list of security protections that apply to an entire object, a set of the object's properties, or an individual property of an object. Each active directory object has two associated ACLs: the discretionary access-control list (DACL) and the system access-control list (SACL).

A DACL is a list of user accounts, groups, and computers that are allowed (or denied) access to the object. A DACL is a list of access-control entries (ACEs) in which each ACE lists the permissions granted or denied to the authentication (EU Annex 11 p12.3). This feature is a challenge-responses exchange with a new key that is used at each log in.

A SACL enables administrators to log attempts to access a secured object. Each ACE specifies the types of access attempts by a specified trustee (27) that cause the system to generate a record in the security event log. An ACE in a SACL can generate audit records when an access attempt fails, when it succeeds, or both.

As an example of access controls in a typical manufacturing room, an operator logs into the system to perform an operation in a process area. After the operator types the user identification (ID) and password, a digital ticket is created that asks the training system to verify the operator's training record and confirm whether the area and equipment were cleaned and released for production. The system returns the appropriate authorization to operate. In this example, authentication, public-key certificate certificates, and ACL are combined to provide the necessary control to operations.

ACLs must be current and reviewed regularly.

Audit Trails Control

As part of the integrity of e-records, audit trails refer to a journal that records modifications to the e-records. The person or automated processes operating on the user's behalf may perform these modifications. An audit trail mechanism provides the capability to reconstruct the modified e-records and therefore does not obscure previously recorded e-record. The tracking mechanism includes a computer-generated timestamp that indicates the time of the entry.

Audit trails are computer generated and can be part of the e-record or an e-record by itself. The controls associated with e-records apply to electronic audit trails.

Controls to the audit trails include: user access rights to audit trial file must be restricted to prevent e-record amendments; the audit trails must be switched off; timestamp must be reliable (refer to "Time Controls"); the system administrator rights should not be assigned to audit trails review or approval; record and audit must be linked; audit trails cannot be modified; access to the audit trials is limited to print-read only.

The combination of authentication, public-key certificates, encryption, and ACLs provides the mechanisms to control the access to audit trail–related files.

Authentication

Authentication is a process in which the credentials provided are compared to those on a file in a database of information on authorized users on a local operating system or within an authentication server. If the credentials match, the process is completed, and the user is granted authorization for access to the applicable computer resources (see Figure 18.5).

There are various ways for authentication a person: user IDs and static passwords; user IDs and dynamic passwords; and biometric devices. Certificate-based authentication includes user IDs and dynamic passwords that use public-key certificates.

Figure 18.6 represents the typical authentication via user ID and static/dynamic password.

The gathering of the identification documentation (EU Annex 11 p2) of a regulated user is typically performed by the regulated entity Human Resources. Similar regulatory requirement is summarized in US FDA 21 CFR Part 11.100(b).

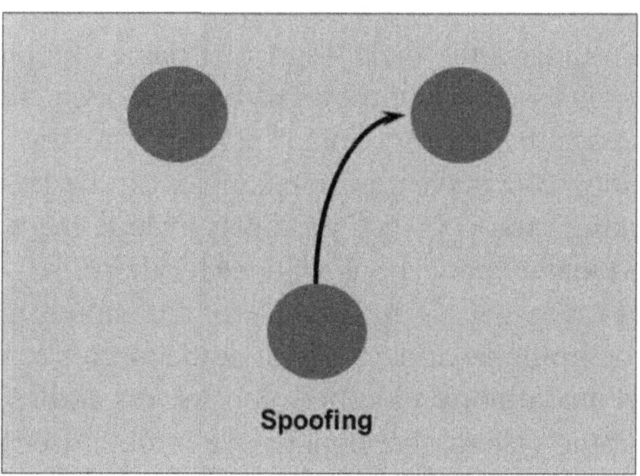

Figure 18.5 Authentication.

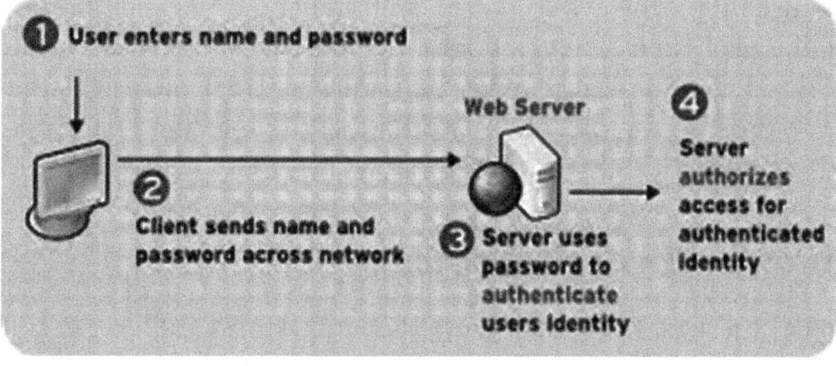

Figure 18.6 Typical authentication.

The authentication of an entity in a PKI-enabled environment is performed by using a CA. The CA issues and manages security credentials and public keys for message encryption and decryption. The objective of a security credential is to associate an identity with a public-key value.

The identity is not of the user but the cryptographic key of the user placed on file in a database of authorized users' information on a local operating system or within a certificate server. Having a less secure key lowers the trust we can place on the identity.

Certificate-based authentication is a technique for strong authentication. A party wishing to be authenticated presents a public-key certificate. If the certified party is still trusted in the organization, then the certificate server trusts that the party is who it claims to be. One benefit of certificate-based authentication is that the entity does not have to have an established relationship with, for example, a server before being authenticated.

The digital signature is another method to authenticate a person. This method prevents denying by the sender that they have sent the message. When the verifier validates the digital signature using a public key of a sender, the verifier is assured that the signature has been created only by the sender who possesses the corresponding secret private key and no one else.

The authentication of a server, as an example, can be performed using a computer networking protocol. Such protocols include mechanisms for servers to identify and make connections with each other.

Secure Sockets Layer (SSL) is an example of a computer networking protocol using cryptographic technologies that authenticates regulated users and performs encrypted communication between servers and regulated users. Using a cryptographic system, the identity of a remote user (or system) can be established. A typical example is the SSL certificate of a web server providing proof to the user that he/she is connected to the correct server.

The SSL protocol establishes an encrypted link between a server and a regulated user, typically a web server (website) and a browser; or a mail server and a mail client (e.g., Outlook). By authenticating a server, the person is assured communication with the correct site. SSL also signs the transmitted e-records, so the person is assured that the e-records have not been changed in transit. Server certificates follow the X.509 certificate format.

Security of the Electronic Signatures

The output of a digital signature hashed data is considered an e-record. All technical controls applicable to e-records are applicable as well to the hashed data.

In digital signature implementations, the integrity and security of the signatures private key must be considered. The degree of confidence in the linkage between a public key and its owner depends on the confidence in the CA that issues the public-key certificate.

Within the cryptographic module, the part of a system or application providing cryptographic services such as encryption, authentication, or digital signature generation and verification, public keys shall be protected against unauthorized modification and substitution. Private keys must be securely managed. These are implemented in various other services, including unauthorized disclosure, modification, and substitution.

Provisions in X.509-compliant public-key certificates enable the identification of policies that indicate the strength of the mechanisms used as well as the criteria for certificate handling. The rules expressed by certificate policies are reflected in security policies that detail the operational rules and system features of CAs and other PKI components. Logical security and proper configuration to the CA, certificate server, and security server help ensure security during the creation and management of public-key certificates.

The private key may be stored in a user's local disk in an encrypted format or as part of a token that interfaces with the computer. Personal cryptographic tokens have been considered to be the obvious secure repository for private keys, and the options for onboard cryptographic processing ensure that a private key is never clear outside of the token.

Signature E-records Linkage

An electronic signature solution must secure electronic signatures through encrypted copy protection and make it impossible to copy, cut, or paste signatures and audit trails from an approved e-record. This requirement is consistent with 21 CFR Part 11.70 and EU Annex 11 p 14(b).

Also, any changes to the e-record after an electronic signature has been assigned should invalidate the signature until the e-record has been reviewed again and re-signed (28).

The above requirements support the integrity of digitally signed e-records. It is vital to consider the integrity and security of the main components of the digital signatures: the PKI components. The level to which the user is confident about the linkage between a public key and its owner depends significantly on how confident the user is about the system that issued the certificate that links them.

In addition to the system issuing public-key certificates, access-control technologies, and procedures, the signature and e-record linkage must have supporting tools to verify the integrity of this link. PKI uses a hashing algorithm and keys to demonstrate the integrity of signed e-records. A digital signature is linked to an e-record by incorporating an encrypted message digest of the e-record into the signature itself. This link is retained for as long as the e-record is kept and provides the trustworthiness of electronically signed e-records for that period.

Time Controls

The DTS issues a secure timestamp that can be used for digital signatures and audit trails. The DTS includes the time, a hash of the e-record being time-stamped, and a time certification.

The DTS gives strong legal evidence that the contents of the time-stamped work existed at a point in time and have not changed since that time. The hashing as part of the DTS maintains complete privacy of the e-records themselves.

The workflow of the digital time-stamping practice consists of a message digest created from the e-record and sent to the DTS. The DTS sends back the time stamp, as well as the date and time the time stamp was received, with a secure signature. The signature proves that the e-record existed on the stated date. The e-record contents remain unknown to the DTS – only the digest is known. The DTS must use lengthy keys because the time stamp may be required for many years.

DTS and public-key certificates provide the mechanism to authenticate the source (device checks) of the time stamp in the audit trails and electronic signatures. Access-right lists and public-key certificates can be used to control access to the DTS.

In addition to DTS, other supporting time controls include an infrastructure that supports time-stamping from a trusted time such as the coordinated universal time. This technology, which in some cases is compliant with X.509, is tied into a time-calibration service. Applications or computer logs may require time-stamping services on the server.

The access controls to the time server and all associated infrastructure must ensure proper security restrictions to protect the time/date settings.

The time controls using cryptographic technologies provide a secure time/date mechanism that cannot be altered by personnel. A minor change in the e-record will result in a change to the message digest.

The Uniqueness of the Electronic Signatures

Electronic signatures replacing handwritten signatures must have appropriate controls to ensure their authenticity and traceability to the specific person who electronically signed the record(s).

The main element for signing e-records and messages in the digital signature is the private key (29). Users of PKI may generate key pairs (private and public). When generated by PKI, key pair is produced by prime numbers, which are created from large, random numbers (e.g., candidate prime numbers). ANSI X9.17 specifies a key generation technique. A private key is uniquely associated with an entity and is not made public.

No matter who generates the key pairs, the CA certifies the public key. However, many organizations mandate that the CA generate the key pair to ensure the keys' quality.

In a certificate-based authentication scheme, a browser generates a session key that is encrypted with a server's public key.

The uniqueness of the electronic signatures is one element of attributable e-records.

E-records in Transit

Records must remain unaltered while in transit. The unauthorized manipulation of records, audit trail records, and replay of transmissions will be reliably identified as errors. The typical cryptographic controls associated with e-records in transit are explained below.

The Integrity of E-records in Transit

The integrity of e-records in transit is required by the US FDA 21 CFR 211.68. A similar requirement can be found as a guideline in EU Annex 11 p4.8 and 5 (see Figure 18.7).

Hash and encryption functions can be used for assuring the integrity of transmitted e-records and for message verification.

Hash protects the integrity and privacy of e-records and prevents their loss. For example, e-records must be protected when confidential patient e-records are sent to other locations.

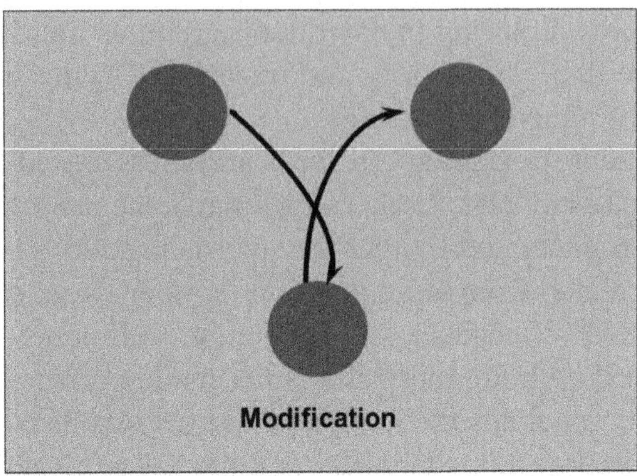

Figure 18.7 Records integrity.

Records and messages authentication provide the means to evaluate the integrity of the e-records and message in transit. It involves technical controls to detect unauthorized modifications to e-records and messages. A recipient can use two approaches to authenticate e-records in transit and messages:

- Encrypt records or messages using the recipient's public key

A cryptographic hash function allows one to easily verify that some input e-records maps to a given hash value, but if the input e-records is unknown; it is deliberately difficult to reconstruct it (or equivalent alternatives) by knowing the stored hash value. This is used for assuring the integrity of transmitted e-records and is the building block for the Hash Message Authentication Code (HMACs (30)), which provide message authentication. Consequently, a way that the recipient can make sure that it is the right file is if by the sender posts the hash value publicly. The recipient can then compute the hash value of the file received and check if it matches the hash value.

Encryption protects the privacy of messages and e-records in transit between networks, including the internet. Tools such as network diagnostics or protocol analyzers can read the information easily as it is transmitted. To mitigate this difficulty, systems such as SSL transport layer security or VPNs can provide the necessary protection of critical e-records across networks.

These solutions use encryption, digital signatures, or public-key certificate to ensure data privacy, identification of the originator of messages, and verification of message integrity.

- Sign the records or message

A digital signature can also confirm the integrity of a message. In case an attacker has access to the digitally signed records and modifies the e-records, the digital signature verification at receiver end fails. The hash of modified data and the output provided by the verification algorithm will not match. Hence, the receiver can safely deny the message if data integrity has been broken.

Device Checks

The device checks are justified where only certain devices have been selected as legitimate sources of e-records input or commands. As an example, in a network environment, it may be necessary for security reasons to limit the issuance of critical commands to any authorized workstation. US FDA 21 CFR 11.10(h) is a regulatory requirement related to device checks.

Public-key certificate can be used to implement any of these verifications. In the above example, the identity of the file server extracting e-records can be determined.

Summary

The cryptographic technologies support e-records integrity in the CGMP of health agencies worldwide. Hashing, e-records encryption, digital signatures, and/or services family (e.g., Virtual Private Network) are a set of tools and techniques that can be implemented to properly control the integrity of e-records.

These technical controls have an important advantage over other controls. These cryptographic set of tools and techniques mitigate threats to and vulnerabilities connected with e-records integrity.

E-records encrypted in transit and at rest provide end-to-end e-records protection.

The following table recaps the cryptographic tools supporting e-records integrity.

	Hashing	*Data encryption*	*Digital signatures*	*Services family*
Access controls				Public-key certificate
Audit trail controls		√		Public-key certificate
Authentication	√		√	Public-key certificate SSL
Device checks				Public-key certificate
Integrity and privacy of e-records in storage.	√	√	√	
Integrity and privacy of e-records in transit.	√	√	√	HMAC VPN
Security of the electronic signature	√			
Signature-e-records linkage		√	√	DSA
Time controls	√			DTS
The uniqueness of the electronic signatures				Private key

The implementation of these technologies should be following a security-by-design approach – that is, design the security into devices and applications from the beginning, including the cost of doing so.

Disclaimer

Any mention of products or references to organizations is intended only to convey information; it does not imply recommendation or endorsement, nor does it imply that the products mentioned are necessarily the best available for the purpose.

The opinions expressed in this chapter are strictly those of the author.

References

1. López, O., "EU Annex 11 and Data Integrity: Designing Data Integrity into your Practices," In: *Paper Presented at the 2014 ISPE Annual Meeting*, Las Vegas, NV, 12–15 October 2014.
2. Integrity – the degree to which a system or component prevents unauthorized access to, or modified of, computer programs or data. (IEEE).
3. Electronic record – information recorded in electronic form that requires a computer system to access or process. (SAG, "A Guide to Archiving of Electronic Records," February 2014).
4. Wechsler, J., "Data Integrity Key to GMP Compliance, Pharmaceutical Technology," September 2014.
5. NIST, *Recommendation for Key Management, Part 1: General.* (Special Publication 800–57 Part 1 Rev 4, July 2015).
6. López, O., "Trustworthy Computer Systems," In: *Data Integrity in Pharmaceutical and Medical Devices Regulation Operations.* (CRC Press, Boca Raton, FL, 1st ed., 2017). pp 101–119.
7. Vibbert, J.M., "The Internet of Things: Data Protection and Data Security," *Global Environment Information Law Journal*, 7(3), Spring 2016.
8. Davis, L., "MHRA: Data Integrity defined?" *PharmOut.* https://www.pharmout.net/mhra-data-integrity-defined/.
9. Information security – is a set of strategies for managing the processes, tools and policies necessary to prevent, detect, document and counter threats to digital and non-digital information. Infosec responsibilities include establishing a set of business processes that will protect information assets regardless of how the information is formatted or whether it is in transit, is being processed or is at rest in storage. (http://searchsecurity.techtarget.com/definition/information-security-infosec).
10. Cryptographic – It is the practice and study of techniques for secure communication in the presence of third parties. (http://searchsoftwarequality.techtarget.com/definition/cryptography).
11. In this chapter "CGMP regulated activities" is defined as the manufacturing-related activities established in the basic legislation compiled in Volume 1 and Volume 5 of the publication "The Rules governing medicinal products in the European Union" http://ec.europa.eu/health/documents/eudralex/index_en.htm, US FDA 21 CFR Part 211, "Current Good Manufacturing Practice In Manufacturing, Processing, Packing or Holding of Drugs; General and Current Good Manufacturing Practice For Finished Pharmaceuticals" or any predicate rule applicable to medicinal products for the referenced country.
12. Digital signature – Digital signature means an electronic signature based upon cryptographic methods of originator authentication, computed by using a set of rules and a set of parameters such that the identity of the signer and the integrity of the data can be verified. (US FDA 21 CFR Part 11.3(5)).

13. Virtual Private Network – Describes the use of encryption to provide a secure telecommunications route between parties over an insecure or public network, such as the internet.
14. López, O., "Electronic Records Lifecycle," *Journal of GxP Compliance*, 19(4), November 2015.
15. IT Infrastructure Library (ITIL), "The Official Introduction to the ITIL Service Lifecycle," 2007.
16. MHRA, "MHRA GxP Data Integrity Guidance and Definitions," March 2018.
17. "NIST SP 800–57P1 – Recommendation for Key Management," (Gaithersburg, MD, January 2016).
18. López, O., "Technologies Supporting Part 11," In: *21 CFR Part 11: Complete Guide to International Computer Validation Compliance for the Pharmaceutical Industry*. (CRC Press, Boca Raton, FL, 1st ed., 2004). pp 141–146.
19. Symmetric-key Algorithm – It is a cryptographic algorithm that uses the same key to encrypt and decrypt data.
20. Alanazi, H., Zaidan, B., Zaidan, A., Jalab, H., Shabbir, M. Al-Nabhani, Y., "New Comparative Study Between DES, 3DES and AES within Nine Factors," *Journal of Computing*, 2(3), March 2010, 152–157. ISSN 2151-9617.
21. A public-key certificate (also known as a digital certificate or identity certificate) is an electronic representation of identification or passport, issued by a certification authority (CA) to a PKI user, stating identification information, validity period, the holder's public key, the identity and digital signature of the issuer, and the purpose for which it is issued.
22. https://searchsecurity.techtarget.com/definition/X509-certificate.
23. López, O., "Trustworthy Computer Systems," In: *Data Integrity in Pharmaceutical and Medical Devices Regulation Operations*. (CRC Press, Boca Raton, FL, 1st ed., 2017). pp 101–119.
24. MHRA, "MHRA GxP Data Integrity Guidance and Definitions," March 2018.
25. EudraLex, The Rules Governing Medicinal Products in the European Union, Volume 4, "EU Guidelines to Good Manufacturing Practice, Medicinal Products for Human and Veterinary Use Part 1, Annex 11 – Computerized Systems," June 2011.
26. MHRA, "MHRA GxP Data Integrity Guidance and Definitions," March 2018.
27. A trustee is the user account, group account, or logon session to which an access control entry (ACE) applies. Each ACE in access (ACL) has one security identifier (SID) that identifies a trustee.
28. PI 041–1, "Good Practices for Data Management and Integrity in Regulated GMP/GDP Environments," *Pharmaceutical Inspection Co-operation Scheme (PIC/S)*, November 2018, (Draft 3).
29. Private key – a cryptographic key that can be obtained and used by anyone to encrypt messages intended for a recipient, such that the encrypted messages can be deciphered only by using a second key that is known only to the recipient.
30. A keyed-hash message authentication code (HMAC) is a specific type of message authentication code (MAC) involving a cryptographic hash function (hence the "H") in combination with a secret cryptographic key.

Chapter 19

Integration Between Computer Systems and E-records Lifecycles

Introduction

Before the current emphasis by the regulatory agencies worldwide and competent authorities on e-records integrity, the focus was on computer systems.

The regulated industry is now providing the same attention to computer systems and e-records as well.

To avoid added work and as part of the computer system workflows, it is pertinent to incorporate integrity-related controls to the e-records and build in the correct management of e-records during the computer systems' Operational Period. This design-related work must be incorporated into the computer system preferably as part of the computer design during the Project Stage. If e-records integrity design controls cannot be implemented to the computer system, then the e-records integrity controls must be established implementing procedural controls.

After the computer system is released to operations, the prominence in the e-records is the management of the e-records since the e-records are created, transformed, access, used, migrated, stored, and destroyed after the system is released. After releasing the computer systems to operations, the typical CGMP controls associated with the operational life of the computer system take over. Comparable CGMP controls applicable to the computer systems apply to the e-records.

Figure 19.1 depicts an approach to the integration of the e-records lifecycle during the system development period and operational life period. The selected system lifecycle is from the EU Annex 11.

An element in e-records governance (1) is the computer validation process. Besides, to demonstrate the quality embedded to the system during the SLC, this process provides the initial assurance of the successful implementation of the e-records integrity controls and the computer systems records management. These record controls are to be maintained through the operation and even after the retirement of the computer system.

Computer systems validation is the formal assessment and reporting of quality and performance measures for all the lifecycle stages of software and system development, its implementation, qualification and acceptance, operation, modification, re-qualification, maintenance, and retirement. This should enable both the regulated user and the competent authority to have a high level of confidence in the integrity of both the processes executed within the controlling computer system(s) and in those processes controlled

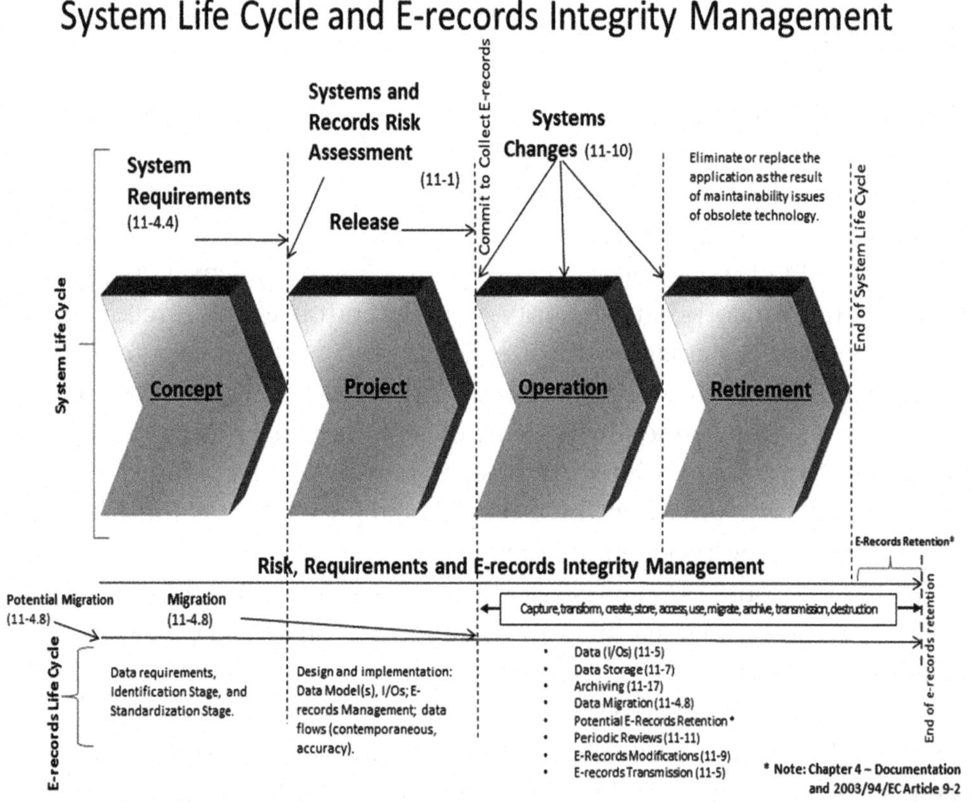

Figure 19.1 Integrated SLC and DI management.

by and/or linked to the computer system(s), within the prescribed operating environment(s) (2).

In the context of worldwide health authority regulations, the validation process applicable to computer systems incorporates the intended purpose of the systems.

The SLC incorporates the computer validation process.

The following sections feature the integration between the computer systems and the e-records lifecycles. The e-records lifecycle is discussed in Chapter 2.

Concept Period

The Concept Period establishes the definition of the project (EU Annex 11 p4.5), including clear data integrity goals and objectives, and the generation of the quality plan (EU Annex 11 p3 and EU Annex 11 p4.5).

In addition to the above activities, during the Concept Period, the process is understood and system requirements (EU Annex 11 p4.4) delineated. The system requirements incorporate the configuration that a system must-have for a hardware and software application to run smoothly and efficiently. Failure to meet these requirements can result in installation, operational, and/or performance challenges. The installation problems may prevent a device or application from getting installed, whereas the performance problems may cause a product to malfunction or perform below expectation or even to hang or crash.

Non-functional requirements should be part of the system requirements as well.

From the context of the e-records lifecycle, two stages defining the planning, requirements, and designing of the e-records model and the functionality to manage the e-records model are incorporated. These are discussed in Chapter 2.

Project Period – Risk Assessment

A mature e-records governance system adopts a "quality risk management" approach across all areas of the quality system (EU Annex 11 p4.5).

During the Project Period, risk assessments are performed on the process, system, and records. The objective of these assessments is to identify risk during the operation. These uncovered risks, if any, will be used to support the technological and procedural controls mitigating the risks.

The critical e-records are identified. The integrity risk to critical e-records will vary depending upon the degree to which the e-records generated by the computer system can be configured, and therefore potentially manipulated (EU Annex 11 p12.2). The other critical area to be considered is transient data during the period of creating the e-records (refer to Chapter 13).

Other areas to be assessed are capture, transformation (as applicable), creation, storing, access, use, transmission, migration, archiving, and final disposition of e-records.

An assessment of the risks to the e-records is performed in the areas described above, uncovering likely e-records manipulations in an unauthorized manner and, via a root analysis, finding a way to mitigate the potential unauthorized manipulation of the e-records. These analyses may lead to architecture and design trade-offs during system design and development.

Refer to Chapter 8, "Vulnerabilities of E-records."

The MHRA guidance (1) suggests ways to mitigate the risk of e-records manipulations in an unauthorized manner.

- Access controls must be enforced to ensure that only authorized individuals can access and use the system based on the job role (EU Annex 11 p12). The access controls are applicable to database servers or any server containing GMP-related e-records.
- The regulated entity must have documentation about users and their access levels (EU Annex 11 p12.3). This documentation must be consistent with the actual access settings in the system.
- In cases that technological or design constraints don't allow unique access to the computer application and/or database server(s), a procedural control must provide access and traceability.
- The access to system administrators should be minimal, unique per administrator, and traceable. The preferred traceability method for actions performed by a system administrator is audit trails (EU Annex 11 p9). EU Annex 11 does not specify if the audit trails must be electronically recorded.
- Separation of roles must be enforced on e-records maintenance.
- E-records maintenance must be controlled (EU Annex 11 p12.4) and an approval method must be implemented (EU Annex 11 p10).

Another area to consider is the risk associated with e-records migration from an existing system(s) over to a new system. Refer to Chapter 15. The risk of e-records migration may be mitigated by verifying "that data is not altered in value and/or meaning during this migration process" (EU Annex 11 p4.8).

As described in Chapter 9 in this book, Annex 20 (3) summarizes an approach to the quality risk management pertinent to computer systems and computer-controlled equipment. The risks uncovered during this activity must be managed through the SLC (EU Annex 11 p1).

The e-records risk management must be performed during the e-records lifecycle (EU Annex 11 p1). Decisions regarding well-known risks must be made before starting the design, as part of the Project Stage, of the computer system and/or the e-records management function.

According to the MHRA guidance (1) "the effort and resource assigned to data governance should be commensurate with the risk to product quality."

Besides, the MHRA has communicated to the regulated user that they must carry out a routine effectiveness review of their governance systems to ensure e-records integrity and traceability is maintained (4). The effectiveness review can be performed during the periodic review.

The requirements document must include a requirement(s) related to the mitigation of the uncovered risks.

Manufacturers must develop and make use of a system which allows an acceptable risk.

Project Period – Requirements

Business requirements are gathered as part of the Concept Phase at the beginning of the computer system project, including the e-records integrity-related requirements. These e-records integrity-related requirements are traced to the regulated entity e-records governance (EU Annex 11 p4.4).

The following e-records integrity requirements are critical:

- Identify critical data and e-records.
- Develop a data flow diagram.
- Establish e-records management requirements (e.g., e-records written contemporaneously).
- Establish the requirements related to transient data (e.g., security).
- Identify interfaces (EU Annex 11 p5) and the data to be entered manually (EU Annex 11 p6).

- Develop data models and databases.
- Based on the data flow diagram and risk assessment, identify the e-records integrity-related controls. The identified risk must be managed through the SLC (EU Annex 11 p1).
- If e-records from a legacy system and/or any other system are migrated to the system under development, there must be a verification to demonstrate that the e-records value and/or meaning have not been altered. This verification must include associated metadata.
- Based on risk assessment, assess the need of audit trails (EU Annex 11 p12.4) and controls to prevent unauthorized access to the application, servers, and the operating systems (EU Annex 11p 7.1, EU Annex 11 p12 and 21 CFR 11.10(g)).
- Identify and protect the reliable time source that is to be used to generate timestamps.
- Identify storage, archiving, and migration needs.

The appropriate methods to prevent unauthorized manipulation of e-records include:

- Use of keys
- Use of passwords
- Use of personal codes
- Restricted access to computer terminals

Of special interest are the system administrator access and the access to the e-records retained by computer storage (EU Annex 11 p7.1). According to the MHRA guidance (1), MHRA expects that each system administrator should have unique access to the computer system appropriate for their job role. Every regulated user with administrative privileges is logged into the computer system with his distinct log attributes. This distinctiveness ensures that there is traceability of actions performed in the computer and the respective user, including an audit trail. This exception may not apply to read-only activities.

During the development period of a new system in which a legacy system is replaced, the requirements stage must consider the e-records migration from the legacy system to the new system. If this is the case, it will require:

- Considering storage and infrastructure requirements
- Mapping source and destination fields
- Specification of the mandatory fields for e-records

- Extracting and loading requirements
- Specifications of the e-records inputs (e.g. format, decimal places, units, ranges, limits, defaults, and the conversion requirements)
- Defining what constitutes an error and how errors must be handled
- Verification requirements to ensure that source e-records are the same as the e-records in the destination.

As the reader can conclude from the above requirements, this is a project by itself.

The business requirements are transformed into user requirements or capabilities needed by a user to solve or achieve an objective. Finally, the user requirements are translated to functional requirements or requirements that specific behavior or functions of the computer system (EU Annex 11 p4.4).

With the information collected until this instant in the project, a supplier may be contemplated to carry out the design.

Project Period – Building, Testing, Documenting, and Installing

As part of the Project Period and based on the solution architecture, the application is built and tested, the built and testing outcomes documented, and then the built installed and deployed.

The requirements are translated into configurations and design controls to manage the identified risks, including e-records integrity risks.

The following is addressed by the EU Annex 11 guideline:

- IT infrastructure must be qualified to ensure capacity, security and e-records integrity (EU Annex 11-Principle b).
- As part of the qualification of the application and associated controls, test the backup and restoration procedure(s), and verify the output of the backup (EU Annex 11 p7.2). Each backup set should be checked to ensure that it is error-free, including the metadata and all configuration-related files.
- The ability to retrieve the e-records and audit trails should be ensured and tested (EU Annex 11 p7.1).
- Verify the accuracy of reports and audit trail reports (EU Annex 11 p8).
- As applicable, and based on the operational sequencing, test accuracy of the e-records (EU Annex 11 p7.1) and workflows.

- The level of access is assigned based on the duties of each user (EU Annex 11 p2).
- Training related to the operational aspect of the system is a relevant element of the proper operation of the system.

Data flows and mappings must be reviewed during the design of the system.

Project Period – E-records Migration and Computer Systems Release to Operations

If e-records are transferred to a new environment changing the format of the e-records, the qualification must include test cases and the associated verifications that the electronic records' new format do not alter the content of the records and associated metadata during the migration process (EU Annex 11 p4.8). The migrated records and the application(s) are integrated, and testing executed to demonstrate such integration. Refer to Chapter 15.

As part of the implementation, one of many e-records integrity-related requirements addressed in the MHRA guideline (1) is the recording of transactions contemporaneously by computer systems. These are typical transactions in which the user agrees, completes by performing certain predefined actions, or acknowledges a deviation. These actions must not be combined into a single computer system transaction with other operations.

The above guideline can be traced to Section 4.8 in Volume 4, Chapter 4 (Documentation) from the EudraLex, "Rules Governing Medicinal Products in the European Union."

> Records should be made or completed at the time each action is taken and in such a way that all significant activities concerning the manufacture of medicinal products are traceable.

Recording e-records contemporaneously is a key factor related to e-records reliability.

Operations Periods

During this stage, e-records are generated, transformed, recorded, accessed, used, integrated, logically deleted, migrated, and retired. It is when the integrity of the e-records can be compromised. The objective of all e-records requirements, and the implementation of such requirements, is to preserve the e-records integrity.

During the operational stage the procedural controls associated with e-records integrity must be enforced:

- Only authorized people can modify the e-records stored on data servers or any other media.
- There is a record of changes made.
- The entry of e-records considered critical is checked by a designated person other than the one who made the records or checked by the system itself.
- A procedural control is available for cancellation changes to the level of approval and for entering or editing e-records, including changing of personal passwords.

To keep the focus on the e-records integrity technical controls mainly during the computer system operational stage, the e-records integrity controls can be categorized into four spaces: e-records created; e-records in storage; e-records during processing; and e-records while in transit (5).

Computer System Retirement – E-records Migration

The activities to migrate e-records as part of a computer system retirement are not different from the migration of e-records as part of the transfer of e-records to a new computer system, discussed previously.

E-records must be preserved as part of the planning to retire the computer system generating e-records.

The e-records preservation plan must include one of the following options:

- Make sure that a new system will be able to retrieve e-records from previous systems.
- Preserve previous applications (not contemplated, the system is to be retired).
- Archive hard copies (when allowed).
- Completion of system documentation and validation dossier.

If archiving hard copies, reproducing computer records in paper copies is the selected method to migrate the e-records; the paper copies must be certified as true copies of the original e-records, and the paper copies are to be signed and dated as verified true copies. All electronic metadata must also be a part of the fixed record. The verified hard copy must then be stored with other paper-based records.

After executing the e-records preservation plan, ensure that the quality assurance (QA) unit of the regulated user performs an audit on the preserved records. The audit will verify the traceability between planning and implementation and will assess the successful execution of the preservation plan.

E-records migration must ensure the protection of e-records from deliberate or inadvertent alteration or loss (refer to Chapter 15).

E-records Archiving

In the context of e-records no longer actively required, these e-records can be archived. This is considered a long retention environment.

E-records archiving is the process of moving e-records that are no longer actively used to a separate records storage device for long-term retention, often disabling the e-records from any further changes. The retention period of these e-records has not been finalized.

The controls applicable to e-records in storage are also applicable to archived records.

The archiving process is an activity that may involve a modification of format, media, and/or physical storage. It must be performed in a controlled manner following a procedural control.

There are multiple types of archiving disposition:

- Extract/migrate – The migration of digital information from one hardware/software configuration to another or from one generation of computer technology to a later one offers one method of dealing with technological obsolescence. Data is extracted from the current system and moved to another location, or the entire instance is migrated elsewhere.
- Host – These are single-instance database systems that are not typically managed by the site and are hosted elsewhere.
- Archive – It contains the following types:

- Report – In this case, the official record is in hard copy currently or the most effective end state will become hard copy.
- Physical to virtual (P2V) (encapsulate) – To be able to access the e-record effectively, in some cases it is necessary to have both the application and the database in a virtual environment. Encapsulation is a technique for grouping together a digital object and anything else necessary to provide access to that object. In this case, the software will be used to encapsulate the data and application and the product housed in a server designated for this purpose.
- Technology emulation creates an environment that behaves in a hardware-like manner. It potentially offers substantial benefits in preserving the functionality and integrity of digital objects.
- Keeping every version of software and hardware – There is a requirement to keep every version of software and hardware, operating systems and manuals, as well as the retention of personnel with the relevant technical skills. This option makes the preservation of obsolete technologies to access the archived e-records unfeasible.

If the e-records in storage are transferred to another format, media, or system, the archiving process must include verifications that the e-records are not altered in value and/or meaning during this migration process. The metadata must be also transferred and verified. Refer to "Data Migration" in this chapter.

The computer system holding the archived records must implement all security-related functions to restrict access to authorized personnel only. Periodically, archived records need to be verified for accessibility, readability, integrity, and the state of security control.

If changes are implemented to the computer infrastructure and/or application, then it is required to ensure and test the ability of the application to access the e-records.

E-records may be retained on archived media for a very long period. The procedure addressing the e-records in storage should also address the stability of the storage media itself.

After completing the specified record retention requirements, the records can be physically deleted.

Each country has its particularity about each best practice discussed in this book. One example of such particularity is the clinical e-records archiving guidelines established in South Africa. In South Africa, e-records must be reproduced in hard copy, which is to be signed and dated as a verified accurate copy of the original data. The verified hard copy should then be stored with other paper-based records. This requirement in South Africa is established to overcome the possibility of loss or inability to read the information due to technological redundancy.

The MHRA guidance (1) recommends that archive e-records should be locked such that they cannot be altered or deleted without detection and audit trail.

The archive arrangements must be designed to permit recovery and readability of the e-records and metadata throughout the required retention period.

E-records Final Disposition

Refer to Chapter 2.

References

1. MHRA, "GXP' Data Integrity Guidance and Definitions," March 2018.
2. PI 011–3, "Good Practices for Computerised Systems in Regulated "GXP" Environments," *Pharmaceutical Inspection Cooperation Scheme (PIC/S)*, September 2007.
3. EudraLex, "The Rules Governing Medicinal Products in the European Union, Volume 4, EU Guidelines to Good Manufacturing Practice Medicinal Products for Human and Veterinary Use, Annex 20 – Quality Risk Management," February 2008.
4. MHRA, "MHRA Expectation Regarding Self-Inspection and Data Integrity," September 2014.
5. López, O., *Data Integrity in Pharmaceutical and Medical Devices Regulation Operations: Best Practices Guide to Electronic Records Compliance.* (CRC Press, Boca Ratón, FL, 2017).

Chapter 20

Miscellaneous E-records Integrity Issues

Introduction

This chapter covers e-records integrity controls to the following technologies: Backup as a service (BaaS), audit trails review, testing audit trails, databases integrity, verification, and testing – retention of e-records, and e-records integrity in wireless environments.

> Without solid data quality and governance, AI, IoT, and BI projects are doomed from the outset.
>
> **Murphy, Leo, "How to Make the Business Case for Data Quality & Data Governance Initiatives," February 2020 (1)**

Backup as a Service

From the context of data integrity, a backup is a true copy of the original record that is maintained securely throughout the record retention period.

Organizations would rather buy IT services from an IT service provider. This trend is commonly referred to as XaaS, anything as a service.

BaaS, also known as an online backup service, is an approach to backing up data that involves purchasing backup and recovery services from an online data backup provider. Instead of performing backup with a centralized, on-premises IT department, BaaS connects systems to a private, public or hybrid cloud managed by the outside provider.

The most important advantage of backup as a service compared to on-premises data backup solutions is the ease of management. There's no need to rotate storage devices, manually move data to off-site locations, or perform integrity checks and deduplication – the BaaS provider takes care of everything.

As any setting of XaaS, the most important elements are the activities to determine the service requirements, the selection of the provider matching the service requirements, the SLA to understand roles and responsibilities, and the periodic audits to verify the fulfillment of the SLA and other contractual agreements.

As a process, e-records integrity verifies that e-records have remained unaltered from the electronic storage device to the backup media.

The regulatory expectation on backups is that backup data are exact and complete, including the metadata and system configuration; secure from alteration, inadvertent erasures, or loss; and checked for accuracy. Backup and restore procedures must be verified periodically (2).

The following are the controls associated with e-records while in transit: qualification of IT infrastructure (3), build-in checks, and accuracy checks. Refer to "E-records Integrity in Wireless Environments" in this chapter for the description of each item.

Audit Trails Review

Introduction

As part of the trustworthiness and reliability of e-records (4), audit trails refer to a journal, paper-based or computer-based or version control, that can trace the records modifications to the records. The audit trail helps to recover or reproduce historical events and records related to the neglect of its media operations including the "who, what, when and why" information.

All computer systems managing medicine-manufacturing-related e-records are required to provide audit trail functionality. Audit trails can be particularly appropriate when users are expected to create, modify, or delete regulated records during normal operation (4).

Audit trails of administrative events records must be regularly reviewed. The scope and extent of the audit trail review should be based on a documented risk assessment (e.g. data criticality, security level, and frequency of use and storage capacity). The audit trails must be reviewed according to the applicable procedures. This procedure must contain the steps to follow in case an investigation is initiated after data integrity issues are identified during the audit trail review.

Systems that cannot provide the audit trail functionality must be controlled through process design and/or procedural controls (e.g., logging, change control, version control, or other combinations of recording paper plus electronic records) that demonstrate equivalence to an electronic audit trail and the documentation traceability requirements.

The US FDA regulatory requirements for audit trails are that it must automatically record:

- Any creation, changes, or deletions of regulated electronic record
- User ID (name of the user)
- Old value
- New value
- Date and time
- Reason for change (if applicable)

EU Annex 11 p 9 provides the following guidelines about audit trails.

> Consideration should be given, based on a risk assessment, to building into the system the creation of a record of all GMP-relevant changes and deletions (a system-generated "audit trail"). For change or deletion of GMP-relevant data, the reason should be documented. Audit trails need to be available and convertible to a generally intelligible form and regularly reviewed.

PICS data integrity guidance (5) states that the audit trail should include the following parameters:

- Who made the change
- What was changed, including old and new values
- When the change was made, including date and time
- Why the change was made (reason)
- Name of any person authorizing the change

If a computer system has the capability, however, to verify its output, such as with audit trials, this could be considered as a check for accuracy (6).

Some typical expectations from the regulators include:

- The system must be designed to permit data changes in such a way that the data changes are documented and that there is no deletion of entered data (i.e., maintain an audit trail, data trail, edit trail) (ICH E6_R2, November 2016).
- Accurate and complete copies of the audit trail must be generated in both human-readable (printout) and electronic form.
- Changes, manipulations, or deletions of the audit trail content by any user must be prevented.
- Audit trails must not be allowed to be disabled or turned off.
- An audit trail must be linked to the record.
- Audit trail records are maintained and available for the entire retention period associated with the related electronic records.
- Timestamp, used in the audit trails, must be controlled and protected.
- Backups must include all relevant raw regulated e-records, metadata, and audit trails.
- Audit trails must be in place for user management and system settings.
- The audit trail should retain the dynamic functionalities found in the computer system.
- The system enforces creating the audit trail at the moment the e-record is updated.

Categories of Manufacturing-Related Audit Trails

In manufacturing environments, there are three main categories of CGMP audit trail records: batch-specific, administrative events, and systems activities. In all cases, audit trails are required.

Product- or Batch-Specific Data

This audit trail information describes changes made to CGMP data that is associated with a specific batch of GMP material.

This information is reviewed at the time the change is made, rather than during the predefined frequency based on criticality and frequency of system use.

Data review, including audit trails, is required before batch release (21 CFR 211.22).

Administration Events

This audit trail information describes alteration to user account permissions, group permissions or roles, account lockout events or alerts, and administrator or privileged user tasks.

This information can be reviewed as part of the system audit trail review process at a predefined frequency based on the risk assessment.

System Activities (7)

It is a record of all administrator changes. The frequency of this review should be determined based on a risk assessment. The system activities audit trails review may be performed as part of the system periodic review as appropriate.

What Are We Looking for in an Audit Review?

The review of audit trails follows a risk-based approach concerning data criticality, security level, and frequency of system uses and storage capacity. System-specific audit trail review frequency, based on risk assessment, should be incorporated in the respective data integrity procedure and should include considerations for the type of audit trail information.

Systematic or significant errors in data collection, potential data manipulation, and modification to the e-records by unauthorized users must be evaluated.

Review of Audit Trail Entries

Guidance for "Regular Review" of Audit Trails

An audit trail is only useful if there is a regular review of the activities that are stored in it.

Audit trails may be reviewed as a list of relevant data, or by an "exception reporting" process. An exception report is a validated search tool that identifies and documents predetermined "abnormal" data or actions that require further attention or investigation by the data reviewer (8).

Depending upon the criticality of the stored regulated e-records, the frequency of the review will increase and should be risk based (7).

The audit trail review frequency of those systems with a history of corruption or data loss issues or data integrity-related observation by a regulatory authority, internal audit, or external audits must be set to the highest frequency established by a procedural control. After the systems have been remediated and the affectivity check successfully concluded, the system may return to its less review frequency.

What Are We Looking for in an Audit Review?

As part of the audit trail review, the following changes should be considered:

- Unauthorized login attempts
- Changes to the original value
- Reasons for change to the value

It will be verified that operations have been performed correctly and whether any change (modification, deletion, or overwriting) has been made to the original information in the associated e-records. All changes must be properly authorized.

Suspected Data Integrity Violation – What Do We Need to Do?

The audit trails must be reviewed according to the applicable procedures.

Any significant variation from the expected outcome found during the audit trail review should be fully investigated and recorded. A procedure should describe the actions to be taken if a review of audit trails identifies serious issues that can impact the quality of the medicinal products or the integrity of data, including escalation processes for the notification of senior management and national authorities where necessary (5).

Testing Audit Trails

Audit trail functionality should be verified during the validation of the system to ensure that all changes and deletions of critical data associated with each manual activity are recorded and meet ALCOA+ principles.

Validation documentation should demonstrate that audit trails are functional and that all activities, changes, and other transactions within the systems are recorded, together with all metadata.

The typical functionality to be tested is briefly discussed under "typical expectations" examined earlier.

In brief, the audit trails testing must verify the specified format of audit trails to ensure that all critical, relevant, and required information is captured.

Databases Integrity

In terms of a database, data integrity refers to the process of ensuring that a database remains an accurate reflection of the universe of discourse it is modeling or representing.

Data integrity is normally enforced in a database system by a series of integrity rules. Three types of integrity rules are an inherent part of the relational database model: entity integrity, referential integrity, and domain integrity.

Entity integrity concerns the concept of a primary key. Entity integrity is an integrity rule which states that every table must have a primary key and that the column or columns chosen to be the primary key should be unique and not null.

Referential integrity concerns the concept of a foreign key. The referential integrity rule states that any foreign-key value can only be in one of two states. The usual is that the foreign-key value refers to a primary key value of some table in the database. Occasionally, and this will depend on the rules of the data owner, a foreign-key value can be null. In this case, we are explicitly saying that either there is no relationship between the objects represented in the database or this relationship is unknown.

Domain integrity specifies that all columns in a relational database must be declared upon a defined domain. The primary unit of data in the relational data model is the data item. Such data items are said to be non-decomposable or atomic. A domain is a set of values of the same type. Domains are therefore pools of values from which actual values appearing in the columns of a table are drawn.

User-defined integrity refers to a set of rules specified by a user, which do not belong to the entity, domain and referential integrity categories.

If a database supports these features, it is the responsibility of the database to ensure data integrity as well as the consistency model for data storage and retrieval. If a database does not support these features, it is the responsibility of the applications to ensure data integrity while the database supports the consistency model for data storage and retrieval.

Having a single, well-controlled, and well-defined data integrity system increases stability (one centralized system performs all data integrity operations), performance (all data integrity operations are performed in the same tier as the consistency model), re-usability (all applications benefit from a single centralized data integrity system), and maintainability (one centralized system for all data integrity administration).

Modern databases support these features, and it has become the effective responsibility of the database to ensure data integrity. Companies, and indeed many database systems, offer products and services to migrate legacy systems to modern databases.

Retention of E-records – Verification

Introduction

E-records may be stored in the processing environment, the same environment in which the e-records were first captured, or migrated to a new location or archived. In any place in which the e-records are stored, the e-records most be retained as required by the applicable regulations (e.g., 21 CFR Part 211.180; Directive 2003/94/EC, Chapter II, Article 9, Section 1, and so on)

Together with the requirements by the worldwide authorities to have access to regulated records "throughout the retention period" (EU Annex 11 p7.1), the controls implemented to retained e-records must guarantee the reliability of such records.

It is not practical to have an open test script to assess the retention of e-records to demonstrate the effectiveness of the controls implemented through the e-records lifecycle. This may take years after loading the e-records to the migration environment.

The design and testing documentation to demonstrate EU Annex 11 p7.1 guidance and compared to other worldwide guidance and regulations are discussed in this chapter.

The extraction of the e-records from the source system(s) and the loading of the e-records to the migration environment can be verified and the results recorded after the execution of such tests. The preservation of the e-records is part of the operational and maintenance controls associated with records in the migrated environment.

Documentation

Documentation constitutes an essential part of the quality assurance system and is key to operating in compliance with CGMP requirements (9).

Design specification or similar document must describe the file structure(s) in which the data are stored, the storage capacity requirements, and how the security scheme is to be implemented. The file structure and security are verified and the verification documented tested during the qualification.

After the e-records are in the storage device, the logical and physical protections must be adequate to the risk (EU Annex 11 p12.2). Logical and physical protections comprise the protection of data storage devices from unauthorized parties (EU Annex 11 p7.1 and p12.1) as well as the environmental impacts influencing the respective data storage devices (EU Annex 11 p7.1).

The migration environment is one in which the e-records are stored as the result of the inactivity, superseded, replaced, or withdrawn for the use of e-records. The e-records may be read-only. Even the records may be read-only, there must be procedural control managing the access to the location of e-records, including access authorization (EU Annex 11 p12.3). During the periodic evaluation (EU Annex 11 p11) the security of the repository holding the retained e-record is to be evaluated.

If the migrated e-records can be modified, as an element of the e-record integrity, there must be a record of modifications made to the e-record that includes the previous entry, who made the change, and when the change was made (9) (EU Annex 11 p9).

To reduce the risk of losing the data in the storage and guarantee e-records readiness to the users, periodic backups must be performed (EU Annex 11 p7.2). The backup must be stored separate from the primary storage location and at a frequency based on an analysis of risk to GMP data and the capacity of the storage device.

All the above must be written in a procedural control. As an example, items to be considered as part of the backup procedure (6) include:

- Backup and restore procedures
- Frequency of backup
- Verification of the ability to retrieve a backup data and files
- At least two generations or two copies of backups, unless other measures are taken to prevent backup versions from damage

- Backup copies stored separately from the system in a way that it is highly unlikely that both the original and the backup copy/copies can be damaged
- Availability of the backup within an appropriate period

Accessibility to and readability and accuracy of the storage device and backups should be checked immediately after copying and periodically thereafter (EU Annex 11 p11). If changes are proposed to the storage-related computer infrastructure (hardware and software) and the application accessing the records in storage, the above-mentioned checks must be performed as part of the qualification of the new component.

The person who owns the stored e-records will also be carrying the accuracy controls of these records.

Finally, when an outside agency is used to provide data storage service, there should be a formal agreement including a clear statement of the responsibilities of that outside agency (EU Annex 11 p3).

Based on the above, it will be required the typical SLC documentation, including the approach to validate all data management functions, qualify the data server(s), and the procedural controls managing the e-records.

Testing Required Concerning the Retention of E-records

The design of the infrastructure to hold e-records must be tested to demonstrate that the implementation is as intended.

The key EU Annex 11 paragraphs related to the verification and testing to the retention of e-records are:

EU Annex 11 p7.1 – The third sentence is the main requirement in this chapter. Access to e-records throughout the retention period must be ensured. This requirement will take verifications, testing, and procedural controls to support the retention of the e-records during the e-records lifecycle.

EU Annex 11 p7.1 – It includes physical and logical security of data server or associated repository.

EU Annex 11 p7.1 – It specifies the need for a procedural control to set the periodic verification for accessibility to and readability and accuracy of the e-records located in the data server or applicable repository. The procedural control must include metadata verification.

EU Annex 11 p7.2 – It involves performing and recording periodic backups of e-records and associated metadata.

EU Annex 11 p11 – It involves performing and recording periodic reviews of data server or repository.

EU Annex 11 p17 –The e-records may be migrated and/or archived. EU Annex 11 p4.8 is applicable; verification and testing are required to check that e-records are not altered in value and/or meaning during the migration/archiving activities.

EU Annex 11 p5 – On those systems in which the application resides in an application server and the e-records in a data server, and these servers are physically distinct, a periodic I/Os verification will be required. I/O errors can result in serious production errors and distribution of adulterated or misbranded products (US FDA CPG 7132a.07, 21 CFR 211.68(b) and EU Annex 11 p7.1).

EU Annex 11 p17 – In the Operational Stage, before changes are implemented to the data server or associated repository the ability to retrieve the e-records must be ensured and tested.

E-records Integrity in Wireless Environments (10)

Introduction to Wireless Environment

Bluetooth, Wi-Fi, radiofrequency, and so on are the typical wireless environments in which manufacturing-related data may be transported.

As an example, in this section, I will use a wireless LAN (WLAN). Refer to Figure 20.1.

WLAN is another type of media used to provide network connectivity to the local LAN and its resources. It serves the same purpose as the typical "wired" LAN environment that most business locations use.

The major difference between the two network environments is that the wireless device accesses the network via a shared radio frequency band instead of using a physical cable and jack that is typical via a switched Ethernet connection.

The implementation of wireless networking also has potential regulatory implications. Validated applications may use the wireless LAN data connectivity for the transmission of CGMP e-records. To protect the reliability of CGMP e-records, wireless security measures such as authentication and

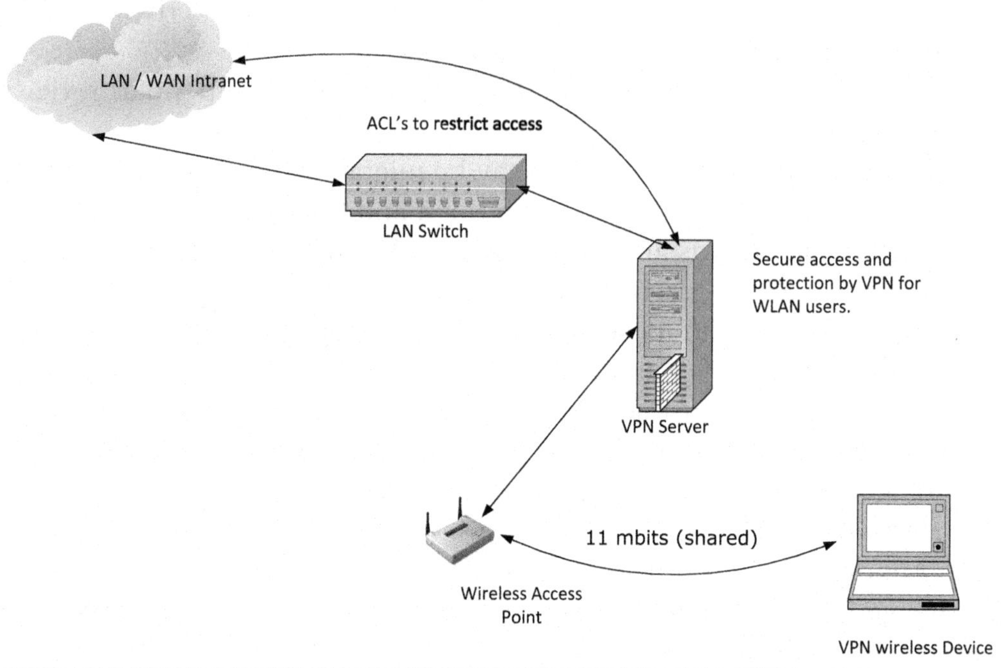

Figure 20.1 WLAN.

encryption must be implemented, and the proper implementation of these security measures shall require documented verification.

Various wireless networking standards are available: 802.11, Bluetooth, and HipeLAN/ 1 and 2.

802.11 and HiperLAN/2 are the most common standards for wireless LANs.

The wireless network still utilizes the existing network topology to accomplish its purpose of providing network connectivity. A wireless access point (AP) is physically cabled to a LAN switch and acts as a translator between the wired and wireless worlds. This access point links the wireless data devices to the physical hardwired network. A wireless data device is one that transmits and receives data between an AP and itself via a radio frequency.

Triple data encryption standard (DES) through a VPN tunnel is the method chosen for enterprise WLANs, which is the same method used for remote access. The VPN tunnel is established between the wireless device and a local VPN server to provide secure protection for all data transferred on VPN secured WLAN.

The intermediary devices (routers and/or switches) that are used to pass the tunnel traffic are typically unaware of the content and pass the data along without performance impact.

The following illustration is a high-level drawing that depicts the key components involved with a basic wireless LAN connection for enterprise WLAN environments. The level of technological complexity can increase by varying amounts depending on the type of facility and the amount of wireless data networking coverage that is being provided.

Data Integrity in Wireless Environments

Data integrity is defined as the "property that data have not been altered in an unauthorized manner" and it "covers data in storage, during processing, and while in transit." The "while in transit" provides the criteria that must be met for data have remained unaltered while moving wireless from one point to another.

The following criteria to consider are the qualification of infrastructure; built-in checks; and accuracy checks (11).

- Qualification of infrastructure

The infrastructure qualification is a process that provides documentary evidence of the design, development, integration, and implementation, operational lifecycle, and retirement of all infrastructure hardware components, products, and/or services. The objective of this process is to ensure that the integrated infrastructure hardware and associated devices are appropriate for the intended use. "Intended use" can be linked with what Joseph M. Juran called the "quality parameters." These parameters are capability, installability, usability, performance, reliability, maintainability, documentation/information, and service.

By approaching the computer infrastructure hardware as equipment, the CGMP regulations applicable to equipment apply to the infrastructure hardware (12). Equipment needs to be qualified once and, when applicable, as part of any modification.

Once the computer infrastructure is qualified, the various application that operates over the computer infrastructure can be validated without repeating the computer infrastructure qualification effort, unless the new application requires new computer infrastructure or system-level software not previously included as part of the computer infrastructure qualification effort.

When a new application will operate over the computer infrastructure, it is always practical to perform an impact analysis of the new application over the computer infrastructure.

The "documentary evidence" is established after several formal and informal activities, many of which must be completed in a predefined order. These activities comprise infrastructure qualification. The work products of each phase in the infrastructure qualification provide the "documentary evidence" that is required to demonstrate that the infrastructure conforms to the needs and intended uses of the user and that all requirements were consistently fulfilled.

- Built-in checks

The correct I/Os ensure the secure exchange of data between systems and correct inputs on the processing of data. These built-in checks maximize the mitigation associated with I/Os errors.

Built-in checks as described in the EU Annex 11 p5, includes transmission integrity and transmission confidentiality. Transmission integrity guards against improper information modification or destruction while in transit. The implementation of the transmission integrity maybe through encryption.

The impact on network-based technologies is that insufficient error checking at the point of transaction entry can result in incorrect transaction processing and data integrity risks. Integrity can be lost when data is processed incorrectly or when transactions are incorrectly handled due to errors or delayed processing.

The built-in check is the mechanism that can ensure the authenticity, integrity, and confidentiality of transmissions, and the mutual trust between communicating parties.

- Accuracy checks

Critical data transferred between computer systems or from a computer system to paper, the verification of accuracy can be performed by a second person or, if the system is properly validated, by the computer system itself.

The impact on network-based technologies is that insufficient error checking at the point of transaction entry can result in incorrect transaction processing and data integrity risks. Integrity can be lost when data is processed incorrectly or when transactions are incorrectly handled due to errors or delayed processing.

In the context of the computer system checks, verification is one that is programmed into the background of the data entry and configured to ensure the accuracy of the data inputs. This could be specific checks on data format, ranges, or values.

References

1. Murphy, L., "How to Make the Business Case for Data Quality & Data Governance Initiative," February 2020. https://www.linkedin.com/pulse/how-make-business-case-data-quality-governance-leo-murphy/?trackingId=78vWhB34RJyL8KnY4zA29w%3D%3D.
2. US FDA, "Data Integrity and Compliance with drug CGMP," December 2018.
3. López, O., *Computer Infrastructure Qualification for FDA Regulated Industries.* (PDA and DHI Publishing, LLC, River Grove, IL, 2006).
4. US FDA, "Guidance for Industry: Electronic Records; Electronic Signatures — Scope and Application," August 2003.
5. PI 041–1, "Good Practices for Data Management and Integrity in Regulated GMP/GDP Environment," *Pharmaceutical Inspection Co-operation Scheme (PIC/S)*, November 2018 (Draft 3).
6. "US Federal Register vol 43 no 45013," September 1978.
7. Conseil Européen des Fédérations de l'Industrie Chimique (CEFIC), "Practical Risk-based Guide for Managing Data Integrity," March 2019 (Rev 1).
8. MHRA, "GxP Data Integrity and Definitions," March 2018.
9. Health Canada, "Good Manufacturing Practices (GMP) Guidelines for Active Pharmaceutical Ingredients (APIs)," GUI-0104, C.02.05, Interpretation #15, December 2013.
10. López, O., "Qualification of Wireless Services," In: *Computer Infrastructure Qualification for FDA Regulated Industries.* (PDA and DHI Publishing, LLC., Bethesda, MD, 1st ed., 2006). pp 129–132.
11. López, O., "A Computer Data Integrity Compliance Model," *Pharmaceutical Engineering*, March/April 2015.
12. US FDA CPG 7132a.11, "Computerized Drug Processing; CGMP Applicability To Hardware and Software," September 1987.

Chapter 21

E-records Remediation Project Revisited – Medicine Manufacturing

Introduction

Chapter 19 in my first book, addressing e-records integrity (1), covers a broad data integrity remediation project.

This chapter describes the e-records integrity remediation project in a typical medicine manufacturing CGMP environment. In this environment, computer systems handle data guided by the related medicine CGMP regulation.

Specifically, in this chapter, the computer systems generating e-records in this CGMP environment are typically stand-alone and the generated CGMP data is not stored in an electronic storage device. The data generated is in transient memory only and displayed on the human–machine interface (HMI).

The CGMP records of the above stand-alone systems supporting the manufacturing operation are paper based. These paper-based records are obtained by periodically manually transferring to paper or printed out the machine-related operation. These paper-based records are considered the raw data and are subject to verification by a second person.

These paper-based systems, there is no CGMP e-records system backing the manufacturing operation. These systems produce CGMP records via a printout or transcribed by an operator. According to the CEFIC DI guide (2), these systems do not store GxP data and manually transfer the data to paper (categorized 2) or a system with some limited manual adjustable input data and the generated GxP data is not stored but printed out (categorized 3). At the end of the remediation explained in this chapter both systems will be systems with some limited manual adjustable input data and the generated GxP data will not be stored but sent via an interface to another system (categorized 4).

The regulatory authorities expect that the length of time that CGMP data is held in transient memory should be minimized. Removing or reducing the time that data is stored in temporary memory reduces the risk of undetected data manipulation (3). The other objective of this remediation project is to implement role-based security and audit trails improving the reliability of the e-records.

Refer to Chapter 13 about the integrity controls associated with these stand-alone systems storing data on memory.

In the EU it is expected that CGMP facilities with industrial automation and control equipment/systems such as programmable logic controllers (PLCs) should be able to demonstrate working towards system upgrades with individual login and audit trails. Refer to Art 23 of Directive 2001/83/EC) (4).

Remediation Project Fundamentals

The integrity of CGMP e-records is accomplished through a process of assessments, all-inclusive procedural controls, implementing e-records integrity services into the system design, and vendor engagement and sustainability. All mentioned activities are integrated with a systematic training and communication program.

The precise automated e-records integrity services integrate the key components to be designed into the system such as identification of the data to be recorded (Chapter 2), the design of the databases holding the e-records (Chapter 2), the management of the e-records functions, and the development of the data flow from capturing, transformation sequencing, transmission, and creation of the CGMP e-record.

The correct design will provide the data quality (Chapter 23) expected by the applicable CGMP regulation.

For this chapter, one option to the remediation project is to connect all stand-alone system to a network, send all transient data to an electronic storage device (e.g., SCADA, Historian) connected to the network as well, and lastly send the e-records to the manufacturing execution system (MES). This may be the most cost-effective approach.

Another option is to connect each system, individually, to an electronic storage device, capture and create the e-records to each associated system, and send the records directly to the MES.

In addition to the added complexity of access management, the second option will create multiple locations with raw data, one per system. The first option will have one location containing the raw data of multiple systems. The design of this first option is more complex than the second option but provides one focal point to all raw data to each isolated system. Managing the access level of this focal point to e-record is easier than multiple repositories.

Figure 21.1 illustrates a complete remediation project. Like any project, the schedule is based on priorities, risks, time, and the availability of resources.

The scope of this chapter includes the technological and regulatory challenges only. People and implementation challenges are out of the scope.

The best guidance about data integrity remediation is contained in the US FDA Warning Letters to KVK-Tech, Inc., (MARCS-CMS 592387) on February 11, 2020.

Evaluate E-records Controls

As part of the remediation process to e-records integrity, a comprehensive evaluation plan and associated execution of the plan to analyze the risks and possible controls to the e-records.

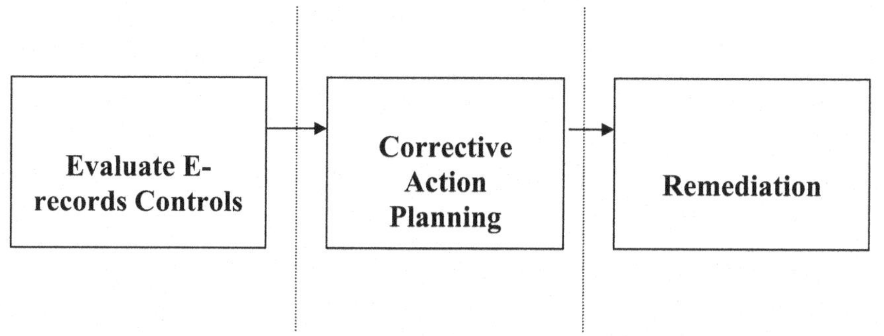

Figure 21.1 Complete remediation project.

An evaluation plan is needed to define the nature, extent, schedule, and responsibilities of the evaluation process. The methodology to evaluate the controls to the e-records should be described. Results should include conclusions about the extent of data integrity deficiencies and their root cause.

The evaluation plan must be based on a data governance document. This governance document briefly describes the technical controls, policies, procedural controls, and behavioral aspects addressing the management of records that, if effectively implemented, assure data quality and integrity.

As part of the evaluation plan, there must be an approach to manage quality risk to data integrity. The effort applied to control measures should be commensurate with this data risk and criticality of the evaluated records. At the moment writing this book, the best source to manage the risk thought the e-record lifecycle is the CEFIC DI guide (2).

This evaluation plan is the first phase to reaching an organized, prioritized, and balanced e-records integrity remediation project approach. The results of the evaluation will determine whether the e-records management practices and security procedures specific to the system will provide a controlled environment, ensuring the integrity of the e-records.

The executed evaluation plan will uncover also the extent of inaccuracies in the e-records, including trustworthy of the computer systems managing these e-records, procedural controls, change management, e-records and system security, the effectiveness of the audit trails, system backups, operator (user) training, inaccuracies in the recorded e-records and reports.

If the evaluation demonstrates that certain e-records do not meet the applicable regulatory requirements, then the evaluation would not in itself support the integrity of the e-records in scope.

In the US FDA CGMP environment the applicable regulatory requirements are as follows: 211.101(d), 211.122, 211.186, 211.188(b)(11), and 212.50(c)(10) for attributable records; 211.180(e) and 212.110(b) for legible records; 211.100(b) and 211.160(a) for contemporaneously records; 211.180 and 211.194(a) for original or a true copy records; and 211.22(a), 211.68, 211.188, and 212.60(g) for accurate records (5).

In Volume 4 of the Rules governing medicinal products in the European Union, Article 9 p2 in the Commission the Directive 2003/94/EC accounts for the e-records integrity requirements. The same requirements can be found in 91/412/EEC, applicable to veterinarian products.

Similar requirements can be found in other regulatory agencies.

As part of the prioritization in the evaluation plan, a risk assessment of how the observed deficiencies may affect the reliability and completeness of quality information available for the drug product. The risk assessment provides the effects of potentially compromised data as well on release decisions that rely on data generated by uncontrolled system and/or repositories.

Each critical e-record must be identified and must be well understood. Data flow diagrams and data process mappings are used as tools for reviewing the movement of data. Other factors to consider during the prioritization process are the components and functions of impacting regulatory requirements.

An evaluation report must be generated for each e-records repository and the computer system(s) managing those e-records. The evaluation report summarizes the current operation of the computer system, allocates its priority, provides a reference to any supporting documentation, and identifies the compliance gaps in each repository and associated computer system managing those records.

The evaluation report also should include any discrepancies between data or information identified in approved applications, and the actual results, methods, or testing conditions. The report should include an explanation of the impact of all discrepancies.

Sample Project and the Evaluation of E-records Controls

The evaluation of each legacy stand-alone system, as is, revealed that the systems do not prevent unauthorized activities. There must be role-based system access in place to control unauthorized access to the system. Each stand-alone system does not create e-records and does not have audit trail capability because there is no durable storage capability.

The evaluation included a complete understanding of the data creation, transformation, processing, and process mapping and dataflow. This breakdown by functionality provides a better understanding of the data activities and the data controls associated with these activities. This analysis uncovered the gaps associated with the data controls. These gaps were inputs to the corrective action planning.

Corrective Actions Planning

Based on the information on each e-record control evaluation report, a corrective action plan is generated describing the specific procedures, technologies, actions, and controls that the regulated entity will implement.

The purpose of the corrective action plan is to investigate the extent of the deficient practices noted during the evaluation. The action plan must include an investigation into the data integrity issue root(s) cause and the associated risk.

The corrective action plan defines the overall activities, schedule, and responsibilities necessary to guide the development and implementation of technological and procedural controls to bring the e-records into compliance with the data integrity-related expectations. The plan should identify any existing technological/procedural controls that may be modified or new technological/procedural controls, which need to be implemented to ensure that the data integrity-related regulatory requirements are completed consistently and uniformly.

Using the evaluation reports, the remediation activities, available resources, project schedule, and the business cost of the remediation approach can be estimated. This will enable a business decision to be made regarding the remediation or replacement of the current system/components surrounding the e-records based on the cost-effectiveness of the system/components and its operational feasibility.

The plan must contain the activities that place emphasis on achieving consistent, high-quality, sustainable data integrity compliance solutions.

For data integrity-related issues found on computer systems performing activities covered by the medicine manufacturing practices regulation, the corrective action plan must describe the broad actions that will be taken to assure product quality and the prevention of the recurrence of breaches of e-records integrity.

Once the corrective action plan has been approved, it can then be executed.

Sample Project and the Corrective Actions Planning

The corrective action plan includes connecting all stand-alone system to the network, as well as sending all transient data to a permanent storage location (e.g., SCADA, Historian) connected to the network. The e-records in a storage media location are to be sent to the manufacturing execution system.

At the SCADA or Historian-level, role-based access was implemented to avoid unauthorized users access to the system. Those regulated users authorized to access the system will access the system based on their role. The remediation will consider the data integrity-related controls on data at rest and data while in transit. Audit trail at the permanent storage location will be implemented as well.

For data traceability purposes, the processes mapping at the SCADA or Historian level will be added to the process mapping at the controller/supervisory level.

As part of the remediation, procedural controls must be developed, including archiving, backup business continuity, incident management, problem management, data retirement, migration, restore, risk management, training, periodic reviews, security, timestamping controls, and so on.

Remediation

The remediation process consists of six major activities. These activities are:

- Interpretation
- Training
- Remediation execution
- New applications assessments
- Application upgrade assessments
- Supplier qualification program

During the remediation phase, the e-records and the associated controls are brought into compliance by implementing the procedural and/or technological controls determined by the corrective action plan. Besides, the processes needed to sustain compliance solutions are implemented.

Interpretation

The ability to evaluate the risks of an e-record with its integrity regulatory expectations requires a thorough understanding of the regulation and guidelines, and a consistent interpretation. The objective of the Interpretation phase in this plan is to provide current, consistent, competent authorities interpretation of e-records integrity to the regulated entity and interested outside parties.

Training

In the context of the e-records integrity, awareness and understanding of the applicable regulation(s) and guidelines are fundamental to the success of the remediation plan. The objective of the e-records integrity training is to ensure that all systems containing e-records and e-records owners have an appropriate level of knowledge on how to preserve the integrity of such records.

Remediation Execution

Once the corrective action plan is approved, the computer technology suppliers and developers are requested to identify products in which deficiencies can be overcome. When appropriate, procedural controls need to be revised and/or developed to address the deficiencies which cannot be solved by technological controls.

The implementation of technological controls will probably require a comprehensive SLC including the recommendation, conceptualization, and implementation of the new technology, the release and early operation of the new technology, and the decommissioning and disposal of old technologies. If the technological implementation fails, the failure should be documented along with details of the corrective action taken. Once this action has been taken, the system must be re-evaluated in the same way as any other system which had been subject to an upgrade or correction.

When all action items applicable to the affected e-records have been implemented, it can be formally released to operation and support under a maintenance agreement.

The corrective action plan should be periodically reviewed since the evolving technology requirements will need to be considered and the plan revised accordingly.

New Applications and Application Upgrade Assessments

The objective of e-records integrity assessments for new repositories, applications managing e-records, and for application upgrades, is to identify the e-records integrity gaps before releasing the system into production. All gaps must be corrected by technological controls and/or procedural controls.

New and upgrades to systems/components, which are released into production must have the highest level of e-records integrity compliance.

Suppliers Qualification Program

A key business strategy has been the outsourcing of work to computer technology suppliers and developers. The objective of qualifying computer technology suppliers and developers is to evaluate and monitor these "strategic" partners for e-records integrity compliance and to provide input to the partner selection and partner relationship management processes.

For each supplier qualification performed, a report must be prepared which describe the results of the qualification.

Sample Project and Remediation

The remediation to each stand-alone system will consist of

- Installation of infrastructure.
- Connection to the SCADA or Historian via a network
- Implementation of the role-based access at the SCADA or Historian level
- Design verification of data flows
- Implementation of application, including implementation of build-in and accuracy checks
- E-records migration, as applicable
- Training and deployment of procedural controls
- Qualification of infrastructure integration

Remediation Project Report

The Remediation Project Report provides evidence of successful project completion. It summarizes the findings, the technological and procedural controls, and associated activities that were necessary to establish the computer technologies compliant with e-records integrity-related requirements. This report and all supporting documentation should be archived.

This report ensures that the remediation project is complete, meaningful, and related to the specific acceptance criteria and/or specifications. The conclusions must be supported by documented evidence.

Once a legacy system has achieved a satisfactory, documented e-records integrity compliant state, any subsequent changes can be prospectively validated.

References

1. López, O., *Data Integrity in Pharmaceutical and Medical Devices Regulation Operations: Best Practices Guide to Electronic Records Compliance.* (CRC Press, Boca Ratón, FL, 2017).

2. Conseil Européen des Fédérations de l'Industrie Chimique (CEFIC), "Practical Risk-Based Guide for Managing Data Integrity,". March 2019 (Rev 1).
3. EU, "Questions and Answers: Good Manufacturing Practice and Good Distribution Practice, Data Integrity," August 2016. https://www.ema.europa.eu/en/human-regulatory/research-development/compliance/good-manufacturing-practice/guidance-good-manufacturing-practice-good-distribution-practice-questions-answers#data-integrity-(new-august-2016)-section.
4. MHRA, "'GxP' Data Integrity Guidance and Definitions,". March 2018.
5. US FDA, "Data Integrity and Compliance with Drug CGMP - Questions & Answers - Guidance for industry," December 2018.

Additional Reading

Eglovitch, J., "How to Remedy Data Integrity Failures: FDA's Step-by-Step Approach,".*The Golden Sheet*, October 2015).

Chapter 22

Designing E-records Integrity into your Practices (1)

Using EU Annex 11, this chapter proposes a model (2) describing the data integrity provisions applicable to new computer system implementations. The model defined the controls on data integrity to computer systems in operation. Based on this context, the data integrity in a computer system can be assessed.

Note that data integrity, by contrast, refers to whether data is trustworthy. It must be trustworthy to be useful.

Introduction EU Annex 11

> Data Integrity – The property that data has not been altered in an unauthorized manner. Data integrity covers data since it was created, in storage, during processing, and while in transit.
>
> **NIST SP 800-57P1**

The European Medicines Agency (EMA) CGMPs legislation applicable tor computer systems performing CGMP-regulated activities (3) are contained in Directives 2003/94/EC (4) and 91/412/EEC (5). These Directives (6) were expanded and explained in EU Annex 11 (7) guidance document. EU Annex 11 provides the consistent criteria for effective implementation, control, and use of computer systems in CGMP-regulated activities. Medicines imported into the EU need to take it into account as an applicable requirement.

Non-EU countries are adopting the content of EU Annex 11. As an example, the Canadian CGMPs requirements for Medicinal Products for Human (8) references the PIC/S Annex 11 (9) as Canada's guideline applicable to computer systems performing CGMP-regulated activities. Also, since May 2013, EU Annex 11 applies to active pharmaceutical ingredients (APIs) in Canada.

Another example of non-EU country embracing the content of EU Annex 11 is the CFDA. The 2014 draft CGMP Annex 2, covering computer systems, incorporates most of the EU Annex 11 clauses.

Other non-EU embracing EU Annex 11 are Argentina, Australia, Brunei Darussalam, Cambodia, Indonesia, Japan, Korea, LAO PDR, Malaysia, Myanmar, Philippines, Singapore, South Korea, Thailand, United States of America, Vietnam, and many more.

The use of EU Annex 11 can be extended to other regulated applications. For example, the EU GCP inspectors agreed to use as the reference for inspection of computer systems the published PIC/S Guidance on "*Good Practices for Computerised Systems in Regulated 'GXP' Environments*" (PI 011-3). This guidance is an internal document helping inspectors with the interpretation of EU Annex 11.

Except for medical device software, the EU Annex 11 may be applicable for software used in the production of a device (e.g., programmable logic controllers in manufacturing equipment) and software used in the implementation of the device manufacturer's quality system (e.g., software that records and maintains the device history record).

Since EU Annex 11 can be correlated with the principal regulations and guidelines (https://drive.google.com/open?id=1EqeWvGAipuuwQJh2qf0v7ru50BiWzov-), it can be used as a computer system compliance model for computer system performing regulated activities.

EU Annex 11 as a Computer Data Integrity Compliance Model

EU Annex 11 is organized in the five areas "Principles," "General," "Project Phase," "Operational Phase," and "Glossary" with altogether 17 sub-chapters.

Sub-chapter EU Annex 11 p4.1 specifically refers to the need for ensuring that the computer system has been developed under a quality model which must incorporate a system lifecycle and associated risk management. As part of the risks associated with computer systems, the issue of record keeping is a relevant one. The computer system must ensure that the methods of record keeping fulfill, at least, the same degree of confidence as that provided with paper systems.

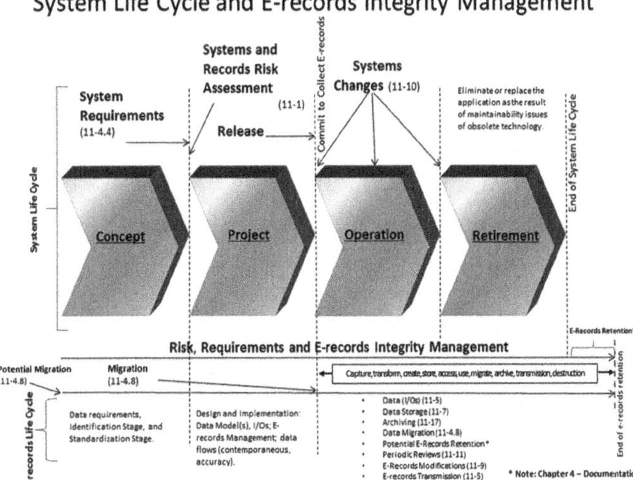

Related to the current issue about record keeping, the provisions on data integrity in EU Annex 11 can be used as a compliance model. These provisions can be used as the rules to build computer systems managing the integrity of the data.

The basic EMA requirement on data integrity comes from EU Council Directives 2003/94/EC and 91/412/EEC.

> The electronically stored data shall be protected, by methods such as duplication or back-up and transfer on to another storage system, against loss or damage of data, and audit trails shall be maintained.

Decisions on the data integrity controls need to start early in the system lifecycle and based on a risk assessment (EU Annex 11 p1). All required controls must be traceable throughout the lifecycle (EU Annex 11 p4.4). From the context of data integrity, this path can be called data integrity management.

Consistent with the definition of data integrity in NIST SP 800-57P1, the data integrity-related chapters in EU Annex 11 are interrelated with the correct and secure entry of data (both manually entered and automatically captured data) and the subsequent data processing, storage, and archiving, as applicable. These controls decrease the risks of a wrong decision based on wrong results. The identity of authorized individuals carrying out work needs to be added to the records including date and time stamps of entries.

Supporting Processes Applicable to the Data Integrity Controls

The following controls maintain data integrity as part of the lifecycle of the system.

- Procedural controls

US FDA 21 CFR Part 11.10(c) requires the employment of procedures for the protection of e-records to enable their accurate and ready retrieval throughout the records retention period.

Procedures should describe:

- How e-records will be maintained
- Storage conditions and precautions
- Retrieval and access restrictions
- The technical approach to long-term electronic record storage (e.g., electronic records migration, as described below)
- Personnel responsibilities for relevant tasks

The regulated user should update the procedures and controls as conditions warrant.

- Risk management (EU Annex 11 p1)

The basis for all these processes enabling the computer data integrity is the initial risk assessment as part of the risk management (EU Annex 11 p1). Integration of the SLC and the risk management must exist to effectively implement and maintain the data integrity controls. Based on the intended use and the risks associated with the computer system, the implementation and maintenance of a computer system should determine the approach, the combination of techniques to be used, and the effort to be applied.

- Personnel (EU Annex 11 p2)

EU Annex 11 p12 establishes restricting the computer systems access to authorized users only. Complementing EU Annex 11 p12, EU Annex 11 p2 establishes the level of access of those allowed to access the computer system based on their assigned tasks.

- Requirements document (EU Annex 11 p4.4)

The requirements document must include both structural and functional analysis (EU Annex 11 p4.1 and EU Annex 11 p4.7). This analysis describes what functionality is required and the data integrity controls (EU Annex 11 p1) to be implemented, and consequently the intended use of the computer system.

It must also include "data flows and interfaces with other systems or processes, and security measures should be available" (EU Annex 11 p4.3). The specifics on these descriptions will be found in the design-related specification. These descriptions are used to implement the controls associated with EU Annex 11 p5 and EU Annex 11 p6.

Based on the requirements and functionality, appropriate data integrity controls are applicable to the application and the infrastructure supporting the application (EU Annex 11 p4.4 and EU Annex 11 – 2nd Principle).

The requirements document is the basis for the final quality of the system to be implemented and the source of all the implementation and maintenance activities.

- Security (EU Annex 11 p12)

> The electronically stored data shall be protected, by methods such as duplication or back-up and transfer on to another storage system, against loss or damage of data, and audit trails shall be maintained.
>
> **Chapter II, Article 9(2), the Commission Directive 2003/94/EC**

A means of ensuring records protection must be established for all computer systems. Computer security is the principal enabler to create the integrity of the e-records.

The system owner (10) is the person responsible for providing the records protection suitable controls over the application and network components. These record protection controls ensure that only authorized personnel can make changes to any component of the computer system and the security of the records residing on the system.

Security must be instituted at several levels (EU Annex 11 p2). Procedural controls must govern physical access to computer systems (*physical security*). As part of physical security, security to devices used to store programs, such as tapes, disks and magnetic strip cards, must be considered. Access to these devices should be controlled.

Access to individual computer system platforms is controlled by network-specific security procedures (*network security*). Finally, application-level security and associated authority checks control the access to the computer system applications (*applications security*).

A defined procedure at network and application levels should be established to record the creation, alteration, and cancellation of access authorizations (EU Annex 11 p12.3).

Periodic (or continuous) reviews must be performed after the initial validation (EU Annex 11 p11). As part of the periodic reviews should be verified stored, backed up, and archived e-records for accessibility, readability, and accuracy. Also, the output of the backup should be verified, as well as accuracy of audit trail. As applicable, the periodic review must verify accurate and reliable records transfer.

Where a record is deleted before meeting its approved retention, an audit trail of the deletion is required until the end of the approved retention period (EU Annex 11 p7.1 and 11 p9).

It should be considered recording activities of unauthorized persons attempting to access the computer system and/or data storage devices.

Regarding data security access, the segregation of duties between analysts, reviewers and administrative tasks is critical. If in the security module, as part of the application, is not possible to implement configurable segregation of duties controls, it will be required to establish these controls in a procedure.

To recap, the security controls in place include restricting access to non-authorized persons, computer equipment, and data storage area.

An example regarding the protection of personal data, the EMA principles related to data quality, including security, are established in Article 6 of Directive 95/46/EC. Many of these principles apply to regulated e-records.

- Incident management (EU Annex 11 p13)

The faults, incorrect documentation, data errors, improper operation, or interface errors of computer system components illustrate some of the incidents which can affect the correct operation of a computer system. These incidents are also known as non-conformances (11).

Effective monitoring of the operation of a computer system involves users or operators trained in the proper operational procedure. This facilitates their ability to recognize unexpected responses and outputs, react to the incident properly, and fully document such incidents to aid in the evaluation and debugging process.

Managed by CAPA, the initial assessment of the incident includes root cause analysis (12).

- Business continuity (EU Annex 11 p16)

Based on risk, the business continuity ensures continuity of the operation in the event of a system breakdown. Business continuity refers to the prepared measures that will secure business operations in case of system failure or trouble. The procedural control employed to restore the system must be adequately documented and tested regularly. All relevant personnel should be made aware of its existence and trained to use it. A copy of the procedure should be maintained off-site.

At the lowest level, the business continuity applies to the accidental deletion of a single file, in which case a procedure should be in place for restoring the most recently backed-up copy. At the other extreme, a disaster such as destruction of the hardware, software, and data files.

- Suppliers and service providers (EU Annex 11 p3)

Service Providers are all parties who provide any services irrespective of whether they belong to an independent (external) enterprise, to the same regulated entity group/structure, or to an internal service unit.

One of the services acquired by a regulated user is the procurement of application software used in CGMP-regulated activities. Such software includes non-configured products, configured products, and custom applications.

The use of vendor-supplied software presents some additional difficulties in acquiring objective evidence of the software's quality. The use of software in production, quality assurance or as a component requires a level of knowledge enough to provide confidence in its accurate, consistent, and reliable behavior when employed by a specific user. In the case of vendor-supplied software, the user must generate some of this documentation, while other necessary documentation is generated by the software developer. This is the basic concept contained in the ASTM E2500-12 (13).

The documentation provided by the supplier must be reviewed by the regulated user to check if the regulated user's requirements are fulfilled (EU Annex 11 p3.3).

The regulated user remains responsible for the quality of the computer systems performing CGMP activities and their production processes and the integrity of the data.

The acquisition of quality software systems from outside sources necessitates a predefined, structured procurement process. The validity of potential suppliers should be evaluated appropriately (EU Annex 11 p4.5) and the evaluation documented. There must be formal agreements with third parties, suppliers, and service providers, including a clear statement of the responsibilities of that outside agency (EU Annex 11 p3.1).

Similar requirements are applicable to cloud environments delivered by the cloud service provider to the regulated user. The performance of the provider must be monitored and reviewed periodically. Any needed improvements need to be identified and the implementation monitored.

Categories of Data Integrity Controls

Based on the data activity in the data handling function, the required data integrity controls can be categorized into four activities: data creation, data storage; data during processing, and data while in transit. Refer to Figure 22.1.

The data integrity controls applicable to data creation include:

- The selected data recording method must ensure the accuracy, completeness, content, and meaning are collected and retained for their intended use. The data must be recorded contemporaneously (211.100(b) and 211.60(a)).

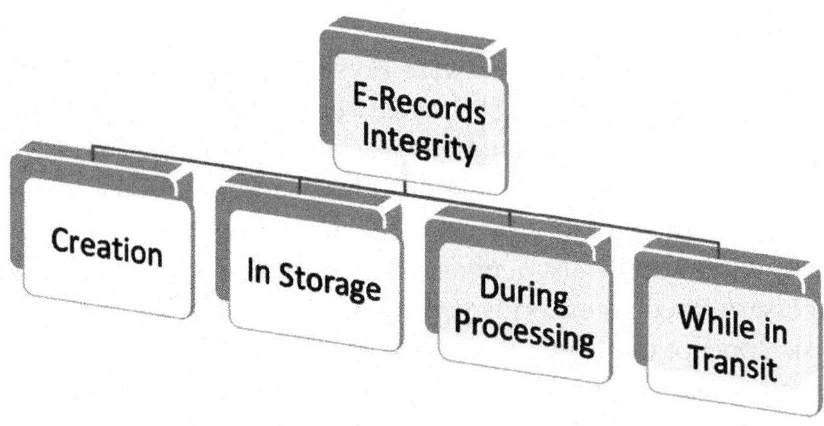

Figure 22.1 Categories of data integrity.

The data integrity controls applicable to data in electronic storage devices include:

- Data migration (EU Annex 11 p4.8)

Data migration is the process of transferring data between storage types, formats, or computer systems. It is a key consideration for any system implementation, upgrade, or consolidation. Data migration is usually performed programmatically to achieve an automated migration, freeing up human resources from tedious tasks. Data migration occurs for a variety of reasons, including server or storage equipment replacements or upgrades; website consolidation; server maintenance; installing a new version of an application or operating system software program, and data center relocation (14).

If data are transferred to another data format or system, the verification of the migrated data should include corroboration that the data are not altered in value, meaning, structure, context, and links (e.g., audit trails), and/or meaning during this migration process.

Some operating systems have a built-in copy verification mechanism, such as a cyclic redundancy check, that could be used to prevent an inaccurate or incomplete copy from being made. A copy process that does not implement such a built-in error checking mechanism (EU Annex 11 p5) to prevent making an inaccurate or incomplete copy should be validated.

Accessibility and readability (EU Annex 11 p7.1) of data after the migration are also applicable to the data migration.

- Data storage (EU Annex 11 p7)

Data storage is a device that records (stores) or retrieves (reads) information (data) from any medium, including the medium itself.

Design specification or similar document must describe the file structure(s) in which the data are stored, the capacity requirements of the storage, and how the security scheme is implemented. The file structure and security are tested during the qualification.

Access to computer systems and electronic storage devices must be restricted. After the data is in the storage device, the integrity of e-records must be ensured. Logical and physical protections must be adequate to the risk (EU Annex 11 p12.2). Logical and physical protections comprise the protection of data storage devices from unauthorized parties (EU Annex 11 p7.1

and 12.1) as well as the environmental impacts influencing the respective data storage devices (EU Annex 11 p7.1).

Authorized persons should be able to enter or modify e-records in the computer and there should be a record of changes and deletions.

As an element of the data integrity, there must be a record of any data change made that includes the previous entry, who made the change, and when the change was made (EU Annex 11 p9).

To reduce the risk of losing the data in the storage and guarantee data readiness to the users, periodic backups must be performed (EU Annex 11 p7.2 and TGA Blood Establishment Regulations (April 2013)). The backup must be stored separate from the primary storage location, and at a frequency based on an analysis of risk to CGMP data and the capacity of the storage device.

The efficacy of the backup and restored processes must be verified (EU Annex 11 p7.2) as part of the qualification process. Also, the capacity level of the storage must be monitored.

The accuracy of the e-records in storage must be periodically checked.

- Archiving (EU Annex 11 p17)

E-records that become inactive, superseded, replaced, or withdrawn from use can be archived.

Data archiving is the process of moving records that are no longer actively used to a separate records storage device for long-term retention, often disabling it from any further changes. In the context of e-records, records that are no longer active, in which the retention period has not been finalized, are archived.

Periodically, archived records need to be verified for accessibility, readability, and integrity. If changes are implemented to the computer infrastructure and/or application, then it is required to ensure and test the ability to retrieve data.

Archiving is also impacted by EU Annex 11 p4.8, 10, 11 and 12.

The data integrity controls applicable to data processing include:

- Process e-records throughout E-records retention

21 CFR 211.180(e) requires that records be maintained so that data in the records can be used for periodically evaluating product quality standards to

determine the need for changes in product specifications, or manufacturing, or control procedures.

Specifically, applicable to e-records in the processing environment, the ability to process information in an e-record should not reduce. By being able to process the information, the regulated user maintains the ability to efficiently reconstruct events, detect and investigate problems, detect trends and assess the need to modify procedures or specifications to improve product quality, safety, and effectiveness.

As explained in Chapter 2, in the retention environment if the e-records are inactive, superseded, replaced, and withdrawn, these e-records may be set for read-only e-records.

Process and retention environments must allow generating copies of e-records.

- Built-in checks (EU Annex 11 p5)

Computer systems exchanging data electronically with other systems should include, if technically feasible, appropriate built-in checks for the correct computer I/Os. The correct I/Os ensure the secure exchange of data between systems and correct inputs on the processing of data. Logical problems can happen because of design flaws, human errors, or software bugs (15).

These built-in checks maximize the mitigation associated with I/O errors. As the system automatically compares data on input with predefined limits, as an example, the user should be warned of potential errors when the data is entered manually or as input from other computer systems. For security purposes, the validity of the source of data input may be determined (21 CFR Part 11.10(h), Device Checks).

An alternative control to the built-in checks when critical data (16) are being entered manually, the check can be done by a second person (EU Annex 11 p6 and ICH Q7 5.45). Refer to "Accuracy Checks" elsewhere.

There should be no difference between manual input by the user and the take-over of data from another system. In the same way, processing operations performed by the system should be checked by the system itself.

Built-in checks should be verified periodically to ensure correct input and output transmission.

- Printouts (EU Annex 11 p8)

Even with the increased use of computer systems in the CGMP-regulated activities and, subsequently, e-records, it is very common to see regulated users relay on printouts as a hardcopy to be attached to the batch record and/or relay on printouts to perform regulated activities.

> All data defined as critical data and associated metadata should be printable.
>
> **Aide Memoire (Ref. #: 07121202) of the German ZLG (Central Authority of the Laender for Health Protection)**

If these printouts are used as quality records, then the design, qualification, and controls of these printouts are critical. The reports are validated as per applicable procedural control.

In cases of internal audits (e.g., self-inspections (Eudralex Volume 4, Chapter 9)) or external audits (e.g., inspections by regulatory agencies or competent authority), it must be possible to obtain printed reports not specified nor validated during the implementation of the normally required reports.

In this particular case, to generate reliable printouts, a report generator can be utilized to take data from a source such as a database or a spreadsheet, and use it to produce a document in a format which satisfies a particular human readership.

If the printout is created by a report generator, then a verification of the printout must be performed before providing the printout to the auditor and/or using the printout as a CGMP record.

In any case, the printout functionality must provide the capability to print audit trails (EU Annex 11 p8.2 and EU Annex 11 p9). Also, EU Annex 11 p8.1 recommends that the printout be clear. "Clear printed" means printouts that apart from the values themselves, the units, and the respective context can also be seen in the printout (17). Units and the respective context are also known as metadata.

Printouts must be verified before hardware and/or software is exchanged. As part of the validation/qualification of the software/hardware, regression testing can be used to check that the data concerned can also be printed in the new configuration.

- Audit trails (EU Annex 11 p9) (18)

As part of data integrity, it is imperative to keep track of all changes made to the information in the e-records that document activities related to all

CGMP-relevant records (audit trails). The use of audit trails or other security measures helps to confirm that only authorized additions, deletions, or alterations of CGMP-relevant e-records have occurred and allow a means to reconstruct significant details about manufacturing activities and data collection. This is necessary to verify the quality and data integrity. Computer-generated, time-stamped audit trails or other security measures can also capture information related to the creation, modification, or deletion of CGMP-relevant e-records and may be useful to ensure compliance with the appropriate regulation.

The need for audit trails should be determined based on a justified and documented risk assessment that takes into consideration circumstances surrounding system use, the likelihood that information might be compromised, and any system vulnerabilities. Should it be decided that audit trails or other appropriate security measures are needed to ensure e-record integrity, personnel who create, modify, or delete e-records should not be able to modify the documents or security measures used to track e-record changes. Computer-generated, time-stamped electronic audits trails are the preferred method for tracking changes to electronic source documentation.

Audit trails or other security methods used to capture e-record activities are:

- All CGMP-relevant e-records are subject to all requirements regarding data integrity.
- They should describe when, by whom, and the reason changes were made to the e-record. Original information should not be hidden through the use of audit trails or other security measures used to capture e-record activities.
- They must be available and, if necessary, convertible to an understandable form (EU Annex 11 p8).
- They must be regularly reviewed (EU Annex 11 p11)

■ Security (EU Annex 11 p12)

Refer to "Security" elsewhere in the book.

■ Electronic signature (EU Annex 11 p14) (19)

EU Annex 11 sees the formalization of electronic signatures in EU CGMP. Many laboratories have implemented electronic signatures based on the US FDA 21 CFR Part 11, but the European regulation does not appear as stringent as the US regulation. Electronic signatures are required to have the same impact as handwritten signatures within the boundaries of the regulated entity, be permanently linked to the respective record, and include the time and date that a signature was applied. There is not the stated bureaucracy and formality of 21 CFR 11 to send letters the FDA, have no repudiation of electronic signature requirements or the three different types of signature. However, many of the same requirements are implicit as the European legislation simply states that electronic signatures have the same impact as handwritten signatures and hence all of the non-repudiation requirements apply immediately.

- Archiving (EU Annex 11 p17)

Refer to "Archiving" elsewhere in the book.

- Operational checks

The objective of operational checks is to enforce the sequencing of steps and events as applicable to the process managed by the computer system. The application-dependent algorithms, sequencing of operations, instructions to the operator, critical embedded requirements, and safety-related precautions to be followed within the computer system are encompassed in the computer program(s) which drive the computer system. These application-dependent and predicate rule requirements are defined in the requirements document, implemented as part of the Project Phase and executed during the Operational Phase.

The above controls applicable to data processing are set in, as appropriate, during the Project Phase and each control is evaluated, after implementation, during the periodic reviews (EU Annex 11 p11).

The data integrity controls applicable to data while in transit are looking for checks for correct and secure entry, both manually entered and automatically captured data. It includes:

- Principle #2 – IT Infrastructure should be qualified.

The integrity of data can be compromised by the physical integrity of the hardware (15). The infrastructure can become compromised due to age, malfunction, maintenance problems, natural disasters, or power outages.

Computer hardware infrastructure is considered as equipment (20). All CGMP controls associated with equipment apply to the computer infrastructure, including the location of the hardware, maintenance, calibration of hardware, and the qualification.

Qualification (20) of the hardware includes:

- Installation
- Evaluation of the system
- Performance
- Change control, maintenance and calibration, security, contingency planning, SOPs, training, performance monitoring, and periodic re-evaluation

The computer infrastructure must be brought into conformance with the regulated entity's established standards through a planned verification process building upon acknowledged good IT practices. Once in conformance, this state must be maintained by established processes and QA controls, the effectiveness of which must be periodically verified (21).

- Data (EU Annex 11 p5)

Refer to "Build-in Checks" elsewhere above.

- Accuracy checks (EU Annex 11 p6)

EU Annex 11 p6 applies to critical data entered manually to the computer system. The intent of EU Annex 11 p6 is to confirm that critical data entered manually by an authorized person was entered accurately and that there is an independent verification record to show this.

The independent verification of the manually entered critical data can be performed by a second authorized person or a computer system.

In the context of the computer system check, verification is one that is programmed into the background of the data entry and configured to ensure the accuracy of the data input. This could be specific checks on data format, ranges, or values.

- Contemporaneous e-records

E-records should be completed at the time each action is taken and in such a way that all significant activities concerning the manufacture and disposition of products are traceable (TGA Blood Establishment Regulations (April 2013) and 21 CFR 211.100 and 211.160).

Summary

EU Annex 11 provides the provisions that can be used to build computer systems with integrity on the data that the computer manages.

To simplify the discussion, the data integrity provisions can be categorized into four areas: data capture, data storage, data during processing, and data while in transit.

As in the management of the risks and requirements, the data integrity must be managed through the computer system lifecycle.

The Project Phase starts with the potential migration issues and the creations of the data integrity requirements. Based on these requirements, an assessment of the risk associated with the data is performed and possible mitigations are established and implemented as part of the project. Issues as data I/Os (EU Annex 11 p5), data storage (EU Annex 11 p7), and data migration (EU Annex 11 p4.8) are addressed.

During the Operational Phase, the key provision is to support changes to the baseline (EU Annex 11 p10) and data archiving (EU Annex 11 p17). The effectiveness of the data integrity provision implemented is evaluated periodically (EU Annex 11 p11).

References

1. López, O., "EU Annex 11 and Data Integrity: Designing Data Integrity into your Practices," In: *Paper Presented at the 2014 ISPE Annual Meeting*, Las Vegas, Nevada, 12–15 October 2014.
2. A model to describe, assess, and/or predict quality.
3. The term "GMP regulated activities" in the EU context is defined as the manufacturing related activities established in the basic legislation compiled in Volume 1 and Volume 5 of the publication "The Rules governing medicinal products in the European Union," http://ec.europa.eu/health/documents/eudralex/index_en.htm.
4. Commission Directive 2003/94/EC laying down the principles and guidelines of good manufacturing practice in respect of medicinal products for human use and investigational medicinal products for human use, October 1994.

5. Commission Directive 91/412/EEC laying down the principles and guidelines of good manufacturing practice for veterinary medicinal products, July 1991.
6. A directive is a legal act of the European Union, which requires member states to achieve a particular result without dictating the means of achieving that result. It can be distinguished from regulations which are self-executing and do not require any implementing measures. Directives normally leave member states with a certain amount of leeway as to the exact rules to be adopted. Directives can be adopted using a variety of legislative procedures depending on their subject matter.
7. EC, "Volume 4 – EU Guidelines to Good Manufacturing Practice: Medicinal Products for Human and Veterinary Use – Annex 11: Computerized Systems," (European Commission, Brussels, June 2011). pp 1–4.
8. Health Canada, "Good Manufacturing Practices (GMP) Guidelines – GUI-0001," February 2018.
9. "Annex 11 to PIC/S Guide to Good Manufacturing Practice for Medicinal Products, Document PE 009–10, PIC/S Secretariat, 14 rue du Roveray, CH-1207 Geneva," January 2013.
10. System owner – The person is responsible for the availability, and maintenance of a computerized system and for the security of the data residing on that system. (EU Annex 11).
11. Non-conformance – A departure from minimum requirements specified in a contract, specification, drawing, or other approved product description or service.
12. EudraLex, "The Rules Governing Medicinal Products in the European Union Volume 4, EU Guidelines for Good Manufacturing Practice for Medicinal Products for Human and Veterinary Use Chapter 1, Pharmaceutical Quality System, Section 1.4A (xiv)," January 2013.
13. ASTM E2500-12, "Standard Guide for Specification, Design, and Verification of Pharmaceutical and Biopharmaceutical Manufacturing Systems and Equipment," 2012.
14. Janssen, C., "Data Migration," http://www.techopedia.com/definition/1180/data-migration (retrieved August 12, 2013).
15. Syncsort Editors, "Data Integrity vs. Data Quality: How Are They Different?" January 2019. https://blog.syncsort.com/2019/01/data-quality/data-integrity-vs-data-quality-different/.
16. Critical data – data with high risk to product quality or patient safety. (ISPE GAMP COP Annex 11 – Interpretation, July/August 2011).
17. Journal for GMP and Regulatory Affairs, "Q&As on Annex 11," Issue 8, April/May 2012.
18. US FDA, "Guidance for Industry Computerized Systems Used in Clinical Investigations," Section IV.D.2, May 2007.
19. McDowall, R.D., "The New GMP Annex 11 and Chapter 4 is Europe's Answer to Part 11," *European Compliance Academy, GMP News*, January 2011.
20. WHO, Technical Report Series No. 937, Annex 4. Appendix 5, "Validation of Computerized Systems," Section 7.1.2, 2006.
21. Cappucci, W., Chris Clark, C., Goossens, T., Wyn, S., "ISPE GAMP CoP Annex 11 Interpretation," *Pharmaceutical Engineering*, 31, July/August 2011.

Chapter 23

Introduction to Data Quality (1)

Introduction

In drug manufacturing, quality is viewed as a required objective to be achieved through the management of the production process. Data are the results of the production process, and the way this process is performed affects data accuracy (2).

Data quality is the extent to which all data (electronic, paper based, or hybrid) are accurate, auditable, in conformance, complete, consistent, with integrity, provenance, and valid throughout the lifecycle of the data. Because the data collected during a manufacturing process characterizes the product quality and provides details on how safe the product may be, data quality is the ability of a given product manufacturing data set to work for product quality and public safety.

US FDA (FDA), as many regulatory agencies, expects that all data be reliable and accurate (3). If data integrity is the "extent to which all data are complete, consistent, and accurate throughout the data lifecycle" (3), is data integrity expectations by the regulatory agencies the knowledge up to date to match with the current CGMP?

CGMP requires companies to use up-to-date technologies to conform to the regulations. When operating under a quality system, manufacturers must develop and document control procedures to capture, create, protect, access, use, migrate, transform, archive, and destroy e-records. The e-records provide evidence of operational and quality system activities. This will provide a quality system approach to fulfilling oversight and review of CGMP records.

A quality management system (QMS) is a set of policies, processes, and procedures required for planning and execution (production/development/service) in the core business area of an organization (i.e., areas that can impact the organization's ability to meet customer requirements) (4). The set of control procedures applicable to data integrity must be sufficiently comprehensive to provide evidence of operational and quality system activities.

Data integrity refers to whether data is trustworthy. Just because data is trustworthy, it does not mean it is also useful (5). The usefulness of data is achieved by implementing data quality into the practices of data handling.

This chapter discusses the significance of data quality and the criteria to collect useful data. The attributes of useful data are accuracy, auditability, conformity, completeness, consistency, integrity, provenance, and availability of valid complete e-records to support quality medicines. Quality data must meet all these criteria. If it is lacking in just one attribute, it could compromise any data-driven initiative (5).

Data Quality

According to the Federal Information Processing Standards (FIPS) (6), data quality is considered the accurate, auditable, in conformance to requirement, complete, consistent, with integrity, provenance, and valid making data both correct and useful (Figure 23.1). The Medicines and Healthcare products Regulatory Agency (MHRA) data integrity guidance highlights that "This guidance primarily addresses data integrity and not data quality since the controls required for integrity do not necessarily guarantee the quality of the data generated" (7).

The above is evident. Only four out of six attributes defined by FIPS are contained in the data integrity guidance documents. Missing attributes in the industry definitions are conformity and validity. Only two out of six attributes defined by FIPS are contained in FDA expectations. Missing attributes in the FDA expectations are the conformity, validity, consistency, and completeness

Data quality cannot exist without data reliability, and data reliability cannot exist without data integrity (see Table 23.1).

The precise collection and management of CGMP data is the total quality of this data. ALCOA (Attributable, Legible, Contemporaneous, Original,

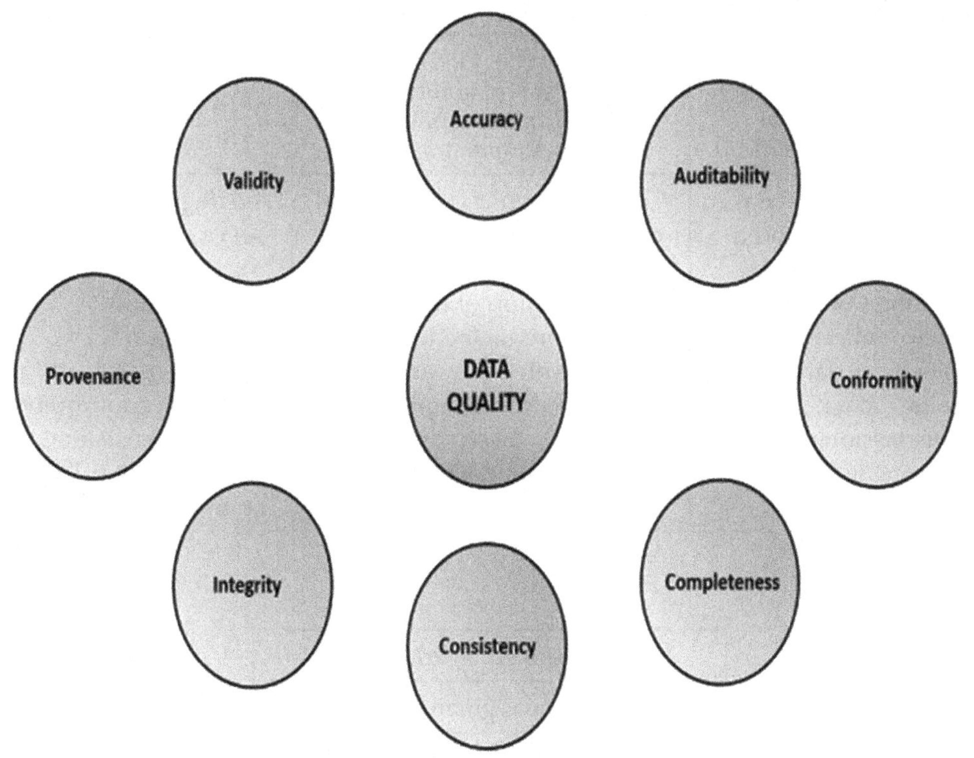

Figure 23.1 Elements of data quality.

Accurate) and ALCOA+ (Attributable, Legible, Contemporaneous, Original, Accurate, Complete Consistent, Enduring, Available) are features related with data reliability, but ALCOA and ALCOA+ fell short of the expectation in the data quality arena.

The following is a brief description of each of the attributes to data quality. On some attributes, simple examples are incorporated. These examples came from https://medium.com/@merwanehamadi/what-is-data-quality-55b7737f1b6e

Data Accuracy

Data accuracy refers to whether the data values stored for an object are the correct values. It describes the real-world context it refers to. To be correct, data values must be the right value and must be represented in a consistent and unambiguous form. One of the dimensions in the data accuracy is data reliability.

Table 23.1 Definitions: Data Integrity, Data Reliability, and Data Quality

Data integrity (NIST SP 800-57P1, ISO 17025, INFOSEC, 44 USC 3542 or ANSI/IEEE)	*Data reliability (US National Archives and Records Administration (8))*	*Data quality (ISO 9000:2015)*
The property that data has not been altered in an unauthorized manner. Data integrity covers data entry or collection, data storage, data transmission, and data processing.	A reliable record is one whose content can be trusted as a full and accurate representation of the transactions, activities, or facts to which they attest and can be depended upon in the course of subsequent transactions or activities.	The degree to which a set of characteristics of data fulfils requirements. Examples of characteristics are accuracy, conformity, validity, consistency, reliability, and completeness.

Example:

	The email address of Paul
Database	paul@gmail.com
Reality	Paul1@gmail.com

The data accuracy is designed to decrease the risks of not preserving of content and meaning of the data. It includes the built-in checks for the correct and secure entry and processing of data (9). EU Annex 11 paragraphs associated with data accuracy are 4.8, 6, 7.2, 10, and 11 (10).

Data accuracy is an element of a workflow that verifies the correctness of the collected data. During the Project Stage in the system life cycle, these accuracy-related workflows are tested and periodically verified during the Operational Stage in SLC as part of the inputs and outputs (I/Os) verifications (11).

Data Auditability

The changes to a set of data need to be traceable. The history of updates is important to track what and when data edits were made and by whom.

The EU Annex 11 paragraph associated with data audibility is 9 (12).

Data Conformity

Conformity means the data are following a set of standard data definitions related to data type, size, and format.

Example:

Name	*Unsubscribed*
Paul	True
John	True
Sam	False

This workflow is designed as part of the Project Stage in the SLC and executed during the transformation occurring subsequently when the signals for sensor(s) are captured and the data are in transient mode. During the Project Stage in the SLC, these workflows are tested. During the Operational Stage in the SLC, these workflows are periodically verified as part of the I/O verifications.

Data Completeness

Completeness is the property that all necessary parts of the entity in question are included. Completeness of a product is often used to express the fact that the product has met all the requirements.

The EU Annex 11 paragraphs associated with data completeness are 4.8, 7.1, and 9 (9).

Data Consistency

Consistency can be expressed as adherence to a given set of rules throughout the dataset. The adherence to a given set of rules among data is designed during the Project Stage in the SLC. The consistency is tested and periodically verified as part of the I/O verifications.

The EU Annex 11 paragraphs associated with data accuracy are 4.8 and 5 (10).

Data Integrity

Integrity is the property that data has not been altered in an unauthorized manner. Data integrity covers data entry or collection, data storage, data transmission, and data processing.

The controls associated with security start early in the lifecycle of the system. The security requirements can be expressed as technical features (e.g., access controls), assurances (e.g., background checks for system developers), or operational practices (e.g., awareness and training). System security requirements, like other system requirements, are derived from several sources including law, policy, applicable standards and guidelines, functional needs of the system, and cost-benefit trade-offs.

A record risk assessment looks at the sensitivity of the information to be processed. The assessment should consider legal implications, organization policy, and the functional needs of the system. Risk assessment is used to support decision-making.

System security testing includes both the testing of the parts of the system that have been developed or acquired and the testing of the entire system. Security management, physical facilities, personnel, procedures, the use of commercial or in-house services (such as networking services), and contingency planning are examples of areas that affect the security of the entire system but may be specified outside of the development or acquisition cycle. Because only items within the development or acquisition cycle will have been tested during system acceptance testing, separate tests or reviews may need to be performed for these additional security elements.

Many security activities take place during the operational phase of a system's life. In general, these fall into three areas: security operations and administration; operational assurance; and periodic re-analysis of the security.

Data Provenance

Data provenance is the assurance of the data source systems. This confidence is established by instituting data quality rules at the source.

This data reliability issue is relevant in the data warehouse environment in which data is extracted from source systems.

Without standards and business processes, likely, the data across all source systems will not line up. When the data is not consistent, we have created non-conformances to the data fields holding the source systems data.

Data quality in source systems involves:

- Data entered or generated directly in computer systems is the raw data and official record for CGMP purposes. It must comply with all requirements related to data. The usage of the source data must comply with the regulated entity procedural control(s) covering the electronic data utilization.
- All entries in data fields, both text and from selection lists, must be:
  - Contemporaneous – Entered at the time the work is done or soon afterwards
  - Reliable – A complete and accurate representation of the transactions, activities, or facts to which they attest
  - Usable – Able to be located, retrieved, presented, and interpreted, separately and when combined with other data
- Audit trails record all changes to electronic data, as applicable.

To uncover the degree of data quality in a source system, data profiling is the technical analysis of data to describe its content, consistency and structure. As soon as a candidate data source is identified, a quick data profiling assessment should be made to provide a go/no-go decision about proceeding with the project. Once the basic strategic decision is made to include a data source in the project, a lengthy tactical data profiling effort should be made to identify as many data problems as possible.

The profile must be used to data standard enforcement across platforms.

Data Validity

Data validity is about the correctness and reasonableness of data conforming to the syntax and structure defined by the business requirements.

Example:

	email
Paul	paul@g@gmail.com

This workflow, as in data accuracy, is designed as part of the Project Stage in the SLC and executed during the transformation occurring subsequently the signals for sensor(s) are captured, and the data are in transient mode.

During the Project Stage in the SLC, these workflows are tested and periodically verified as part of the I/O verifications.

Data Quality Design

The e-records lifecycle incorporates two stages defining the planning, requirements, and designing of the e-records model and the functionality of managing the e-records model.

During the Project Stage in the SLC, it should be designed for the detection and prevention of data defects before they corrupt databases or end-user applications.

The controls to be instituted as part of the design may include the following:

- Data design must be reviewed.
- Accuracy checks for data entered must be performed manually (13).
- Built-in checks should be available for the correct and secure entry and processing data (8).
- Until the transient data are recorded to durable media, the transient data must be ensuring that the transient data may be subject to transformation, but not manipulation (7).
- During the Operational Stage in the SLC, it must be implemented controls in which error/defect data are collected and stored for future or real-time evaluation.
- During the Operational Stage in the SLC, periodically cleansing data ensures data quality. Refer to the next section reviewing "data cleansing."
- During the Operational Stage in the SLC, the correctness of data loaded to the data storage area must be periodically reconciled. The technique and tools to be used in the data reconciliation process, the frequency of data reconciliation, the rationale for the choice of subsets of data to reconcile, and the documentation of results of data reconciliation must be defined during the design and implemented according to the specifications.

The software may be designed to reject or adjust certain I/Os data that does not conform to some predetermined criterion or else fall within certain pre-established limits. It can be a useful way of reducing, especially, manual data entries errors. This type of edit is called accuracy checks (9). Edits can also be used to falsify information and give the erroneous impression that a function is under control (14). Edits by software applications that alter e-records might be a vulnerability to e-records.

Quality Control to Data

There must be recovery mechanism to detect and correct corrupt or inaccurate e-records from an e-record set, table, or database; this process should identify incomplete, incorrect, inaccurate, or irrelevant parts of the data and then replace, modify, or delete dirty or coarse data (15). The process to correct damaged e-records provides a mechanism for creating an accurate reproduction of an original e-record that is discovered to be stained, marred, or otherwise damaged.

Data cleansing or scrubbing is the process used to ensure data quality. To correct any error, the error should be investigated to prevent it from happening again.

When an e-record is discovered to be unreadable, the record can be restored from a true copy of the record. If a true copy is not available, a trustworthy backup copy of the record must be identified and restored from the backup set.

If the data set being cleansed consists of CGMP-relevant e-records, then any changes and deletions must generate an audit trail. The reason for the modification must be documented as part of the e-record. Audit trails need to be available and convertible to a generally intelligible form and regularly reviewed (12).

Damaged e-records may be considered an incident and investigated.

Summary

A data quality assurance and data security program must ensure operations and decision-making are supported with data meeting needs of accuracy, conformity, validity, consistency, reliability, and completeness.

Instead of regulated companies emphasizing data integrity, it is suggested companies concentrate on data quality to meet quality requirements, as contained in the respective medicine manufacturing practices regulations.

References

1. López, O., "Introduction to Data Quality," *Journal of Validation Technology*, 26(2), April 2020.
2. Veregin, H., "Data Quality Parameters," *Geographical Information Systems*, 1999.
3. FDA, "Data Integrity and Compliance with Drug CGMP – Questions and Answers, Guidance for Industry," December 2018.
4. ISO 9001:2015 Quality Management Systems – Requirements.
5. Syncsort Editors, "Data Integrity vs. Data Quality: How Are They Different?" January 2019. https://blog.syncsort.com/2019/01/data-quality/data-integrity-vs-data-quality-different/.
6. Federal Information Processing Standards (FIPS), Publication 11-3, "American National Dictionary for Information Systems," *Windrowed*, July 1979.
7. MHRA, "GxP Data Integrity and Definitions," March 2018.
8. US NARA, "Records Management Guidance for Agencies Implementing Electronic Signature Technologies," October 2000.
9. EU GMP Annex 11 p5, "Computerised Systems," June 2011.
10. PI 041–1, "Good Practices for Data Management and Integrity in Regulated GMP/GDP Environment," *Pharmaceutical Inspection Co-operation Scheme (PIC/S)*, November 2018 (Draft 3).
11. US FDA, "21 Code of Federal Regulations Part 211.68(b)," December 2008.
12. EU GMP Annex 11 p9, "Computerised Systems," June 2011.
13. EU GMP Annex 11 p6, "Computerised Systems," June 2011.
14. US FDA, "Guide to Inspection of Computerized Systems in the Food Processing Industry," April 2003.
15. CEFIC, "Practical Risk-Based Guide for Managing Data Integrity," March 2019 (Rev 1).

Additional Reading

McDowall, R.D.., "Data Quality and Data Integrity Are the Same, Right? Wrong!" *Spectroscopy*, 34(11), November 2019, 22–29.

Chapter 24

Summary

To keep the focus on data integrity, data-related technical controls can be categorized in four activities: data creation; data in storage; data during processing; and data while in transit (Figure 22.1). The flow of data on any data handling system can be reduced to these four activities.

To be able managing properly the activities referenced above, the e-records lifecycle (Figure 2.1) needs to be understood. It provides the controls over loaded data, transient data, raw data, and e-records. Chapter 22 provides a model for the implementation of the data integrity controls based on four referenced activities.

Failure to address just one element of the data lifecycle will weaken the effectiveness of the controls implemented to the data handling system and the e-records integrity-related controls.

Data flow and data process mappings are tools to identify the data integrity controls based on the activity performed by the data. The workflows of each critical data are employed to assess the risks to the data during each activity. Also, the workflows are used to track potential issues for investigation and resolution.

If an electronic handling system is used to handle e-records required under the applicable regulation, the system must be validated and the associated e-records storage devices qualified for its applicable regulatory requirements.

The validation of an e-records handling system and the qualification of the electronic storage devices:

- Ensure all access and user rights in electronic management systems and storage devices are properly controlled to prevent system users from compromising data integrity (1).
- Control e-records in a way that ensures the e-records (1):
  - Can only be created and modified by authorized personnel
  - Are protected against intentional or accidental deletion
  - Are traced through an audit trail when created or modified
  - Are backed up at regular intervals to protect against potential data loss due to system issues or data corruption
  - Are available for review during an inspection and are readily retrievable in a suitable format
  - Include all necessary metadata
- Confirm the accuracy and reliability of e-records (2).

After the deployment to operations, the following controls will maintain the integrity of the e-records:

- Built-in checks are executed to verify the accuracy of correct entries and the processing of transient data, raw data, and e-records. Built-in checks are executed as well between the interfaces to the electronic storage devices.
- Periodic verification is performed to e-records for accessibility, readability, accuracy, access authorization list and verification, backups, audit trails, final disposition activities, incidents, availability of contingency plan, availability of recovery procedures, and so on.
- Changes to the e-records storage devices (processing and retention environments) and associated software are evaluated to ensure the ability to record and retrieves the e-records from the storage device.

References

1. Canadian Health Care GMPs C.02.024.1 – 6.
2. TGA, "Australian Code of Good Manufacturing Practice for Human Blood and Blood Components, Human Tissues and Human Cellular Therapy Products,". Version 1.0 April 2013.

Appendix I
Glossary of Terms

For additional terms, refer to the *Glossary of Computerized System and Software Development Terminology;** *A Globally Harmonized Glossary of Terms for Communicating Computer Validation Key Practices;*† EudraLex – Volume 4 Good Manufacturing Practice (GMP) Guidelines – Glossary;‡ and the MHRA GMP Data Integrity Definitions and Guidance for Industry (March 2015).

For the purpose of this glossary, the terms and definitions given in 9000-3 and ISO 12207 are applicable. In the event of a conflict in terms and definitions, the terms and definitions specified in this glossary and the references in the first paragraph above apply.

Abstraction: A basic principle of software engineering and enables understanding of the application and its design, and the management of complexity.

Acceptance Criteria: The criteria that a system or component must satisfy to be accepted by a user, customer, or other authorized entity. (IEEE)

Acceptance Test: Testing conducted to determine whether a system satisfies its acceptance criteria and to enable the customer to determine whether to accept the system. (IEEE)

---

* FDA, "*Glossary of Computerized System and Software Development Terminology,*" Division of Field Investigations, Office of Regional Operations, Office of Regulatory Affairs, Food and Drug Administration, August 1995.

† Herr, Robert R. and Wyrick, Michael L., "*A Globally Harmonized Glossary of Terms for Communicating Computer Validation Key Practices,*" PDA Journal of Pharmaceutical Science and Technology, March/April 1999.

‡ http://ec.europa.eu/health/files/eudralex/vol-4/pdfs-en/glos4en200408_en.pdf

Access: The ability or opportunity to gain knowledge of stored information. (DoD 5015.2-STD)

Accuracy: Indicator of whether the data values stored for an object are the correct values. To be correct, a data value must be the right value and must be represented in a consistent and unambiguous form.

Accurate Data: Correct, true, valid, and reliable data that reflect the recorded events/activities.

Acquirer: An organization that acquires or procures a system, software product or software service from a supplier. (ISO 12207:1995*)

Application: Software installed on a defined platform/hardware providing specific functionality. (EMA Annex 11)

Application Developer: See Software Developer.

Approver(s): In the context of configuration management, the person(s) responsible for evaluating the recommendations of the reviewers of deliverable documentation, and for rendering a decision on whether to proceed with a proposed change and initiating the implementation of a change request.

Archive: Long-term, permanent retention of completed data and relevant metadata in its final form for the purpose of reconstruction of the process or activity.

Assessment: Investigation of processes, systems, or platforms by a subject matter expert or by IT Quality and Compliance. An assessment does not need to be independent in contrast to audit.

Audit: An independent examination of a software product, software process, or set of software processes to assess compliance with specifications, standards, contractual agreements, or other criteria. (IEEE)

Auditor: In the context of configuration management, the person responsible for reviewing the steps taken during a development or change management process to ensure that the appropriate procedures have been followed.

Audit Trail: An electronic means of auditing the interactions with records within an electronic system so that any access to the system can be documented as it occurs for identifying unauthorized actions in relation to the records, e.g., modification, deletion, or addition. (DOD 5015.2-STD) (2) GMP audit trails are metadata that are a record of GMP critical information (for example the change or deletion of GMP relevant data). (MHRA)

* Note: The 1995 revision is not the most recent version.

Authentication: Verifying the identity of a user, process, or device, often as a prerequisite to allowing access to resources in an information system. (NIST Special Publication 800-18)

Authenticity: The property of being genuine and being able to be verified and trusted; confidence in the validity of a transmission, a message, or message originator. See Authentication. (NIST Special Publication 800-18)

Automated Systems: Include a broad range of systems including, but not limited to, automated manufacturing equipment, automated laboratory equipment, process control, manufacturing execution, clinical trials data management, and document management systems. The automated system consists of the hardware, software, and network components, together with the controlled functions and associated documentation. Automated systems are sometimes referred to as computerized systems. (PICS CSV PI 011-3*)

Availability: Ensuring timely and reliable access to and use of information. (44 U.S.C., SEC. 3542)

Backup: A copy of current (editable) data, metadata and system configuration settings (variable settings which relate to an analytical run) maintained for the purpose of disaster recovery. (MHRA)

Baseline: An agreed-upon description of the attributes of a product, at a point in time, which serves as a basis for defining change. A "change" is a movement from this baseline state to a next state.

Bespoke Computerized System: A computerized system individually designed to suit a specific business process. (EMA Annex 11)

Best Practices: Practices established by experience and common sense.

Biometrics: Methods of identifying a person's identify based on physical measurements of their physical characteristics or repeatable actions. Some examples of biometrics include identifying a user based on a physical signature, fingerprints, and so on.

Business Continuity Plan: A plan describing how business processes will continue, respond, or recover in the event of a disruption. The plan will include preparedness to meet and address emergencies and threats based on the business' prioritization of those business processes.

---

* PI 011-3. "Good Practices for Computerised Systems in Regulated 'GXP' Environments," Pharmaceutical Inspection Cooperation Scheme (PIC/S), September 2007.

Business Process: A set of structured activities or tasks that produce a specific service for a particular customer or customers. It is often visualized as a flowchart of a sequence of activities with decision points. (CEFIC)

Calibration: Set of operations that establish, under specified conditions, the relationship between values of quantities indicated by a measuring instrument or measuring system, or values represented by a material measure or a reference material, and the corresponding values realized by standards. (PICS CSV PI 011-3)

Centrally Managed Security System: Computer system authentication with a centralized domain. These systems use the regulated entity network user security configuration.

Capture: The process of placing an object under records management control for disposition and access purposes. Objects are not necessarily moved from the system they reside in when they are captured. Records can be imported from other sources, manually entered the system, or linked to other systems. (36 CFR 1236.20)

Certificate: Used to verify the identity of an individual, organization, web server, or hardware device. They are also used to ensure non-repudiation in business transactions, as well as enable confidentiality using public-key encryption.

Certification Authority: As part of a public key infrastructure (PKI), an authority in a network that issues and manages from a Certificate Server security credentials and public key for message encryption and decryption. (NARA)

Certified Copy: (1)A copy of original information that has been verified, as indicated by a dated signature, as an exact copy having all of the same attributes and information as the original. (FDA, Electronic Source Data in Clinical Investigations, September 2013) (2) A copy of original information that has been verified as an exact (accurate and complete) copy having all of the same attributes and information as the original. The copy may be verified by dated signature or by a validated electronic process. (CDISC (Clinical Data Interchange Standards Consortium) Clinical Research Glossary Version 8.0, December 2009)

Change: Any variation or alteration in form, state, or quality. It includes additions, deletions, or modifications impacting the hardware or software components used that affect operational integrity, service level agreements, or the validated status of applications on the system.

Change Control: A formal system by which qualified representatives of appropriate disciplines review proposed or actual changes that might affect the validated status of facilities, systems, equipment or processes. The intent is to determine the need for action that would ensure and document that the system is maintained in a validated state. (EMA Annex 15, Qualification and Validation)

Cipher: Series of transformations that converts plaintext to cipher text using the cipher key.

Cipher Key: Secret cryptography key that is used by the key expansion routine to generate a set of round keys.

Cipher Text: Data output from the cipher or input to the inverse cipher.

Clear Printed: Printouts that apart from the values themselves, the units and the respective context can also be seen in the printout. (Journal for GMP and Regulatory Affairs, "*Q&As on Annex 11*", Issue 8, April/May 2012)

Cloud Computing: The practice of using a network of remote servers hosted on the internet to store, manage, and process data, rather than a local server or a personal computer.

Cloud Services: Technology that allows users to access and use shared data and computing services via the internet or a virtual private network (VPN). It gives users access to resources without having to build infrastructure to support these resources within their own environment or network. E-records can reside in a cloud environment hosted by a third service provider (e.g., DaaS).

Code Audit: An independent review of source code by a person, team, or tool to verify compliance with software design documentation and programming standards. Correctness and efficiency may also be evaluated. (IEEE)

Code of Federal Regulations: The codification of the general and permanent rules published in the Federal Register by the executive departments and agencies of the federal government.

Code Inspection: A manual [formal] testing [error detection] technique where the programmer reads source code, statement by statement, to a group who ask questions analyzing the program logic, analyzing the code with respect to a checklist of historically common programming errors, and analyzing its compliance with coding standards. This technique can also be applied to other software and configuration items. (Myers/NBS)

Code Review: A meeting at which software code is presented to project personnel, managers, users, customers, or other interested parties for comment or approval. (IEEE)

Code Walkthrough: A manual testing [error detection] technique where program [source code] logic [structure] is traced manually [mentally] by a group with a small set of test cases, while the state of program variables is manually monitored, to analyze the programmer's logic and assumptions. (FDA Glossary of Computerized System and Software Development Technology (8/95), FDA)

Commercial of the Shelf Software: Software commercially available, whose fitness for use is demonstrated by a broad spectrum of users. (EMA Annex 11)

Commissioning: Refer to Site Acceptance Testing (SAT).

Competent: Having the necessary experience and/or training to adequately perform the job.

Completeness: The property that all necessary parts of the entity in question are included. Completeness of a product is often used to express the fact that all requirements have been met by the product.

Complexity: In the context of this book, the degree to which a system or component has a design or implementation that is difficult to understand and verify.

Compliance: Covers the adherence to application-related standards or conventions or regulations in laws and similar prescriptions, and fulfillment of regulatory requirements.

Compliant System: A system that meets applicable guidelines and predicate rule requirements.

Computer: (1) A functional unit that can perform substantial computations, including numerous arithmetic operations and logical operations without human intervention. (2) Hardware components and associated software design to perform specific functions.

Computer System: (1) A system including the input of data, electronic processing and the output of information to be used either for reporting or automatic control. (PICS CSV PI 011-3) (2) A functional unit, consisting of one or more computers and associated peripheral input and output devices, and associated software, that uses common storage for all or part of a program and also for all or part of the data necessary for the execution of the program; executes user-written or user-designated programs; performs user-designated data manipulation, including arithmetic operations and logic operations; and that can execute programs that modify themselves during their execution. A computer system may be a stand-alone unit or may consist of several interconnected units. (ANSI)

Computer Systems Validation: (1) The *formal assessment and reporting* of quality and performance measures for all the life-cycle stages of software and system development, its implementation, qualification and acceptance, operation, modification, re-qualification, maintenance and retirement. This should enable both the regulated user, and competent authority to have a high level of confidence in the integrity of both the processes executed within the controlling computer system(s) and in those processes controlled by and/or linked to the computer system(s), within the prescribed operating environment(s). (PICS CSV PI 011-3*) (2) Documented evidence which provide a high degree of assurance that a computerized system analyses, controls, and records data correctly and that data processing complies with predetermined specifications. (WHO)

Computerized Process: A process where some or all the actions are controlled by a computer.

Computerized System: (1) A system controlled partially or totally by a computer. (2) See Automated Systems.

Computer Validation: Refer to Computer Systems Validation.†

Concurrent Validation: In some cases, a drug product or medical device may be manufactured individually or on a one-time basis. The concept of prospective or retrospective validation as it relates to those situations may have limited applicability. The data obtained during the manufacturing and assembly process may be used in conjunction with product testing to demonstrate that the instant run yielded a finished product meeting all its specifications and quality characteristics. (FDA)

Confidentiality: Preserving authorized restrictions on information access and disclosure, including means for protecting personal privacy and proprietary information. (44 U.S.C., SEC. 3542)

Configurable Software: Application software, sometimes general purpose, written for a variety of industries or users in a manner that permits users to modify the program to meet their individual needs. (FDA)

---

* PI 011-3. "*Good Practices for Computerised Systems in Regulated 'GXP' Environments,*" Pharmaceutical Inspection Cooperation Scheme (PIC/S), September 2007.

† PI 011-3. "*Good Practices for Computerised Systems in Regulated 'GXP' Environments.*" Pharmaceutical Inspection Cooperation Scheme (PIC/S), September 2007.

Configuration Item: Entity within a configuration that satisfies an end use function and that can be uniquely identified at a giving reference point. (ISO 9000-3)

Contemporaneous E-records: E-records recorded at the time they are generated.

Control System: Included in this classification are Supervisory Control and Data Acquisition Systems (SCADA), Distributed Control Systems (DCS), Statistical Process Control systems (SPC), Programmable Logic Controllers (PLCs), intelligent electronic devices, and computer systems that control manufacturing equipment or receive data directly from manufacturing equipment PLCs.

Consistency: The property of logical coherency among constituent parts. Consistency may also be expressed as adherence to a given set of rules.

Correctness: The extent to which software is free from design and coding defects, i.e., fault free. It is also the extent to which software meets its specified requirements and user objectives.

Criticality: In the context of this book, the regulatory impact to a system or component. See Critical System.

Critical: Describes a process step, process condition, test requirement, or other relevant parameter or item that must be controlled within predetermined criteria to ensure that the product/process meets its specification.

Critical Electronic Records: In this book, the e-records with high risk to product quality or patient safety. (ISPE GAMP COP Annex 11 – Interpretation, July/August 2011)

Critical Data: In this book, data with high risk to product quality or patient safety. (ISPE GAMP COP Annex 11 – Interpretation, July/August 2011)

Critical Deficiency: A deficiency in a practice or process that has produced, or may result in, a significant risk of producing a product that is harmful to the user. Also occurs when it is observed that the manufacturer has engaged in fraud, misrepresentation or falsification of products or data. (TGA, Code of GMPs, 2013)

Critical Process Parameter: A parameter which if not controlled will contribute to the variability of the end product. (Health Canada GUI-0029)

Critical Requirement: A requirement that, if not met, has an adverse impact on any of the following: patient safety, product quality, requirements satisfying health authority regulation, cGxP data integrity, or security.

Critical Step: It is a parameter that must be within an appropriate limit, range, or distribution to ensure the safety of the subject or quality of the product of data. (MHRA)

Critical Systems: Systems that directly or indirectly influence patient safety, product quality, and data integrity.

Cryptography or Cryptology: The practice and study of techniques for secure communication in the presence of third parties called adversaries. (http://searchsoftwarequality.techtarget.com/definition/cryptography)

Custom-Built Software: Also known as a Bespoke System, Custom-Built Software is software produced for a customer, specifically to order, to meet a defined set of user requirements. (GAMP)

Customized Computerized System: See Bespoke Computerized System.

Data: Data is defined as the contents of a record. It is the basic unit of information that has a unique meaning and can be transmitted. (ISO/IEC 17025)

Information derived or obtained from raw data (e.g. a reported analytical result). (MHRA)

Database: In electronic records, a set of data, consisting of at least one file or of a group of integrated files, usually stored in one location and made available to several users at the same time for various applications. (36 CFR 1234.2, reference (ii))

Databases refer to structured repositories of indexed information that allow information retrieval, analysis, and output. (NARA)

Database Field: It is a place for a piece of information in a record or file.

Data Base Management System (DBMS): A software system used to access and retrieve data stored in a database. (36 CFR 1234.2, reference (ii))

Data Collection: The process of gathering and measuring information on variable of interest.

Data Conformity: Conformity means the data is following the set of standard data definitions like data type, size, and format.

Data Elements: Individual GxP data items that are part of raw data or metadata. (CEFIC)

Data Flow: Diagram that maps the flow of information of any process or system (inputs, outputs, storage points and routes) between each destination. (CEFIC)

Data Governance: The sum of arrangements to ensure that data, irrespective the format in which it is generated, is recorded, processed, retained, and used to ensure a complete, consistent, and accurate record throughout the data lifecycle.

Data Handling: The process of ensuring that data is stored, archived, or disposed in a safe and secure manner during the data lifecycle.

Data Integrity: The property that data has not been altered in an unauthorized manner since it was created, while in transit, during processing or stored. (NIST SP 800-57P1). The extent to which all data are complete, consistent and accurate throughout the data lifecycle. (IEEE and MHRA)

Data Lifecycle: All phases in the life of the data from generation and recording through processing (including analysis, transformation or migration), use, data retention, archive/retrieval and destruction. (MHRA)

Data Mart: A data mart is a structure/access pattern specific to data warehouse environments, used to retrieve client-facing data.

Data Migration: The process of transferring data between storage types, formats, or computer systems. It is a key consideration for any system implementation, upgrade, or consolidation. (Wikipedia)

Data Process Mapping: Generation of a visual representation of the creation and movement of data through the business process including documentation of the systems used.

Data Ownership: The possession of and responsibilities for information.

Data Quality: Data quality is considered the accurate, auditable, in conformance to requirement, complete, consistent, with integrity, provenance, and valid making data both correct and useful. (FIPS, Publication 11-3, "*American National Dictionary for Information Systems*," Windrowed, July 1979.)

Data Selection: The process of determining the appropriate data type and source, as well as suitable instruments to collect data.

Data Source: Origin where data is collected.

Data Steward: The person or group that manages the development, approval, and use of data within a specified functional area, ensuring that it can be used to satisfy data requirements throughout the organization. (DoD 8320.1-M-1, "Data Standardization Procedures," April 1998)

Data Warehousing: An architected, periodic, and coordinated process of copying from numerous sources into an optimized environment capable of analytical and informational processing.

Data Validity: The correctness and reasonableness of data.

Decommissioning: A planned, systematic process to disassemble and retire from service a facility system and equipment without altering the integrity (validation state) of any other facility, system, or equipment previously connected to the facility, system, or equipment being decommissioned. The decommissioning is done via inspection, testing, and documentation.

Decryption: The transformation of unintelligible data ("ciphertext") into original data ("clear text").

Delete: The process of permanently removing, erasing, or obliterating recorded information from a medium, especially an electronic medium.

Deliverable: A tangible or intangible object produced as a result of project execution, as part of an obligation. In Validation Projects, deliverables are usually documents.

Design Qualification: The documented verification that the proposed design of the facilities, systems and equipment is suitable for the intended purpose. Also known as Design Verification. (EMA Annex 15, Validation and Qualification)

Derived Data: Data that was originally supplied in one form but was converted to another form using some automated process.

Developer: An organization that performs development activities (including requirements analysis, design, testing through acceptance) during the software lifecycle process.

Development: Software lifecycle process that contains the activities of requirements analysis, design, coding, integration, testing, installation and support for acceptance of software products. (ISO 9000-3)

Deviation: When a system does not act as expected.

Digital: Pertaining to data [signals] in the form of discrete [separate/pulse form] integral values.

Digital Certificate: A digital certificate (also known as a public key certificate or identity certificate) is a credential issued by a trusted authority. An entity can present a digital certificate to prove its identity or its right to access information. It links a public-key value to a set of information which identifies the entity associated with the use of the corresponding private key. Certificates are authenticated, issued, and managed by a trusted third party called a CA. See also Public-key Certificates.

Digital Signature Standard (DSS): A National Institute of Standards and Technology (NIST) standard for digital signatures, used to authenticate both a message and the signer. DSS has a security level comparable to RSA (Rivest-Shamir-Adleman) cryptography, having 1,024-bit keys.

Disaster Recovery: The activities required to restore one or more computer systems to their valid state in response to a major hardware or software failure or destruction of facilities.

Disaster Recovery Plan: The written and approved plan associated with a disaster recovery.

Discrepancy: Any problem or entry into the Problem Reporting System. Includes all bugs and may include design issues.

Destruction: In records management, the major type of disposal action. Methods of destroying records include selling or salvaging the record medium and burning, pulping, shredding, macerating, or discarding with other waste materials.

Disposition: Those action taken regarding after they are no longer in office space to conduct current business. (41 CFR 201-4 and RM Handbook, references (kk) and (w))

Documentation: (1) Manuals, written procedures or policies, records, or reports that provide information concerning the uses, maintenance, or validation of a process or system involving either hardware or software. This material may be presented from electronic media. Documents include but are not limited to Standard Operating Procedures (SOPs), Technical Operating Procedures (TOPs), manuals, logs, system development documents, test plans, scripts and results, plans, protocols, and reports. Refer to *Documentation* and *Documentation, level of* in the *Glossary of Computerized System and Software Development Terminology,* August 1995.

(2) Any written or pictorial information describing, defining, specifying, reporting or certifying activities, requirements, procedures, or results. (ANSI N45.2.10-1973)

Efficacy: The measurement of a medicine's desired effect under ideal conditions, such as in a clinical trial.

Electronic Archive: The designated electronic storage device in which electronic records are retained for their long-term preservation. (SAG, "A Guide to Archiving of Electronic Records," February 2014)

Electronic Record: Information recorded in electronic form that requires a computer system to access or process. (SAG, "A Guide to Archiving of Electronic Records", February 2014)

In this book, based on the MHRA definitions, raw data and data are considered e-records. When refer to both, electronic raw data and data, it will be used the term e-records.

Electronic Record Lifecycle: All phases in the life of the electronic record from initial generation and recording through processing (including transformation or migration), use, electronic records retention, archive/retrieval, and destruction.

Electronic Records Management: Electronic records management (ERM) is the management of electronic files and documents as records.

Electronic Source Data: Data initially recorded in electronic format. (FDA, Electronic Source Data in Clinical Investigations, September 2013)

Electronic Storage Device: Hard drives and any form of fixed or portable storage media (e.g., network drives, CD's/DVD's, USB jump/flash drives, and other peripherals).

End User: Personnel who use the validated computer system.

Emergency Change: A change to a validated system that is determined to be necessary to eliminate an error condition that prevents the use of the system and interrupts the business function.

Emulation: Refers to the process of mimicking, in software, a piece of hardware or software so that other processes think that the original equipment/function is still available in its original form. Emulation is essentially a way of preserving the functionality of and access to digital information which might otherwise be lost due to technological obsolescence.

Encryption: (1) The process of converting information into a code or cipher so that people will be unable to read it. A secret key, or password, is required to decrypt (decode) the information. (2) Transformation of confidential plaintext into ciphertext to protect it. An encryption algorithm combines plaintext with other values called keys, or ciphers, so the data becomes unintelligible. [45 CFR 142.304]

Entity: A software or hardware product which can be individually qualified or validated.

Establish: To define, document, and implement.

Evaluation: A systematic determination of the extent to which an entity meets its specified criteria.

Expected Result: What a system should do when a particular action is performed.

Factory Acceptance Test: An Acceptance Test in the Supplier's factory, usually involving the Customer. (IEEE)

Failure Analysis: The process of collecting and analyzing data to determine the cause of a failure. One of the software-based fault location techniques is the Automatic Test Pattern Generation.

FDA Guidance Documents: FDA guidance documents represent the FDA current thinking on a subject. These documents do not create or confer any rights for or on any person and do not operate to bind FDA or the public. An alternative approach may be used if such approach satisfies the requirements of the applicable statutes, regulations, or both.

Federal Register: A daily issuance of the US government which provides a uniform system for making available to the public regulations and legal notices issued by federal agencies.

Field Devices: Hardware devices that are typically located in the field at or near the process, and which are needed to bring information to the computer or to implement a computer-driven control action. Devices include sensors, analytical instruments, transducers, and valves.

File: An arrangement of records. The term is used to denote papers, photographs, photographic copies, maps, machine-readable information, or other recorded information regardless of physical form or characteristics, accumulated or maintained in filing equipment, boxes, or machine-readable media, or on shelves, and occupying office or storage space. (Noun) (41 CFR 201-4 and 36 CFR 1220.14, references (kk)) and (11))

Final Rule: The regulation finalized for implementation, published in the FR (preamble and codified), and codified in the CFR.

Format: For electronic records, the computer file format described by a formal or vender standard or specification. For non-electronic records, the physical form: e.g., paper, microfilm, video, and so on.

Function: A set of specified, ordered actions that are part of a process.

Functional Requirements: This specification describes how the system must technically operate to meet the requirements document.

Functional Testing: Application of test data derived from the specified functional requirements without regard to the final program structure.

GMP: Good Manufacturing Practice means the part of quality assurance which ensures that products are consistently produced and controlled in accordance with the quality standards appropriate to their intended use. (Commission Directive 2003/94/EC)

Current Good Manufacturing Practice (CGMP) refers to requirements in the Federal Food, Drug, and Cosmetic Act (FD&C Act), section 501(a)(2)(B), for all drugs and active pharmaceutical ingredients (APIs). For finished human and animal drugs, the term includes applicable requirements under 21 CFR parts 210 and 211. For biologics, the term includes additional applicable requirements under 21 CFR parts 600-680. (US FDA)

GMP Controls: Set of controls that provide assurance of consistently continued process performance and product quality.

GMP Regulated Activities: The manufacturing-related activities established in the basic legislation compiled in Volume 1 and Volume 5 of the publication The Rules governing medicinal products in the European Union, US FDA 21 CFR Part 211, "Current Good Manufacturing Practice in Manufacturing, Processing, Packing or Holding of Drugs; General and Current Good Manufacturing Practice For Finished Pharmaceuticals" or any predicate rule applicable to medicinal products for the referenced country.

Good Documentation Practices: Good documentation practices are those measures that collectively and individually ensure documentation, whether paper or electronic, is secure, attributable, legible, traceable, permanent, contemporaneously recorded, original and accurate. (WHO)

GxP Application: Software entities which have a specific user-defined business purpose that must meet the requirements of the corresponding GxP regulation.

Guidelines: A document providing guidance on the scientific or regulatory aspects of the development of medicines and applications for marketing authorization. Although guidelines are not legally binding, applicants need to provide justification for any deviations. (EMA)

Guidelines are departmental policy and recommended standards or statements that derive from Legislation. They do not have the force of law or regulation.

GxP Computerized Systems: A computer system that performs a regulated operation which is required to be formally controlled under a GXP international life science requirements.

GxP Regulation: A global abbreviation intended to cover GMP, GCP, GLP, and other regulated applications in context.

The underlying international life science requirements such as those set forth in the US FD&C Act, US PHS Act, FDA regulations, EU Directives, Japanese MHL.W regulations, Australia TGA, or other applicable national legislation or regulations under which a company operates. (GAMP Good Practice Guide, IT Infrastructure Control and Compliance, ISPE 2005)

Human Readable: An electronic record, data or signature that can be displayed in a viewable form, e.g. on paper or computer screen and has meaning (words in a written language).

Hybrid Systems: Hybrid computer systems, including combinations of paper records (or other non-electronic media) and electronic records, paper records and electronic signatures, or handwritten signatures executed to electronic records.

Ingestion: The process that accepts electronic records for archiving. (SAG, "A Guide to Archiving of Electronic Records," February 2014)

Information: Facts provided or learned about something or someone.

Information Security: A set of strategies for managing the processes, tools, and policies necessary to prevent, detect, document, and counter threats to digital and non-digital information. Infosec responsibilities include establishing a set of business processes that will protect information assets regardless of how the information is formatted or whether it is in transit, is being processed, or is at rest in storage.

Information Technology: Any equipment or interconnected system or subsystem of equipment that is used in the automatic acquisition, storage, manipulation, management, movement, control, display, switching, interchange, transmission, or reception of data or information by the executive agency. For purposes of the preceding sentence, equipment is used by an executive agency if the equipment is used by the executive agency directly or is used by a contractor under a contract with the executive agency which: (i) requires the use of such equipment; or (ii) requires the use, to a significant extent, of such equipment in the performance of a service or the furnishing of a product. The term information technology includes computers, ancillary equipment, software, firmware and similar procedures, services (including support services), and related resources. (40 U.S.C., SEC. 1401)

Infrastructure: The hardware and software, such as networking software and operation systems, which makes it possible for the application to function. (EMA Annex 11)

Interface: A shared boundary. To interact or communicate with another system component. (ANSI/IEEE)

Impact of Change: The impact of change is the effect of the change on the GXP computer system. The components by which the impact of change is evaluated may include, but not be limited to, business considerations; resource requirements and availability; application of appropriate regulatory agency requirements; and criticality of the system.

Inspection: (1) A manual testing technique in which program documents [specifications (requirements, design), source code or user's manuals] are examined in a very formal and disciplined manner to discover any errors, violations of standards or other problems. Checklists are typical vehicles used in accomplishing this process. (2) A visual examination of a software product to detect and identify software anomalies, including errors and deviations from standards and specifications. Inspections are peer examinations led by impartial facilitators who are trained in inspection techniques. Determination of remedial or investigative action for an anomaly is a mandatory element of a software inspection, although the solution should not be determined in the inspection meeting.

Installation Qualification: Establishing confidence that process equipment and ancillary systems are capable of consistently operating within established limits and tolerances. (FDA)

Integration Testing: Orderly progression of testing in which software elements, hardware elements, or both, are combined and tested, until all inter-module communication links have been integrated.

Integrity: (1) Guarding against improper information modification or destruction and includes ensuring information non-repudiation and authenticity. (44 U.S.C., Sec. 3542). (2) Protection against unauthorized changes to information. (3) Condition existing when data is unchanged from its source and has not been accidentally or maliciously modified, altered, or destroyed. (National Information System Security (INFOSEC) Glossary) (4) The degree to which a system or component prevents unauthorized access to, or modification of, computer programs or data. (ANSI/IEEE)

Intended Use: Use of a product, process or service in accordance with the specifications, instructions and information provided by the manufacturer. (ANSI/AAMI/ISO 14971) (2) Refer to the objective intent of the persons legally responsible for the labeling of devices. The intent is determined by such persons' expressions or may be shown by the circumstances surrounding the distribution of the article. This objective intent may, for example, be shown by labeling claims, advertising matter, or oral or written statements by such persons or their representatives. It may be shown by the circumstances that the article is, with the knowledge of such persons or their representatives, offered and used for a purpose for which it is neither labeled nor advertised. The intended uses of an article may change after it has been introduced into interstate commerce by its manufacturer, if, for example, a packer, distributor, or seller intends an article for different uses than those intended by the person from whom he received the devices. (US FDA Draft Guidance for Industry and Food and Drug Administration Staff - Mobile Medical Applications, July 2011)

IT Infrastructure: The hardware and software such as networking software and operation systems, which makes it possible for the application to function. (EMA Annex 11)

Key Practices: Processes essential for computer validation that consists of tools, workflow, and people. (PDA)

Legacy Systems: Production computer systems that are operating on older computer hardware or are based on older software applications. In some cases, the vendor may no longer support the hardware or software. (2) These are regarded as systems that have been established and in use for some considerable time. For a variety of reasons, they may be generally characterized by lack of adequate GMP compliance related documentation and records pertaining to the development and commissioning stage of the system. Additionally, because of their age there may be no records of a formal approach to validation of the system. (PICS CSV PI 011-3*)

Lifecycle Model: A framework containing the processes, activities, and tasks involved in the development, operation, and maintenance of a software product, spanning the life of the system from the definition of its requirements to the termination of its use. (ISO 9000-3)

Lifecycle (Record): The life span of a record from its creation to its final disposition is considered its lifecycle. There are four stages in a record lifecycle: Creation, Maintenance, Retention Management, and Disposal.

Limited Security System: Computer system with limited security functionality, such as but not limited to: non-individual accounts, limited number of users, and security based on group-passwords.

* PI 011-3. *"Good Practices for Computerised Systems in Regulated "GXP" Environments"*, Pharmaceutical Inspection Cooperation Scheme (PIC/S), September 2007.

Living Document: A document (or collection of documents) revised as needed throughout the life of a computer system. Only the most recent version(s) is effective and supersedes prior versions.

Locally Managed Security System: Computer system locally authenticated (e.g., with a local domain or a stand-alone system), in which the security process. These systems use equipment specific user security configuration and do not use the regulated entity network user security configuration.

Logically Secure and Controlled Environment: A computing environment, controlled by policies, procedures, and technology, which deters direct or remote unauthorized access which could damage computer components, production applications and/or data.

Lifecycle: All phases in the life of the system from initial requirements until retirement including design, specification, programming, testing, installation, operation, and maintenance. (EMA Annex 11)

Lifecycle Model: Framework containing the processes, activities, and tasks involved in the development, operation, and maintenance of a software product, spanning the life of the system from the definition of its requirements to the termination of its use. (ISO 9000-3)

Maintainer: An organization that performs maintenance activities. (ISO 12207:1995[4])

Major Change: A change to a validated system that is determined by reviewers to require the execution of extensive validation activities.

Manufacture: All operations of purchase of materials and products, production, quality control, release, storage, dispatch of medicinal products, and the related controls.

Manufacturer: An entity that engages in CGMP activities, including implementation of oversight and controls over the manufacture of drugs to ensure quality.

Manufacturing: All operations of receipt of materials, production, packaging, repackaging, labeling, relabeling, quality control, release, storage and distribution of medicinal products and the related controls.

Manufacturing Systems: Elements of pharmaceutical and biopharmaceutical manufacturing capability, including manufacturing systems, facility equipment, process equipment, supporting utilities, associated process monitoring and control systems, and automation systems, that have the potential to affect product quality and patient safety. (ASTM E 2500 – 07)

May: This word, or the adjective "optional," mean that an item is truly optional. Statements use "may" for permissible actions.

Metadata: Data describing stored data: that is, data describing the structure, data elements, interrelationships, and other characteristics of electronic records. (DOD 5015.2-STD) Data that describe the attributes of other data and provide context and meaning. Typically, these are data that describe the structure, data elements, interrelationships and other characteristics of data. It also permits data to be attributable to an individual. (MHRA)

Migration: The act of moving records from one system to another.

Minor Change: A change to a validated system that is determined by reviewers to require the execution of only targeted qualification and validation activities.

Model: A model is an abstract representation of a given object.

Module Testing: Refer to *Testing, Unit* in the *Glossary of Computerized System and Software Development Terminology*, August 1995.

Native File Format: A method used by the computer operating system or file management to arrange data.

NEMA Enclosure: Hardware enclosures (usually cabinets) that provide different levels of mechanical and environmental protection to the devices installed within it.

Non-Conformance: A departure from minimum requirements specified in a contract, specification, drawing, or other approved product description or service.

Non-Custom Purchased Software Package: A generally available, marketed software product, which performs specific data collection, manipulation, output, or archiving functions. Refer to *Configurable, off-the-shelf software* in the *Glossary of Computerized System and Software Development Terminology*, August 1995.

Non-Repudiation: Strong and substantial evidence of the identity of the signer of a message and of message integrity, enough to prevent a party from successfully denying the origin, submission, or delivery of the message and the integrity of its contents.

Objective Evidence: Qualitative or quantitative information, records, or statements of fact pertaining to the quality of an item or service or to the existence of a quality system element, which is based on observation, measurement, or test and which can be verified.

Operator: An organization that operates the system. (ISO 12207:1995[4])

Operating Environment: All outside influences that interface with the computer system. (GAMP)

Ongoing Evaluation: The dynamic process employed after a system's initial validation that can assist in maintaining a computer system in a validated state.

Operational Testing: Refer to *Operational Qualification* in the *Glossary of Computerized System and Software Development Terminology*, August 1995.

Operating System: Software that controls the execution of programs and that provides services such as resource allocation, scheduling, input/output control, and data management. Usually, operating systems are predominantly software, but partial or complete hardware implementations are possible. (ISO)

Original Record: Data as the file or format in which it was originally generated, preserving the integrity (accuracy, completeness, content and meaning) of the record, e.g. original paper record of manual observation, or electronic raw data file from a computerized system (MHRA)

Part 11 Records: Records that are required to be maintained under predicate rule requirements and that are maintained in electronic format in place of paper format, or records that are required to be maintained under predicate rules, that are maintained in electronic format in addition to paper format, and that are relied on to perform regulated activities. Part 11 records include records submitted to FDA, under predicate rules (even if such records are not specifically identified in Agency regulations) in electronic format (assuming the records have been identified in docket number 92S-0251 as the types of submissions the Agency accepts in electronic format). (FDA guidance: Part 11 Scope and Application)

Password: A character string used to authenticate an identity. Knowledge of the password that is associated with a user ID is considered proof of authorization to use the capabilities associated with that user ID. (CSC-STD-002-85)

Packaged Software: Software provided and maintained by a vendor/supplier, which can provide general business functionality or system services. Refer *to Configurable, off-the-shelf software* in the *Glossary of Computerized System and Software Development Terminology*, August 1995.

Periodic Review: A documented assessment of the documentation, procedures, records, and performance of a computer system to determine whether it is still in a validated state and what actions, if any, are necessary to restore its validated state. (PDA) The review is performed at a regular interval. The timing of intervals is left flexible.

Persisted Data/E-record: E-records residing in the diverse data warehouses acquired from a source system(s).

Person: "Person" refers to an individual or an organization with legal rights and duties.

Personal Identification Number: A PIN is an alphanumeric code or password used to authenticate the identity of an individual.

Physical Environment: The physical environment of a computer system that comprises the physical location and the environmental parameters in which the system physically functions.

Planned Change: An intentional change to a validated system for which an implementation and evaluation program is predetermined.

Policy: A directive which usually specifies what is to be accomplished.

Preamble: Analysis preceding a proposed or final rule that clarifies the intention of the rulemaking and any ambiguities regarding the rule. Responses to comments made on a proposed rule are published in the preamble preceding the final rule. Preambles are published only in the FR and do not have a binding effect.

Predicate Regulations: Federal Food, Drug, and Cosmetic Act, the Public Health Service Act or any FDA Regulation, except for 21 CFR Part 11. Predicate regulations address the research, production, and control of FDA regulated articles.

Preservation: Ensuring that electronic records held in the archive remain accessible through the application of appropriate preservation policies and processes. In the context of electronic archiving this means maintenance of the authenticity and integrity of e-records. (SAG, "A Guide to Archiving of Electronic Records," February 2014)

Primary Record: The record which takes primacy in cases where collected or retained concurrently by more than one method fail to concur. (MHRA)

Principles: A foundation of believes, truths, and so on, upon which others are based.

Procedural Controls: (1) Written and approved procedures providing appropriate instructions for each aspect of the development, operations, maintenance, and security applicable to computer technologies. In the context of regulated operations, procedural controls should have QA/QC controls that are equivalent to the applicable predicate regulations. (2) A directive usually specifying how certain activities are to be accomplished. (PMA CSVC)

Process: (1) A set of specified, ordered actions required to achieve a defined result.

(2) A set of interrelated or interacting activities that transform input into outputs. (ISO 9000-3)

Process Owner: The person responsible for the business process. (EMA Annex 11)

Process Mapping: Activities involved in defining what a business entity does, who is responsible, to what standard a business process should be completed, and how the success of a business process can be determined. (CEFIC)

Process System: The combination of the process equipment, support systems (such as utilities), and procedures used to execute a process.

Processable Electronic Records: Records in native file formats that can be read, analyzed, interpreted, and manipulated by current and future hardware and software that can be read the native file structure.

Processing Environment: The environment in which the e-records were initially created. (ISPE/PDA, "*Technical Report: Good Electronic Records Management (GERM)*," July 2002)

Production Environment: The operational environment in which the system is being used for its intended purpose, i.e. not in a test or development environment.

Production Verification (PV): Documented verification that the integrated system performs as intended in its production environment. PV is the execution of selected Performance Qualification (PQ) tests in the production environment using production data.

Project: A project is an activity which achieves specific objectives through a set of defining tasks and effective use of resources.

Project Management: Project management is the application of knowledge, skills, tools, and techniques to project activities to meet the project requirements. (ANSI)

Prospective Validation: Validation conducted prior to the distribution of either a new product, or product made under a revised manufacturing process, where the revisions may affect the product's characteristics. (FDA)

Public-Key Certificate: A public key certificate (a.k.a. a digital certificate or identity certificate) is an electronic representation of an identification or passport, issued by a certification authority (CA) to a PKI user, stating identification information, validity period, the holder's public key, the identity and digital signature of the issuer, and the purpose for which it is issued. (GERM)

Qualification: (1) Action of proving that any equipment works correctly and leads to the expected results. The word validation is sometimes widened to incorporate the concept of qualification. (PIC/S) (2) Qualification is the process of demonstrating whether a computer system and associated controlled process/operation, procedural controls, and documentation can fulfill specified requirements. (3) The process of demonstrating whether an entity can fulfill specified requirements. (ISO 8402: 1994, 2.13.1)

Qualification Protocol: A prospective experimental plan stating how qualification will be conducted, including test parameters, product characteristics, production equipment, and decision points on what constitutes an acceptable test. When executed, a protocol is intended to produce documented evidence that a system or subsystem performs as required.

Quality and Technical Records: Registered evidence about activities on the QMS and/or the process of performing tests (e.g. work sheets, logbooks, control graphs, documentation of equipment qualification, test requests, test reports, reports from audits, training records, records of corrective and preventive actions, and so on). (OMLC – Management of Documents and Records (Rephrased))

Qualification Reports: These are test reports which evaluate the conduct and results of the qualification carried out on a computer system.

Quality: The totality of features and characteristics of a product or service that bears on its ability to satisfy given needs.

Quality Assurance: All planned and systematic activities implemented within the quality system and demonstrated as needed to provide adequate confidence that an entity will fulfill requirements for quality.

Quality Management: All activities of the overall management function that determine the quality policy, objectives, and responsibilities and implement them by such means as quality planning, quality control, quality assurance, and quality improvement within the quality system.

Quality System: To establish policy and objectives and to achieve those objectives to direct and control an organization regarding quality. (ISO 9000:2015)

Raw Data: All data on which quality decisions are based should be defined as raw data. It includes data which is used to generate other records. (Volume 4, EU Good Manufacturing Practice Medicinal Products for Human and Veterinary Use, Chapter 4: Documentation)

Original records and documentation, retained in the format in which they were originally generated (i.e. paper or electronic), or as a "true copy." Raw data must be contemporaneously and accurately recorded by permanent means. In the case of basic electronic equipment which does not store electronic data or provides only a printed data output (e.g. balance or pH meter), the printout constitutes the raw data. (MHRA) The raw data must be permanent, protected against unauthorized modification, written to durable storage location contemporaneously, and must reflect the actual observation.

pAny laboratory worksheets, records, memoranda, notes, or exact copies thereof that are the result of original observations and activities of a nonclinical laboratory study and are necessary for the reconstruction and evaluation of the report of that study. If exact transcripts of raw data have been prepared (e.g., tapes which have been transcribed verbatim, dated, and verified accurate by signature), the exact copy or exact transcript may be substituted for the original source as raw data. Raw data may include photographs, microfilm or microfiche copies, computer printouts, magnetic media, including dictated observations, and recorded data from automated instruments. (Source: US FDA 21 CFR 58.3(k))

Record: A collection of related data treated as a unit. (GERM)

The record provides evidence of various actions taken to demonstrate compliance with instructions, e.g. activities, events, investigations, and in the case of manufactured batches a history of each batch of product, including its distribution. Records include the raw data which is used to generate other records. For electronic records regulated users should define which data are to be used as raw data. At least, all data on which quality decisions are based should be defined as raw data. (Eudralex Vol 4 Ch 4)

A record consists of information, regardless of medium, detailing the transaction of business. Records include all books, papers, maps, photographs, machine-readable materials, and other documentary materials, regardless of physical form or characteristics, made or received by an Agency of the United States Government under Federal law or in connection with the transaction of public business and preserved or appropriate for preservation by that Agency or its legitimate successor as evidence of the organization, functions, policies, decisions, procedures, operations, or other activities of the Government or because of the value of data in the record. (44 U.S.C. 3301, reference (bb))

Record Keeping: The field of management responsible for the efficient and systematic control of the creation, receipt, maintenance, use and disposition of records, including the processes for capturing and maintaining evidence of and information about business activities and transactions in the form of records. (ISO 15489: 2001)

Record Management: The planning, controlling, directing, organizing, training, promoting, and other managerial activities involving the lifecycle of information, including creation, maintenance (use, storage, retrieval), and disposal, regardless of media. Record management procedures are used to achieve adequate and proper documentation of Federal policies and transactions and effective and economical management of Agency/organizational operations. (44 U.S.C. 2901)

Record Owner: A person or organization who can determine the contents and use of the data collected, stored, processed, or disseminated by that party regardless of whether the data was acquired from another owner or collected directly from the provider.

Record Reliability: A reliable record is one whose contents can be trusted as a full and accurate representation of the transactions, activities, or facts to which they attest and can be depended upon in the course of subsequent transactions or activities. (NARA)

Record Retention Period: Length of time the electronic record is to be retained, as mandated by the requirement of the record type, based on regulations or documented policies.

Record Retention Schedule: A list of record types with the required storage conditions and defined retention periods. The time (retention) periods are established based upon regulatory, legal, and tax compliance requirements as well as operational need and historical value.

Reengineering: The process of examining and altering an existing system to reconstitute it in a new form. May include reverse engineering (analyzing a system and producing a representation at a higher level of abstraction, such as design from code), restructuring (transforming a system from one representation to another at the same level of abstraction), documentation (analyzing a system and producing user or support documentation), forward engineering (using software products derived from an existing system, together with new requirements, to produce a new system), retargeting (transforming a system to install it on a different target system), and translation (transforming source code from one language to another or from one version of a language to another). (DOD-STD-498)

Regulated Data: (1) Information used for a regulated purpose or to support a regulated process (GAMP). (2) Data used for GMP purposes as required by the Rules GMP related to operations that may affect patient safety and product quality. (Russian SIDGP Data Integrity Guidance (August 2018))

Regulated Record: It is a record required to be maintained or submitted by GxP regulations.

Regulated Electronic Records: It is a regulated record maintained in electronic format.

Regulations: Regulations are rules for following and enforcing the law. US FDA enforces the regulations contained in Title 21 CFR.

Reports: Document the conduct of exercises, projects or investigations, together with results, conclusions and recommendations. (Eudralex Vol 4 Ch 4) A report containing regulated data is considered a regulated record.

Reliability: A record is reliable if its content can be trusted as a full and accurate representation of the transaction, activities, or facts to which it attests, and it can be depended upon in the course of subsequent transactions and activities. (NARA)

Repository for Electronic Records: A direct access device on which the electronic records and metadata are stored.

Regression Testing: Regression testing is the process of testing changes to computer programs to make sure that the older programming still works with the new changes. Regression testing is a normal part of the program development process and, in larger companies, is done by code testing specialists. Test department coders develop code test scenarios and exercises that will test new units of code after they have been written. These test cases form what becomes the *test bucket.* Before a new version of a software product is released, the old test cases are run against the new version to make sure that all the old capabilities still work. The reason they might not work is because changing or adding new code to a program can easily introduce errors into code that is not intended to be changed.

Regulated Operations: Process/business operations carried out on a regulated agency product that is covered in a predicated rule.

Regulated User: The regulated Good Practice entity, that is responsible for the operation of a computerized system and the applications, files and data held thereon. (PIC/S PI 011-3) See also User and Operator.

Regulation: Regulations are rules for following and enforcing the law. FDA enforces all the regulations contained in Title 21 CFR.

Regulatory Authorities: Bodies having the statutory power to regulate. The expression "regulatory authorities" includes the authorities that review submitted products data and consult inspections.

Regulatory Requirements: Any part of a law, ordinance, decree, or other regulation which applies to the regulated article.

Release: Version of a configuration item that is made available for a specific purpose. (ISO 9000-3)

Reliability: The ability of a system or component to perform its required functions under stated conditions for a specified period. (American National Standards Institute/The Institute of Electrical and Electronics Engineers, Inc. (IEEE) Std 610.12-1990, IEEE Standard Glossary of Software Engineering Terminology)

Reliable Records: Records that are a full and accurate representation of the transactions, activities, or facts to which they attest and can be depended upon in the course of subsequent transactions or activities.

Remediate: In the context of this book, the software, hardware and/or procedural changes employed to bring a system into compliance with the applicable GXP rule.

Remediation Plan: A documented approach on bringing existing computer systems into compliance with the regulation/s.

Replacement: The implementation of a new compliant system after the retirement of an existing system.

Re-qualification: Repetition of the qualification process or a specific portion thereof.

Requirement: A condition or capability that must be met or possessed by a system or system component to satisfy a contract, standard, specification, or other formally imposed document. The set of all requirements forms the basis for subsequent development of the system or system component. (ANSI/IEEE)

Retention Environment: The environment used for subsequent safe keeping and preservation of the e-records. (GERM)

Retention Period: The length of time specified for data on a data medium to be preserved. (ISO)

The duration for which records are retained. Retention periods are defined in a retention schedule document. These retention schedules are based on business, country-specific regulatory, and legal requirements.

Retirement Phase: The period in the SLC in which plans are made and executed to decommission or remove a computer technology from operational use.

Retrospective Evaluation: Establishing documented evidence that a system does what it purports to do based on an analysis of historical information. The process of evaluating a computer system, which is currently in operation, against standard validation practices and procedures. The evaluation determines the reliability, accuracy, and completeness of a system.

Retrospective Validation: See Retrospective Evaluation.

Revision: Different versions of the same document. Can also be used in reference to software, firmware, and hardware boards. Implies a fully tested, fully functional, and released unit/component/document.

Risk: A measure of the extent to which an organization is threatened by a potential circumstance or event, and typically a function of the following:

a. The adverse impacts that would arise if the circumstance or event occurs; and
b. The likelihood of occurrence. Likelihood is influenced by the ease of exploit(s) required and the frequency with which an exploit or like-objects are being attacked at present. (K. Dempsey, P. Eavy and G. Moore, "*Automation Support for Security Control Assessments Volume 1: Overview*," Draft NISTIR 8011, February 2016)

Risk Assessment: A comprehensive evaluation of the risk and its associated impact.

Risk Management: The tasks and plans that help avoid risk and helps minimize damage.

Review: A process or meeting during which a software product is presented to project personnel, managers, users, customers, user representatives, or other interested parties for comment or approval. (IEEE)

SAT: Inspection and/or dynamic testing of the systems or major system components to support the qualification of an equipment system conducted and documented at the manufacturing site.

Secure Repository: A repository or application that, in accordance with specific country laws and regulations, permits users to securely store records and limits the ability to edit and delete documents.

Security Controls: The management, operational, and technical controls (i.e., safeguards or countermeasures) prescribed for an information system to protect the confidentiality, integrity, and availability of the system and its information.

Self-inspection: An audit carried out by people from within the organization to ensure compliance with GMP and regulatory requirements.

Segregation of Duties: A process that divides roles and responsibilities so that a single individual cannot subvert a critical process.

Service Provider: An organization supplying services to one or more internal or external customers. (ITIL Service Design, 2011 Edition)

Shall: Used to express a provision that is binding, per regulatory requirement. Statements that use "shall" can be traced to a regulatory requirement and must be followed to comply with such requirements.

Should: Used to express a non-mandatory provision. Statements that use "should" are best practices, recommended activities, or options to perform activities to be considered in order to achieve quality projects results. Other methods may be used if it can be demonstrated that they are equivalent.

SIPOC Diagram: It is a tool used to identify all significant elements of a process. The representation of such process is a high-level process map.

Signature, Handwritten: The scripted name or legal mark of an individual handwritten by that individual and executed or adopted with the present intention to authenticate a writing in a permanent form. (21 CFR 11.3(8))

Site: In this book, indicates where local guidelines, standards, procedures, and organizations underpin a global policy.

Site Acceptance Test: An Acceptance Test at the Customer's site, usually involving the Customer. (IEEE)

Software Developer: Person or organization that designs software and writes the programs. Software development includes the design of the user interface and the program architecture as well as programming the source code. (TechWeb Network, http://www.techweb.com/encyclopedia/)

Software Development Standards: Written policies or procedures that describe practices a programmer or software developer should follow in creating, debugging, and verifying software.

Software Item: Identifiable part of a software product. (ISO 9000-3)

Software Product: Set of computer programs, procedures, and possibly associated documentation and data. (ISO 9000-3)

Source Code: The human-readable version of the list of instructions (programs) that enables a computer to perform a task.

Source Data: All information in original records and certified copies of original records of clinical findings, observations, or other activities in a clinical trial necessary for the reconstruction and evaluation of the trial. Source data are contained in source documents (original records or certified copies). (EMA/INS/GCP/454280/2010 GCP Inspectors Working Group (GCP IWG). Reflection paper on expectations for electronic source data and data transcribed to electronic data collection.

All information in original records and certified copies of original records of clinical findings, observations, or other activities (in a clinical investigation) used for the reconstruction and evaluation of the trial. Source data are contained in source documents (original records or certified copies). (FDA, Electronic Source Data in Clinical Investigations, September 2013)

Specification: A document that specifies, in a complete, precise, verifiable manner, the requirements, design, behavior, or other characteristics of a system or component, and often, the procedures for determining whether these provisions have been satisfied. (IEEE)

Stakeholder: In this book, anyone who has a stake in the successful outcome of the project – system owner(s), business managers, regulated end-users, quality assurance, software engineers, support people, and so forth.

Static Analysis: (1) Analysis of a program that is performed without executing the program. (NBS) (2) The process of evaluating a system or component based on its form, structure, content, documentation. (IEEE)

Standard Instrument Software: These are driven by non-user-programmable firmware. They are configurable. (GAMP)

Standard Operation Procedures: See Procedural Controls

Standard Software Packages: A complete and documented set of programs supplied to several users for a generic application or function. (ISO/IEC 2382-20:1990)

Structured Data: Refers to data that is stored in defined fields. Categories for structured data include database formats, spreadsheets, statistical data that is the result of quantitative research and analysis, and scientific data collected by instrumentation tools during the scientific process.

Subject Matter Experts: Individuals with specific expertise and responsibility in a particular area or field. (ASTM, E 2500 – 07 Standard Guide for Specification, Design, and Verification of Pharmaceutical and Biopharmaceutical Manufacturing Systems and Equipment)

Supplier: An organization that enters into a contract with the acquirer for the supply of a system, software product or software service under the terms of the contract. (ISO 12207:1995[4])

System: (1) People, machines, and methods organized to accomplish a set of specific functions. (ANSI) (2) A composite, at any level of complexity, of personnel, procedures, materials, tools, equipment, facilities, and software. The elements of this composite entity are used together in the intended operational or support environment to perform a given task or achieve a specific purpose, support, or mission requirement. (DOD) (3) A group of related objects designed to perform or control a set of specified actions.

System Backup: The storage of data and programs on a separate media and stored separately from the originating system.

System Documentation: The collection of documents that describe the requirements, capabilities, limitations, design, operation, and maintenance of an information processing system. See: specification, test documentation, user's guide. (ISO)

System Integrity: The quality that a system has when it performs its intended function in an unimpaired manner, free from unauthorized manipulation. (NIST SP 800-33, Withdrawn: August 2018)

System Lifecycle: All phases in the life of the system from initial requirements until retirement including design, specification, programming, testing, installation, operation, and maintenance. (EMA Annex 11)

System Owner: The person responsible for the availability, and maintenance of a computerized system and for the security of the data residing on that system. (EMA Annex 11)

System Retirement: The removal of a system from operational usage. The system may be replaced by another system or may be removed without being replaced.

System Software: See Operating System.

System Specification: In this book, corresponds to requirements, functional and/or design specifications. Refer to Specification.

System Test: Process of testing an integrated hardware and software system to verify that the system meets its specified requirements.

Technological Controls: Are program enforcing compliance rules.

Templates: Guidelines that outline the basic information for a specific set of equipment. (JETT)

Test Report: Document that presents test results and other information relevant to a test. (ISO/IEC Guide 2:2004)

Test Script: A detailed set of instructions for execution of the test. This typically includes the following:

- Specific identification of the test
- Prerequisites or dependencies
- Test objective
- Test steps or actions
- Requirements or instructions for capturing data (e.g. screen prints, report printing)
- Pass/fail criteria for the entire script
- Instructions to follow if a non-conformance is encountered
- Test execution date
- Person(s) executing the test
- Review date
- Person reviewing the test results

For each step of the test script, the item tested, the input to that step, and the expected result are indicated prior to execution of the test. The actual results obtained during the steps of the test are recorded on or attached to the test script. Test scripts and results may be managed through computer-based electronic tools. Refer to *Test case* in the *Glossary of Computerized System and Software Development Terminology*, August 1995.

Test Non-Conformance: Occurs when the actual test result does not equal the expected result or an unexpected event (such as a loss of power) is encountered.

Testing: Examining the behavior of a program by executing the program on sample data sets.

Third Party: Parties not directly managed by the holder of the manufacturing and/or import authorization.

Threat: The potential for a "threat source" to exploit (intentional) or trigger (accidental) a specific vulnerability. (NIST SP 800-33, Withdrawn: August 2018)

Threat Source: Either (1) intent and method targeted at the intentional exploitation of a vulnerability or (2) the situation and method that may accidentally trigger a vulnerability. (NIST SP 800-33, Withdrawn: August 2018)

Timestamp: A record mathematically linking a piece of data to a time and date.

Traceability: (1) The degree to which a relationship can be established between two or more products of the development process, especially products having a predecessor-successor or master-subordinate relationship to one another; e.g., the degree to which the requirements and design of a given software component match. (IEEE) (2) The degree to which each element in a software development product establishes its reason for existing; e.g., the degree to which each element in a bubble chart references the requirement that it satisfies.

Traceability Analysis: The tracing of (1) Software Requirements Specifications requirements to system requirements in concept documentation, (2) software design descriptions to software requirements specifications and software requirements specifications to software design descriptions, (3) source code to corresponding design specifications and design specifications to source code. Analyze identified relationships for correctness, consistency, completeness, and accuracy. (IEEE)

Traceability Matrix: A matrix that records the relationship between two or more products; e.g., a matrix that records the relationship between the requirements and the design of a given software component. (IEEE)

Training Plan: Documentation describing the training required for an individual based on his or her job title or description.

Training Record: Documentation (electronic or paper) of the training received by an individual that includes, but is not limited to, the individual's name or identifier; the type of training received; the date the training occurred; the trainer's name or identifier; and an indication of the effectiveness of the training (if applicable).

Transfer: The act or process of moving records from one location to another.

True Copy Record: (1) An exact copy of an original record, which may be retained in the same or different format in which it was originally generated, e.g. a paper copy of a paper record, an electronic scan of a paper record, or a paper record of electronically generated data. (MHRA) (2) Accurate reproduction of the original record regardless of the technology used to create the reproduction (for example, printing, scanning, photocopying, microfilm, or microfiche). A true copy of an electronic record must contain the entire record, including all associated metadata, audit trails, and signatures, as applicable, to preserve content and meaning.

Trust: In the network security context, trust refers to privacy (the data is not viewable by unauthorized people), integrity (the data stays in its true form), non-repudiation (the publisher cannot say they did not send it), and authentication (the publisher – and recipient – are who they say they are).

Transient Memory: Memory that must have a constant supply of power or the stored data will be lost.

Trustworthy Computer Systems: Trustworthy computer systems consist of computer infrastructure, applications, and procedures that:

- Are reasonably suited to performing their intended functions
- Provide a reasonably reliable level of availability, reliability and correct operation
- Are reasonably secure from intrusion and misuse
- Adhere to generally accepted security principles

Trustworthy Records: Reliability, authenticity, integrity, and usability are the characteristics used to describe trustworthy records from a record management perspective. (NARA)

Unplanned (Emergency) Change: An unanticipated necessary change to a validated system requiring rapid implementation.

Usable Records: Records that can be located, retrieved, presented, and interpreted.

User: The company or group responsible for the operation of a system. (GAMP) (see also "Regulated User"). The GxP customer, or user organization, contracting a supplier to provide a product. In the context of this document it is, therefore, not intended to apply only to individuals who use the system and is synonymous with "Customer." (EMA Annex 11)

User Backup/Alternative Procedures: Procedure which describe the steps to be taken for the continued recording and control of the raw data in the event of a computer system interruption or failure.

Unit: A separately testable element specified in the design of a computer software element. Synonymous to component, module. (IEEE)

Unit Test: Test of a module for typographic, syntactic, and logical errors, for correct implementation of its design, and for satisfaction of its requirements.

Usability: A useable record is one which can be located, retrieved, presented, and interpreted. (NARA)

Users: People or processes accessing a computer system either by direct connections (i.e., via terminals) or indirect connections (i.e., prepare input data or receive output that is not reviewed for content or classification by a responsible individual).

User ID: A sequence of characters which is recognized by the computer and which uniquely identifies one person. The UserID is the first form of identification. UserID is also known as a PIN or identification code.

Walk-through: A static analysis technique in which a designer or programmer leads members of the development team and other interested parties through a software product, and the participants ask questions and make comments about possible errors, violation of development standards, and other problems. (IEEE)

Workflows: The intended steps, sequencing, specifications, calculations, or other processes through which a piece of work passes from initiation to completion. E.g., operational checks, authority checks, device checks, built-in checks, accuracy checks, and so on.

Validated: It is used to indicate a status to designate that a system or software complies with applicable GMP requirements.

Validation: Action of proving, in accordance with the principles of Good Manufacturing Practice, that any procedure, process, equipment, material, activity or system actually leads to the expected results (see also Qualification). (PIC/S)

Validation Coordinator: A person or designee responsible for coordinating the validation activities for a specific project or task.

Validation Protocol: A written plan stating how validation will be conducted, including test parameters, product characteristics, production equipment, and decision points on what constitutes acceptable test results. (FDA)

Validation Plan: A multidisciplinary strategy from which each phase of a validation process is planned, implemented, and documented to ensure that a facility, process, equipment, or system does what it is designed to do. May also be known as a system or software Quality Plan.

Validation Summary Report: Documents confirming that the entire project planned activities have been completed. On acceptance of the Validation Summary Report, the user releases the system for use, possibly with a requirement that continuing monitoring should take place for a certain time. (GAMP)

Verification: (1) The process of determining whether the products of a given phase of the SLC fulfil the requirements established during the previous phase. (2) A systematic approach to verify that manufacturing systems, acting singly or in combination, are fit for intended use, have been properly installed, and are operating correctly. This is an umbrella term that encompasses all types of approaches to assuring systems are fit for use such as qualification, commissioning and qualification, verification, system validation, or other. (ASTM 5200) (3) Confirmation by examination and provision of objective evidence that specified requirements have been fulfilled. (FDA Medical Devices) (4) In design and development, verification concerns the process of examining the result of a given activity to determine conformity with the stated requirement for that activity.

Verification (Validation) of Data: The procedures carried out to ensure that the data contained in the final report match original observations. These procedures may apply to raw data, data in case-report forms (in hard copy or electronic form), computer printouts and statistical analysis and tables. (WHO)

Virtual Private Network: Describes the use of encryption to provide some secure a secure telecommunications route between parties over an insecure or public network, such as the internet.

Vulnerability: Weakness in system security procedures, design, implementation, internal controls, and so on, that could be accidentally triggered or intentionally exploited and results in a violation of the systems' security policy. (NIST SP 800-33, Withdrawn: August 2018)

Warehouse: A facility or location where things are stored.

Will: This word denotes a declaration of purpose or intent by one party, not a requirement.

Work Products: The intended result of activities or processes. (PDA)

Worst Case: A set of conditions encompassing upper and lower processing limits and circumstances, including those within standard operating procedures, which pose the greatest chance of process or product failure when compared to ideal conditions. Such conditions do not necessarily induce product or process failure. (FDA)

Written: In the context of electronic records, the term "written" means "recorded, or documented on media, paper, electronic or other substrate" from which data may be rendered in a human-readable form. (EMA GMP Chapter 4, 2011)

Appendix II
Abbreviations and/or Acronyms

ABA American Bar Association
ACE Access-Control Entry
ACL Access-Control List
ADP Automated Data Processing
AES Advanced Encryption Standard
AGV Automated Guidance Vehicle
AKA Also Known As
ALCOA Attributable, Legible, Contemporaneous, Original and Accurate
ALCOA+ ALCOA + Complete, Consistent, Enduring and Available
ANDAs Abbreviated New Drug Applications
ANSI American National Standard Institute
API Active Pharmaceutical Ingredients
ASEAN Association of Southeast Asian Nations
ASN.1 Abstract Syntax Notation One
ASTM American Society for Testing and Materials
BaaS Backup as a Service
BI Business Intelligence
BPaaS Business Process as a Service
CA Certification Authority
CAPA Corrective and Preventive Actions
CEFIC Conseil Européen des Fédérations de l'Industrie Chimique
CFDA China Food & Drug Administration
CFR Code of Federal Regulation
cGMP Current Good Manufacturing Practices
CMC Chemistry, Manufacturing, and Controls

CNSSI Committee on National Security Systems Instruction
CPG US FDA Compliance Policy Guide
CPU Central Processing Unit
CPV Continued Process Verification
CRC Cyclic Redundancy Check
CRL Certificate Revocation List
CROs Contract Research Organizations
CSV Computer Systems Validation
DaaS Data as a Service
DACL Discretionary Access Control List
DCS Distributed Control System
DES Data Encryption Standard
DI Data Integrity
DIQbD Data Integrity/Quality by Design'
DM Data Marts
DMZ Website's Demilitarized Zone
DN Distinguished Name
DoD Department of Defense
DQ Design Qualification
DRM Device Master Record
DSA Digital Signature Algorithm
DSHEA Dietary Supplement Health and Education Act
DSS Digital Signature Standard
DTS Digital Time-Stamping Service
DW Data Warehouse
EC European Commission
ECA European Compliance Academy
EDMS Electronic Document Management System
EEA European Economic Area
EEC European Economic Community
EFS Encrypting File System
EMA European Medicines Agency
EMEA European Medicines Agency
ENISA European Union Agency for Network and Information Security
ERM Electronic Records Management
ERP Enterprise Resource Planning
ETSI European Telecommunications Standards Institute
EU European Union
EVM Earned Value Management

FAT Factory Acceptance Test
FD&C Act US Food Drug and Cosmetic Act
FDA Food and Drug Administration
FIPS Federal Information Processing Standards
FR US Federal Register
FTP File Transfer Protocol
GAMP Good Automated Manufacturing Practices
GCP Good Clinical Practices
GDP Good Documentation Practices
GEIP Good E-records Integrity Practices
GERM Good Electronic Records Management
GLP Good Laboratory Practices
GMPs Good Manufacturing Practices
GXP Refers to the various good practices regulated by the regulatory authorities. These are Good Clinical Practice (GCP), Good Distribution Practice (GDP), Good Laboratory Practice (GLP), Good Manufacturing Practice (GMP), Good Pharmacovigilance Practice (GPP), and other regulated applications in context GXP can refer to one specific set of practices or to any combination of the GXP.
HMA Heads of Medicines Agencies
HMAC Hash Message Authentication Code
HMI Human–Machine Interface
IaaS Infrastructure as a Service
ICH International Conference for Harmonization of Technical Requirements for Registration of Pharmaceuticals for Human Use
ICS Industrial Control System
ID Identification
IDA Interchange of Data between Administrations
I/Os Inputs and outputs
IEC International Electrotechnical Commission
IEEE Institute of Electrical and Electronic Engineers
IIS Internet Information Services
IMDRF International Medical Device Regulators Forum
IoT Internet of Things
ISA International Society of Automation
ISO International Organization for Standardization
ISPE International Society for Pharmaceutical Engineering

IT Information Technologies
ITIL IT Infrastructure Library
ITSM IT Service Management
KMS Key Management Service
LAN Local Area Network
LIMS Laboratory Information Management System
MA Marketing Authorization
MES Manufacturing Execution System
MHRA Medicines and Healthcare Products Regulatory Agency (United Kingdom medicines and medical devices regulatory agency)
MRA Mutual Recognition Agreements
MTBF Mean Time Between Failures
MTTR Mean Time to Repair or Mean time to recovery
NARA National Archives and Records Administration
NBS National Bureau of Standards
NDAs New Drug Applications
NEMA National Electrical Manufacturers Association
NIST National Institutes of Standards and Technology
NMPA National Medical Products Association (former CFDA)
NTP Network Time Protocol
OECD Organization for Economic Co-operation and Development
OLAs Operational Level Agreements
OMCL Official Medicines Control Laboratories
OSHA US Occupational Safety & Health Administration
OTC Over the Counter
OTS Off-the-Shelf
P&ID Process and Instrumentation Drawings
PaaS Platform as a Service
PAI Pre-Approval Inspections
PAT Process Analytical Tools
PDA Parenteral Drug Association
PFD Process Flow Diagram
PIC/S Pharmaceutical Inspection Co-Operation Scheme http://www.pic-scheme.org/
PIN Personal Identification Number
PKCS Public-Key Cryptography Standards
PKI Public Key Infrastructure
PLC Programmable Logic Controller
PQS Pharmaceutical Quality System

QA Quality Assurance
QbD Quality by Design
QC Quality Control
QMS Quality Management System
QP Qualified Person
R&D Research and Development
RAM Random Access Memory
RFP Request for Proposal
RIPEMD Race Integrity Primitives Evaluation Message Digest
RTU Remote Terminal Unit
SaaS Software as a Service
SACL System Access Control List
SAG Scientific Archivists Group
SAP Systems, Application and Products
SAS The Statistical Analysis System licensed by the SAS Institute, Inc.
SAT Site Acceptance Test
SCADA Supervisory Control and Data Acquisition
SDLC Software Development Life Cycle
SHA-1 Secure Hash Algorithm 1
SIDGP Russia Federal State Institute of Drugs and Good Practices
SIPOC Suppliers, Inputs, Process, Outputs, Customers
SLA Service Level Agreement
SLC System Lifecycle
SME Subject Matter Experts
SOPs Standard Operating Procedures
SPC Statistical Process Control
SQA Software Quality Assurance
SQE Software Quality Engineering
SSA US Social Security Administration
SSL Secure Sockets Layer
SWEBOK Software Engineering Body of Knowledge
TGA Therapeutic Goods Administration
TLS Transport Layer Security
UCs Underpinning Contracts
UK United Kingdom
UPS Uninterruptable Power Supply
US United States
US FDA United States Food and Drugs Administration

VPN Virtual Privates Network
WAN Wide Area Network
WBS Work Breakdown Structure
WL Warning Letter
WLAN Wireless Local Area Network
WHO World Health Organization
XaaS Anything as a Service

Appendix III
References

"Aide-mémoire of German ZLG regarding EU GMP Annex 11nnex 11," September 2013.

Alanazi, H., Zaidan, B., Zaidan, A., Jalab, H., Shabbir, M. Al-Nabhani, Y., "New Comparative Study Between DES, 3DES and AES within Nine Factors," *Journal of Computing*, 2(3), March 2010, 152–157. ISSN 2151-9617.

Amy, L. T., "Automation Systems for Control and Data Acquisition," *ISA*, 1992.

Appel, K., "How Far Does Annex 11 Go Beyond Part 11?" *Pharmaceutical Processing*, September 2011.

APV, "The APV Guideline "Computerized Systems" based on Annex 11 of the EU-GMP Guideline," Version 1.0, April 1996.

"ASTM, E 2500 – 13 Standard Guide for Specification, Design, and Verification of Pharmaceutical and Biopharmaceutical Manufacturing Systems and Equipment," 2013.

Boogaard, P., Haag, T., Reid, C., Rutherford, M., Wakeham, C., "Data Integrity," *Pharmaceutical Engineering Special Report*, March-April, 2016.

Brown, A., "Selecting Storage Media for Long-Term Preservation," *The National Archives, DPGN-02*, August 2008.

Cappucci, W., Clark, C., Goossens, T., Wyn, S., "Annex 11 Interpretation," *Pharmaceutical Engineering*, 31(4), Jul/August, 2011, pp. 1–7.

CEFIC, "Computer Validation Guide," *API Committee of CEFIC*, January 2003.

CEFIC, "Practical Risk-based Guide for Managing Data Integrity," March 2019 (Rev 1).

Center for Technology in Government University at Albany, SUNY, "Practical Tools for Electronic records Management and Preservation," July 1999.

National Medical Products Association (NMPA (former CFDA)), "Drug Data Management Practices Guidance," December 2020.

Cloud Service Alliance, "Cloud Control Matrix," Rev 3.0.1, July 2014.

Cloud Service Alliance, "Security Guidance for Critical Areas of Focus in Cloud Computing," Rev 3.0, November 2011.

Committee on National Security Systems Instruction (CNSSI), "Glossary," CNSSI 4009, April 2015.
Commission Directive 91/412/EEC, "Laying Down the Principles and Guidelines of Good Manufacturing Practice for Veterinary Medicinal Products," July 1991.
Commission Directive 95/46/EC of the European Parliament and of the Council of 24 October 1995 on the protection of individuals with regard to the processing of personal data and on the free movement of such data. http://eur-lex.europa.eu/LexUriServ/LexUriServ.do?uri=CELEX:31995L0046:en:HTML.
Commission Directive 2003/94/EC, laying down the principles and guidelines of good manufacturing practice in respect of medicinal products for human use and investigational medicinal products for human use, October 2003.
Commission Directive 2017/1572, supplementing Directive 2001/83/EC of the European Parliament and of the Council as regards the principles and guidelines of good manufacturing practice for medicinal products for human use, September 2017.
Council of Europe, "Handbook on European Data Protection Law," December 2013.
Churchward, D., "Good Manufacturing Practice (GMP) Data Integrity: A New Look at an Old Topic, Part 1 of 3," June 2015.
Churchward, D., "Good Manufacturing Practice (GMP) Data Integrity: A New Look at an Old Topic, Part 2 of 3," July 2015.
Churchward, D., "Good Manufacturing Practice (GMP) Data Integrity: A New Look at an Old Topic, Part 3 of 3," August 2015.
Churchward, D., "GMP Compliance and Data Integrity," In: *Paper Presented at the PDA/PIC's Quality and Regulations Conference*, Brussels, Belgium, June 2015.
Cuddy, B., "EMA's Guidance on Data Integrity," In: *Presented at the Indian Pharmaceutical Alliance Annual Congress*, Mumbai, India, 23–24 February 2017.
Department of Defense (DoD) 8320.1-M-1, "Data Standardization Procedures," April 1998.
European Compliance Academy (ECA), "Deletion of Data: Does It Have to be Regulated In an SOP?" June 2019. https://www.gmp-compliance.org/gmp-news/deletion-of-data-does-it-have-to-be-regulated-in-a-sop.
ECA, "Ensuring the Data Integrity of Cloud Service Providers," August 2019. https://www.it-compliance-group.org/icg_news_7259.html.
ECA IT Compliance Working Group, "Shared Platform and Cloud Services Implications for Information Governance and Records Management," http://www.it-compliance-group.org/icg_downloads.html.
Eglovitch, J., "How to Remedy Data Integrity Failures: FDA's Step-by-Step Approach," *The Golden Sheet*, October 2015.
EMA/INS/GCP/454280/2010, GCP Inspectors Working Group (GCP IWG), "Reflection Paper on Expectations for Electronic Source Data and Data Transcribed to Electronic Data Collection Tools in Clinical Trials," August 2010.
EMA, "Reflection Paper on the Expectations for Electronic Source Documents Used in Clinical Trials," August 2010.
European Union Agency for Network and Information Security (ENISA), "Cloud Security Guide for SMEs," April 2015.

ETSI, "CLOUD; Cloud Private-Sector User Recommendations," November 2011.
ETSI, "Identification of Cloud User Needs," ETSI SR 003 381 V2.1.1, February 2016.
European Compliance Academy (ECN), "GMP Data Governance and Data Integrity Guidance," Version 2, January 2018.
European Commission (EC), "General Data Protection Regulation (GDPR)," January 2012 (Proposed regulation to replace EU Data Protection Directive 95/46/EC).
"EU Annex III to Guidance for the Conduct of Good Clinical Practice Inspections Computer Systems," May 2008. http://ec.europa.eu/health/files/eudralex/vol-10/chap4/annex_iii_to_guidance_for_the_conduct_of_gcp_inspections_-_computer_systems_en.pdf
"EU, Questions and Answers: Good Manufacturing Practice and Good Distribution Practice, Data Integrity," September 2019. https://www.ema.europa.eu/en/human-regulatory/research-development/compliance/good-manufacturing-practice/guidance-good-manufacturing-practice-good-distribution-practice-questions-answers#data-integrity-(new-august-2016)-section
"EU, Questions and Answers: Good Manufacturing Practice and Good Distribution Practice, Annex 11," https://www.ema.europa.eu/en/human-regulatory/research-development/compliance/good-manufacturing-practice/guidance-good-manufacturing-practice-good-distribution-practice-questions-answers#eu-gmp-guide-annexes:-supplementary-requirements:-annex-11:-computerised-systems-section.
EudraLex, The Rules Governing Medicinal Products in the European Union, Volume 4, "EU Guidelines to Good Manufacturing Practice, Medicinal Products for Human and Veterinary Use Part 1, Annex 11 – Computerized Systems," June 2011. http://ec.europa.eu/health/files/eudralex/vol-4/annex11_01-2011_en.pdf.
EudraLex, The Rules Governing Medicinal Products in the European Union, Volume 4, "EU Guidelines to Good Manufacturing Practice, Medicinal Products for Human and Veterinary Use, Annex 15 – Validation and Qualification," October 2015.
EudraLex, The Rules Governing Medicinal Products in the European Union, Volume 4, "EU Guidelines to Good Manufacturing Practice, Medicinal Products for Human and Veterinary Use, Annex 16 – Certification by a Qualified Person and Batch Release," 2001.
EudraLex. The Rules Governing Medicinal Products in the European Union, Volume 4, "EU Guidelines for Good Manufacturing Practices for Medicinal Products for Human and Veterinary Use, Annex 20 – Quality Risk Management," February 2008.
EudraLex, The Rules Governing Medicinal Products in the European Union, Volume 4, "EU Guidelines to Good Manufacturing Practice, Medicinal Products for Human and Veterinary Use – Glossary," February 2013.
EudraLex, The Rule Governing Medicinal Products in the European Union, Volume 4, "EU Guidelines for Good Manufacturing Practices for Medicinal Products for Human and Veterinary Use, Part 1, Chapter 2 – Personnel," February 2014.
EudraLex, The Rules Governing Medicinal Products in the European Union Volume 4, "Good Manufacturing Practice, Medicinal Products for Human and Veterinary Use, Chapter 3: Premises and Equipment," 2007.

EudraLex, The Rules Governing Medicinal Products in the European Union Volume 4, "Good Manufacturing Practice, Medicinal Products for Human and Veterinary Use, Chapter 4: Documentation," June 2011.

EudraLex, The Rules Governing Medicinal Products in the European Union Volume 4, "Good Manufacturing Practice, Medicinal Products for Human and Veterinary Use, Chapter 7: Outsourced Activities," January 2013.

EudraLex, The Rule Governing Medicinal Products in the European Union, Volume 4, "EU Good manufacturing practice (GMP) Medicinal Products for Human and Veterinary Use, Chapter 9: Self Inspections," 2001.

EudraLex, The Rules Governing Medicinal Products in the European Union Volume 4, "Good Manufacturing Practice, Medicinal Products for Human and Veterinary Use : Glossary," 2007.

European Agencies Agency, Questions and Answers: Good Manufacturing Practice, "EU GMP Guide Annexes: Supplementary Requirements: Annex 11: Computerised Systems," http://www.ema.europa.eu/ema/index.jsp?curl=pages/regulation/general/gmp_q_a.jsp&mid=WC0b01ac058006e06c#section8.

European Directorate for the Quality of Medicine and Healthcare, "OMCL Validation of Computerised Systems Core Documents," May 2009. http://www.edqm.eu/medias/fichiers/Validation_of_Computerised_Systems_Core_Document.pdf.

European Medicines Agency (EMA), "Q&A: Good Manufacturing Practices (GMP)," February 2011.

Federal Information Processing Standards (FIPS), Publication 11-3, "American National Dictionary for Information Systems," *Windrowed*, July 1979.

GAMP® Good Practice Guide: A Risk-based Approach to Compliant Electronic Records and Signatures, 2005.

GAMP® Good Practice Guide: Electronic Data Archiving, 2007.

GAMP® Good Practice Guide: Global Information Systems Control and Compliance – Appendix 2 – Data Management Considerations, 2005.

GAMP® Good Practice Guide: IT Control and Compliance, International Society of Pharmaceutical Engineering, Tampa FL, 2005.

GAMP® Good Practice Guide: Risk Based Approach to Operation of GXP Computerized Systems, 2010.

GAMP®/ISPE, "A Risk-Based Approach to Compliant GxP Computerized Systems, International Society for Pharmaceutical Engineering (ISPE), Fifth Edition," February 2008.

GAMP®/ISPE, "Risk Assessment for Use of Automated Systems Supporting Manufacturing Processes – Part 2 – Risk to Records," *Pharmaceutical Engineering*, 23(6), November/December 2003.

GAMP®/ISPE, "Records and Data Integrity Guide," 2017.

GAMP®/ISPE, "Risk Assessment for Use of Automated Systems Supporting Manufacturing Process – Functional Risk," *Pharmaceutical Engineering*, May/June 2003, pp. 16–26.

GHTF, "Implementation of Risk Management Principles and Activities Within a Quality Management System," May 2005.

GMP Journal, "Q&As on Annex 11 (1–4) at the Computer Validation in Mannheim, Germany, in June 2011," Issue 7, October/November 2011.

GMP Journal, "Q&As on Annex 11 (5–11) at the Computer Validation in Mannheim, Germany, in June 2011," Issue 8, April/May 2012.

GMP Journal, "Q&As on Annex 11 (12–16) at the Computer Validation in Mannheim, Germany, in June 2011," Issue 9, October/November 2012.

Grigonis, Jr, George J.., Subak, Jr., Edward J., and Wyrick, Michael L., "Validation Key Practices for Computer Systems Used in Regulated Operations," *Pharmaceutical Technology*, 74–98, June 1997.

Graham, L., "Compliance Matters, Good Laboratory Practice," *Blog MHRA Inspectorate*, September 2015.

Hart, S., "Data Integrity: TGA Expectations," In: *Paper Presented at the PDA Conference*, Tel Aviv, Israel, July 2015.

Health Canada, "Good Manufacturing Practices (GMP) Guidelines for Active Pharmaceutical Ingredients (APIs)," GUI-0104, C.02.05, Interpretation No.15, December 2013.

Health Canada, "Good Manufacturing Practices Guide for Drug Products, GUI-0001," February 2018.

ICH Harmonized Tripartite Guideline, "Good Manufacturing Practice Guidance for Active Pharmaceutical Ingredients, Q7," November 2000.

ICH Harmonized Tripartite Guideline, "Quality Risk Management, Q9," November 2005.

ICH Harmonized Tripartite Guideline, "Pharmaceutical Quality Systems, Q10," June 2008.

ICH Harmonized Tripartite Guideline, "Good Clinical Practice, E6," Rev 2, June 2016.

Interchange of Data between Administrations (IDA) Programme of the European Commission, "Model Requirements for the Management of Electronic Records," October 2002. http://www.cornwell.co.uk/moreq.html.

IEEE, "Guide to the Software Engineering Body of Knowledge," Rev 3.0, 2014.

ISO 9001:2015, "Quality Management Systems – Requirements."

ISO 11799: 2003(E), "Information and Documentation – Document Storage Requirements for Archive and Library Materials."

ISO 12207:1995, "Information Technology – Software Life Cycle Processes." [*Note:* The 1995 revision is not the most recent version.]

ISO 13485:2012, "Medical Devices – Quality Management Systems – Requirements for Regulatory Purposes."

ISO 8601:2004, "Data Elements and Interchange Formats – Information Interchange – Representation of Dates and Times."

ISO/IEC 1799:2005, "Information Technology – Security Techniques – Code of Practice for Information Security Management."

ISO/IEC 27001: 2013, "Information Technology – Security Techniques – Information Security Management Systems – Requirements."

ISPE GAMP Forum, "Risk Assessment for Use of Automated Systems Supporting Manufacturing Processes – Part 2 – Risk to Records," *Pharmaceutical Engineering*, 23(6), November/December 2003.

ISPE, "Regulatory Framework – EMEA," Dr. Kate McCormick, 2009.

ISPE, "Regulatory Framework – PIC/S and ICH," Dr. Kate McCormick, 2009.

ISPE GAMP®, "A Risk Approach to Compliant GxP Computerized Systems," International Society for Pharmaceutical Engineering (ISPE), 5th ed., February 2008.

ISPE/PDA, "Good Practice and Compliance for Electronic Records and Signatures. Part 1 Good Electronic Records Management (GERM)," July 2002.

Information Security Committee American Bar Association (ABA), "Digital Signature Guidelines," August 1996.

IT Infrastructure Library (ITIL), "The Official Introduction to the ITIL Service Lifecycle," 2007.

ITIL Service Design, "Section 5.2 – Management of Data and Information," 2011 Edition.

Journal for GMP and Regulatory Affairs, "Q&As on Annex 11," Issue 8, April/May 2012.

Kane, A., the sidebar to "Designing Optimized Formulations," *Pharmaceutical Technology*, 41(4), 2017, pp. 16–21.

López, O., *21 CFR Part 11: Complete Guide to International Computer Validation Compliance for the Pharmaceutical Industry*, (CRC, Boca Raton, FL, 1st ed., 2004).

López, O., "A Computer Data Integrity Compliance Model," *Pharmaceutical Engineering*, 35(2), March/April 2015.

López, O., "A Historical View of 21 CFR 211.68," *Journal of GxP Compliance*, 15(2), May 2013.

López, O., "Annex 11: Progress in EU Computer Systems Guidelines," *Pharmaceutical Technology Europe*, 23(6) June, 2011. http://www.pharmtech.com/pharmtech/article/articleDetail.jsp?id=725378.

López, O., "Annex 11 and 21 CFR Part 11: Comparisons for International Compliance," *MasterControl*, January 2012.

López, O., "An Easy to Understand Guide to Annex 11," Premier Validation, Cork, Ireland, 2011. http://www.askaboutvalidation.com/1938-an-easy-to-understand-guide-to-annex-11.

López, O., "CGMP E-Records Risk Assessments," *Journal of GXP Compliance*, September 2018.

López, O., "Comparison of Health Authorities Data Integrity Expectations," In: *Paper Presented at the 4th Annual Data Integrity Validation*, Cambridge, MA, 15–16 August 2018.

López, O., *Computer Infrastructure Qualification for FDA Regulated Industries*. (PDA and DHI Publishing, LLC, River Grove, IL, 2006).

López, O., *Computer Technologies Security Part I – Key Points in the Contained Domain*. (Sue Horwood Publishing Limited, West Sussex, UK, 2002, ISBN 1-904282-17-2).

López, O., "Computer Systems Validation," In: *Encyclopedia of Pharmaceutical Science and Technology*. (Taylor and Francis, New York, NY, 4th ed., Published online: 23 Aug 2013), pp. 615–619.

López, O., "Data Integrity and your E-recs During Processing," *LinkedIn*, July 2017.

López, O., "Data Integrity Expectations of EU GMP Inspectors," *Pharmaceutical Engineering Europe*, 29(7), July 2017.
López, O., *Data Integrity in Pharmaceutical and Medical Devices Regulation Operations: Best Practices Guide to Electronic Records Compliance*. (CRC Press, Boca Ratón, FL, 2017).
López, O., "Defining and Managing Raw Manufacturing Data," *Pharmaceutical Technology*, 21(6), July 2019.
López, O., "Digital Date and Time Stamps," *LinkedIn*, June 2017.
López, O., "Electronic Records Integrity in the Data Warehouse Environments," *Journal of Validation Technology*, 22(2), April 2006.
López, O., "Electronic Records Lifecycle," Journal of GxP Compliance, 9(4), December 2015.
López, O., "EU Annex 11 and the Integrity of Erecs," *Journal of GxP Compliance*, 18(2), May 2014.
López, O., "EU Annex 11 – Changes to Computer Systems Guidelines in the EU," *LinkedIn*, August 2017.
López, O., *EU Annex 11 Guide to Computer Validation Compliance for the Worldwide Health Agency GMP*. (CRC, Boca Raton, FL, 1st ed., March 2015).
López, O., "Introduction to Data Quality," *Journal of Validation Technology*, April 2020.
López, O., "Maintaining the Validated State in Computer Systems," *Journal of GxP Compliance*, 17(2), August 2013.
López, O., "Maxims Electronic Records Integrity," *Pharmaceutical Technology*, 43(6), June 2019.
López, O., "Overview of Technologies Supporting Security Requirements in 21 CFR Part 11 – Part I," *Pharmaceutical Technology*, February 2002.
López, O., "Overview of Technologies Supporting Security Requirements in 21 CFR Part 11 – Part II," *Pharmaceutical Technology*, March 2002.
López, O., *Pharmaceutical and Medical Devices Manufacturing Computer Systems Validation*. (CRC Press, Boca Raton, FL, September 2018).
López, O., "Points be Considered when Validating Big Data Environments," *Journal of Validation Technology*, October 2019.
López, O., "Regulations and Regulatory Guidelines of Computer Systems in Drug Manufacturing 25 Years Later," *Pharmaceutical Engineering*, 33(4), July/August 2013, pp. 68–81.
López, O., "Requirements Management," *Journal of Validation Technology*, May 2013.
López, O., "Requirements for Electronic Records Contained in 21 CFR 211," *Pharmaceutical Technology*, 36(7), July 2008.
López, O., "Technologies Supporting Electronic Records Integrity – Part I," *GXP Journal Articles*, 21(5), May 2017.
López, O., "Technologies Supporting Electronic Records Integrity Part II," *GXP Journal Articles*, 21(5), September 2017.
López, O., "The Importance of Computer Systems I/Os Accuracy Checks," *GxP Lifeline*, June 2012.

López, O., "Trustworthy Computer Systems," *Journal of GxP Compliance*, 19(2), July 2015.
McDowall, R.D., "Comparison of FDA and EU Regulations for Audit Trails," *Journal of Scientific Computing*, January 2014.
McDowall, R.D., "Computer Validation: Do All Roads Lead to Annex 11?" *Spectroscopy* 29(12), December 2014, pp. 10–13.
McDowall, R.D., "Data Quality and Data Integrity Are the Same, Right? Wrong!" *Spectroscopy*, 34(11), November 2019, 22–29.
McDowall, R.D., "Ensuring Data Integrity in a Regulated Environment," *Journal of Scientific Computing*, March/April 2011.
McDowall, R.D., "Maintaining Laboratory Computer Validation – How to Conduct Periodic Reviews?" *European Compliance Academy (ECA), GMP News*, April 2012. http://www.gmp-compliance.org/pa4.cgi?src=eca_new:news_print_data.htm&nr=3085.
McDowall, R.D., "The New GMP Annex 11 and Chapter 4 is Europe's Answer to Part 11," *European Compliance Academy (ECA), GMP News*, January 2011. http://www.gmp-compliance.org/eca_news_2381_6886,6885,6738,6739,6934.html.
Mell, P., Grance, T., *The NIST Definition of Cloud Computing*, NIST Special Publication 800–145. (National Institute of Standards and Technology, Gaithersburg, MD, 2011).
MHRA, "GMP/GDP Consultative Committee Note of Meeting," October 2015. https://www.gov.uk/government/uploads/system/uploads/attachment_data/file/483846/GMP-GDP_CC_minutes_Oct_2015_FINAL.pdf.
MHRA, "Good Manufacturing Practice (GMP) Data Integrity: A New Look at an Old Topic, Part 1," June 2015. https://mhrainspectorate.blog.gov.uk/2015/06/25/good-manufacturing-practice-gmp-data-integrity-a-new-look-at-an-old-topic-part-1/.
MHRA, "Good Laboratory Practice: Guidance on Archiving," March 2006.
MHRA, "MHRA Expectation Regarding Self Inspection and Data Integrity," May 2014.
MHRA, "GxP Data Integrity Guidance and Definitions," Rev 1, March 2018.
Murphy, L., "How to Make the Business Case for Data Quality & DATA GOVERNANCE INITIATIVE," February 2020. https://www.linkedin.com/pulse/how-make-business-case-data-quality-governance-leo-murphy/?trackingId=78vWhB34RJyL8KnY4zA29w%3D%3D.
NARA, "Records Management Guidance for Agencies Implementing Electronic Signature Technologies," October 2000.
NIST, "An Introduction to Computer Security: The NIST Handbook, Chapter 7, Computer Security Risk Management," (Special Publication 800–12), June 2017.
NIST, "Guidelines for Media Sanitization," (Special Publication 800-88r1), December 2014
NIST, "Managing Information Security Risk," (Special Publication 800–39), March 2011.
NIST, "Recommendation for Key Management, Part 1: General," (Special Publication 800–57 Part 1 Rev 4), July 2015.

NIST, "Recommendation for Key Management: Part 2 – Best Practices for Key Management Organizations," (Special Publication 800-57 Part 2), May 2019.

NIST, "Systems Security Engineering: Considerations for a Multidisciplinary Approach in the Engineering of Trustworthy Secure Systems," (Special Publication 800-160 Vol 1), June 2004.

NIST, "Underlying Technical Models for Information Technology Security," December 2001, (Special Publication 800–33, withdrawn: August 2018).

OECD, "The Application of GLP Principles to Computerized Systems," OECD Guidance Document (Draft), September 2014.

PDA, Technical Report No. 31, "Validation and Qualification of Computerized Laboratory Data Acquisition Systems," *PDA Journal of Pharmaceutical Science and Technology*, 53(4), September 1999, Section 4.5.

PDA, Technical Report No. 32, "Auditing of Supplier Providing Computer Products and Services for Regulated Pharmaceutical Operations," *PDA Journal of Pharmaceutical Science and Technology*, 58(5), September/October 2004, Release 2.0.

PI 011–3, "Good Practices for Computerised Systems in Regulated "GXP" Environments," *Pharmaceutical Inspection Cooperation Scheme (PIC/S)*, September 2007.

PI 041–1, "Good Practices for Data Management and Integrity in Regulated GMP/GDP Environment," *Pharmaceutical Inspection Co-operation Scheme (PIC/S)*, November 2018 (Draft 3).

Pressman, Roger S., *Software Engineering – A Practitioner's Approach*. (McGraw Hill, 2010).

Roemer, M., "New Annex 11: Enabling Innovation," *Pharmaceutical Technology*, 23(6), June 2011.

"Safe Harbor US –EU Agreement on Meeting Directive 95/46/EC," http://www.expo rt.gov/safeharbor/index.asp.

Sampson, K., "Data Integrity," Update, Issue 6, pp. 6–10 (2014). http://www.nxtb ook.com/ygsreprints/FDLI/g46125_fdli_novdec2014/index.php#/0.

Scientific Archivists Group (SAG), "A Guide to Archiving of Electronic Records," February 2014.

Schmitt, S., "Data Integrity," *Pharmaceutical Technology*, 38(7), July 2014.

Schmitt, S., "Data Integrity – FDA and Global Regulatory Guidance," IVT, October 2014.

Russia Federal State Institute of Drugs and Good Practices (SIDGP), "Data Integrity & Computer System Validation Guideline," September 2018 (Draft).

Stenbraten, A., "Cost-effective Compliance: Practical Solutions for Computerised Systems," In: *Paper Presented at the ISPE Brussels Conference, GAMP – Cost Effective Compliance*, Brussels, Belgium, 2011-09-19/20.

Stokes, D., "Compliant Cloud Computing – Managing the Risks," *Pharmaceutical Engineering*, 33(4), 2013, 1–11.

Stokes, T., "Management's View to Controlling Computer Systems," *GMP Review*, 10(2), July 2011.

Syncsort Editors, "Data Integrity vs. Data Quality: How Are They Different?" January 2019. https://blog.syncsort.com/2019/01/data-quality/data-integrity-vs-data-quality-different/.

TGA, "Australian Code of Good Manufacturing Practice for Human Blood and Blood Components, Human Tissues and Human Cellular Therapy Products," Version 1.0, April 2013.

TGA, "Data Management and Data Integrity (DMDI)," April 2017, https://www.tga.gov.au/data-management-and-data-integrity-dmdi.

US FDA, 21 CFR Part 11, "Electronic Records; Electronic Signatures; Final Rule," *Federal Register*, 62(54), March 1997, 13429.

US FDA 21 CFR Part 58, "Good Laboratory Practice for Non-Clinical Laboratory Studies."

US FDA 21 CFR Part 110, "Current Good Manufacturing Practice in Manufacturing, Packing, or Holding Human Food."

US FDA 21 CFR Part 211, "Current Good Manufacturing Practice for Finished Pharmaceuticals," December 2007.

US FDA 21 CFR Part 312, "Investigational New Drug Application."

US FDA 21 CFR Part 606, "Current Good Manufacturing Practice for Blood and Blood Components."

US FDA 21 CFR Part 803, "Medical Device Reporting."

US FDA 21 CFR 1271, "Human Cells, Tissues, and Cellular and Tissue-Based Products."

US FDA, "Data Integrity and Compliance with Drug CGMP, Q&A," December 2018.

US FDA, "FDA PAI Compliance Program Guidance, CPG 7346.832, Compliance Program Manual," May 2010. http://www.ipqpubs.com/wp-content/uploads/2010/05/FDA_CPGM_7346.832.pdf.

US FDA, "CPG Section 425.100 – Computerized Drug Processing; CGMP Applicability to Hardware and Software (CPG 7132a.11)," September 1987.

US FDA, "CPG Section 425.200 – Computerized Drug Processing; Vendor Responsibility (CPG 7132a.12)," September 1987.

US FDA, "CPG Section 425.300 – Computerized Drug Processing; Source Code for Process Control Application Programs (CPG 7132a.15)," April 1987.

US FDA, "CPG Section 425.400 – Computerized Drug Processing; Input/Output Checking (CPG 7132a.07)," September 1987.

US FDA, "CPG Section 425.500 Computerized Drug Processing; Identification of "Persons" on Batch Production and Control Records (CPG 7132a.08)," September 1987.

US FDA, "General Principles of Software Validation; Final Guidance for Industry and FDA Staff," *CDRH and CBER*, January 2002.

US FDA, "Guidance for Industry: Blood Establishment Computer System Validation in the User's Facility," April 2013.

US FDA, "Guidance for Industry: Computerized Systems in Clinical Investigations," May 2007.

US FDA, "Guidance for Industry: Contract Manufacturing Arrangements for Drugs: Quality Agreements," November 2016.

US FDA, "Guidance for Industry: Electronic Records; Electronic Signatures – Scope and Application," August 2003.

US FDA, "Guidance for Industry: Electronic Source Data in Clinical Investigations," September 2013.

US FDA, "Guidance for Industry – Process Validation: General Principles and Practices," January 2011.

US FDA, "Guide to Inspection of Computerized Systems in the Food Processing Industry," April 2003.

Veregin, H., "Data Quality Parameters," *Geographical Information Systems*, 1999.

Vibbert, J.M., "The Internet of Things: Data Protection and Data Security," *Global Environment Information Law Journal*, 7(3), Spring 2016.

Wechsler, J., "Data Integrity Key to GMP Compliance," *Pharmaceutical Technology*, September 2014.

WHO, "Guideline on Data Integrity," QAS/19.819, October 2019 (Draft).

WHO, Technical Report Series No. 981, Annex 2, "WHO Guidelines on Quality Risk Management," 2013.

WHO, Technical Report Series No. 937, Annex 4. Appendix 5, "Validation of Computerized Systems," 2006.

Wingate, G., *Validating Automated Manufacturing and Laboratory Applications: Putting Principles into Practice.* (Taylor & Francis, Boca Raton, FL, 1997).

Yves, S., "New Annex 11, Evolution and Consequences," January/February, 2012. http://www.pharma-mag.com.

Appendix IV
Things That Can Go Wrong when Validating Big Data Environments

Introduction Big Data (1)

The term "big data" refers to extremely large sets of information which require specialized computational tools to enable their collection, analysis, and exploitation.

- The data set is so large and complex that traditional means of processing are ineffective.
- Additional challenges include analyzing, capturing, collecting, searching, sharing, storing, transferring, visualizing, and so on.
- Protection of personal data is an issue.
- The size to accommodate the entire process has been steadily increasing to be able to collect and integrate all the information.

Big data requires specialized computational tools to enable their analysis and exploitation.

In the context of Figure IV.1, e-records are stored in the big data level. This level hosts central repositories (e.g., databases (DBs)) of data from one or more disparate sources. These sources are depicted in the figure as operational applications.

From the context of the big data, the raw data (2) is extracted from its operational application or source repositories locations; maybe processed/

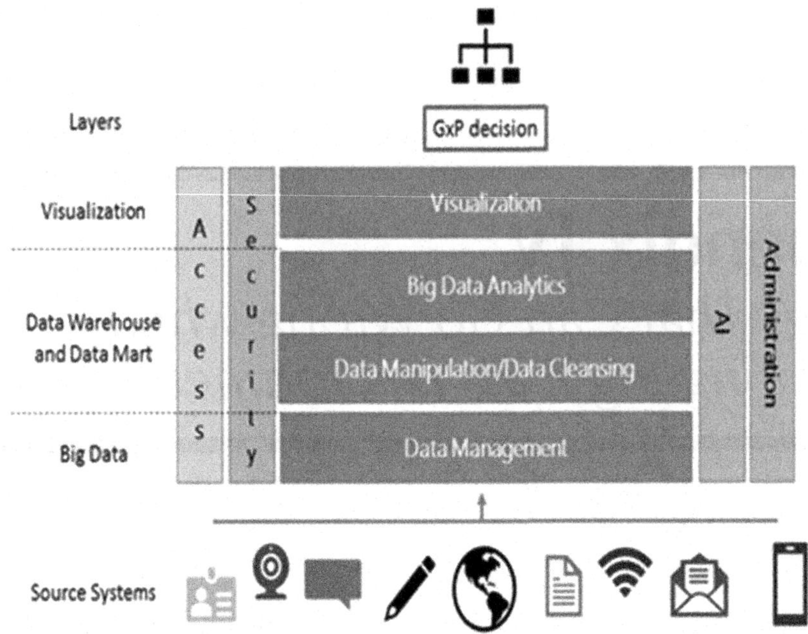

Figure IV.1 Sample big data environment.

transformed by applying a series of rules or functions; is converted to data (3); and then the data loaded into a final set of tables, Data Marts, for the consumption by the users.

The relevance of big data has motivated to the EMA to establish on March 23, 2017, a task force to evaluate the use of big data to support pharmaceutical research, innovation, and development (4).

What Can Go Wrong During the Validation Process?

From the context of the big data functionality, the infrastructure, repository mappings, and the integration sequencing are critical elements to consider during the design process and subsequent application validation.

The e-records acquisition process for big data storage uses standard technologies and procedures that automatically replicate every single byte of data in several locations. One simple error in the manipulation of data can generate errors affecting the results loaded to the Data Marts (DM). At worst, errors can result in serious production errors and distribution of adulterated or misbranded products.

The topic of e-records integrity is key as well and discussed elsewhere in this book.

Infrastructure

The capability to manage large bulk of data is provided by the hardware infrastructure, a great amount of memory and data servers large capacity.

In this case, a critical issue in big data environments withstands the performance, usage, and scalability requirements for big data analyses and integrations with the distributed storage and processing of big data infrastructures.

Some topics to be considered during the design are (5):

- Technology specific – network architecture, and so on
- Monitoring tools
- Definition of logical, physical, and/or security configurations needed to effectively manage the usage and maintenance of the system and data
- Operating parameters
- Interfaces/Connectivity/Interoperability between hardware components and hardware modules of the hardware unit
- Assumptions and constraints of the infrastructure
- Support skills, training, and reporting requirements
- Backup and restore timeframes
- Capacity planning such as storage and memory needs
- Performance requirements
- Security compliance
- Identification of suppliers
- Evaluation of the risk assessment

To demonstrate the suitability of a given piece infrastructure component, product, and/or service to the intended use and, consequently, the qualification state of the infrastructure the main work products that it is expected includes:

- Written design specification that describes what the hardware is intended to do and how it is intended to do it.
- A written test plan and procedures based on the design specification.
- Test results and an evaluation of how these results demonstrate that the predetermined design specification has been met.

The information obtained from the executed test plan and procedure is used to establish written procedures covering equipment calibration, maintenance, monitoring, and control. It is pertinent to highlight that automated systems exchanging data with other systems should include appropriate built-in checks for the correct processing of data (EU Annex 11 p5). The built-in checks are critical to establish data reliability in the multiple interfaces in the big data environment.

The primary concern of the computer infrastructure engineers is to design reliable infrastructure supporting the big data environment.

Developing an unreliable infrastructure enables a slow computing environment not meeting the performance related requirements and instances of unreliable data.

Data Process Mapping (6)

Big data requires the consolidation of various structures and sources into one cohesive dataset for analysis.

This consolidation requires defining the planning, requirements, and designing of the e-records model and the functionality to manage the e-records model. The planning provides the information requirements of the function necessary to collect the e-records and implements a technology-independent set of techniques to arrive at a set of e-records and activity models that represent the CGMP process.

Data mapping is used as the first step for a wide variety of data integration tasks. It is a process of defining how individual fields are mapped, modified, joined, filtered, aggregated, and so on to produce the final desired output. Depending on the number, schema, and primary keys, and foreign keys of the relational databases data sources, database mappings can have a varying degree of complexity.

A data mapping specification is a special type of data dictionary that shows how data from one source repository location flows to target data repository (ies). This document is developed during the data loads design.

As part of the design verification process, the data mapping specification is verified. The results of the design qualification (DQ) to the data mapping specification must be documented. It focuses on ensuring that the proposed design is suitable for the intended purpose.

After clearly understanding the files structure and their relationships, the e-records integrity risk assessment must be revisited (7).

It is pertinent to highlight that automated systems exchanging data with other systems should include appropriate built-in checks for the correct processing of data. (EU Annex 11 p5)

The primary concern of DBAs in this environment is solving the specific problem of getting the right data from point A to point B with the appropriate transformations.

Not developing a Data Mapping Specification and not performing the associated DQ will probably cause an exceptionally long period of debugging the data flows and the associated mapping.

Integration Sequencing

Data integration involves combining and transforming data residing in different sources and providing users with a unified view of them.

It is essential for a real-time transformation of dissimilar data types from multiple sources inside and outside a regulated Good Practice entity. This real-time integration provides a universal data access layer (e.g., Data Marts), using pull technology or on-demand capabilities.

The capability to manage large bulk of data is provided by the infrastructure, including a great amount of memory, robust databases, and a large capacity of data servers.

ETL is not the only integration method for managing big data. ETL is the integration method that applies large volumes, complex transformations, efficiency, and periodic runs.

The ETL is an application often estimated to consume 70% of the time and effort of building a data warehouse. The complexity of the ETL is the reason why the system consuming computer resources intensive. The ETL products include over 40 subsystems that are needed in almost every data warehouse.

These subsystems are configurable software connected to the databases individually record field designed in the data mapping specification.

Two typical transformations are derivation and aggregations.

Derivation comprises the creation of a new field whose value is calculated from one or more fields within an input record. The algorithm that outlines derivation should be completely defined.

Aggregation involves the creation of a new field whose value is calculated to form one or more fields across several input records. As in the derivation, the algorithm that defines the aggregation should be completely defined.

Many of these transformations require assurance that the operations are completed, following the proper sequence, as applicable. The correct e-records integration sequencing provides the correct information to be stored at the corresponding visualization intelligence repository. The use of operational checks is required to enforce permitted sequencing of events, as appropriate (21 CFR Part 11.10(f)). The operational checks usually fall in the category of operation sequencing and are built into the software.

An acceptable method for the validation operational checks is (8):

- The documentation of the program, including a requirements specification which describes what the software is intended to do
- The performance of inspections and testing so that no step or specification can be missed or poorly executed/assigned
- Documentation of the initial and final steps

The primary concern of integrating and transforming erroneously is to obtain incorrect data value(s) and deviations of executed protocols.

References

1. López, O., "Electronic Records Integrity in a Data Warehouse and Business Intelligence," *Journal of Validation Technology Compliance*, 22(2), April 2016.
2. Raw Data – Raw data is defined as the original record (data) which can be described as the first capture of information, whether recorded on paper or electronically. Information that is originally captured in a dynamic state should remain available in that state. (MHRA)
3. Data – Facts, figures and statistics collected for reference or analysis. All original records and true copies of original records, including source data and metadata and all subsequent transformations and reports of these data, that are generated or recorded at the time of the GXP activity and allow complete reconstruction and evaluation of the GXP activity. (MHRA)
4. http://www.pharmtech.com/ema-creates-taskforce-big-data-0 and http://www.ema.europa.eu/ema/index.jsp?curl=pages/news_and_events/news/2017/03/news_detail_002718.jsp&mid=WC0b01ac058004d5c1.
5. López, O., "Infrastructure Lifecycle Approach," In: *Computer Infrastructure Qualification for FDA Regulated Industries.* (Davis Healthcare International Publishing, L.L.C., River Grove, IL, 1st ed., 2006). pp 5–23.
6. Data Process Mapping – It is a generation of a visual representation of the creation and movement of data through the business process including documentation of the systems used. (CEFIC, "*Practical Risk-based Guide for Managing Data Integrity*," March 2019 (Rev 1)).
7. MHRA, "MHRA GxP Data Integrity Definitions and Guidance for Industry," March 2018. https://mhrainspectorate.blog.gov.uk/2018/03/09/mhras-gxp-data-integrity-guide-published/.
8. FDA, "Guide to Inspection of Computerized Systems in Drug Processing," February 1983.

Appendix V
Data Integrity for Analytical Instruments connected to a LIMS

Introduction

An interesting article published in the ECA's GMP News on November 13, 2019, https://www.gmp-compliance.org/gmp-news/data-integrity-for-analytical-instruments-connected-to-a-lims-via-a-middleware

The objective of the article published in ECA's GMP News is to explain how to manage data integrity to analysis devices connected to a Laboratory Information Management System (LIMS) via a middleware.

According to the issue discussed in the article: "The first data (raw data) is generated internally, processed in the middleware and sent to the LIMS. However, the manufacturer does not allow access to the original data in the automated analyzer." Note that the details of the processing functionality residing in the middleware were not provided.

The objective of this appendix is to provide the authors of this book the point of view to the advice provided in the ECA's GMP News article. It will be used, as an example, a typical manufacturing architecture.

Definitions

Before providing the evaluation, let's provide critical definitions that will facilitate understanding the authors' points of view.

- Archive – A designated secure area or facility (e.g. cabinet, room, building, or computerized system) for the long-term retention of data and metadata for verification of the process or activity (1)
- Data – The contents of the record is the basic unit of information that has a unique meaning and can be transmitted (2)
- Data Elements – Individual GxP data items that are part of raw data or metadata (3)
- Data integrity – A property whereby data has not been altered in an unauthorized manner since it was created, transmitted, processed, or stored (4)
- Middleware – Middleware is any software that allows other software to interact; it connects different parts of an application or a series of applications and provides a transparent means of accessing information between clients and servers. For example, several middleware products link a database system to a web server. This allows users to request data from the database using forms displayed on a web browser, and it enables the web server to return dynamic web pages based on the user's requests and profile (5).
- Migration – The transfer of data from a source format or system to a target format or system (6).
- Original record – The first or source capture of data or information, e.g. an original paper record of manual observation or electronic raw data file from a computerized system, and all subsequent data required to fully reconstruct the conduct of the GXP activity (7).
- Processing Environment – The environment in which the e-records were initially created (8).
- Raw Data – Original records and documentation, retained in the format in which they were originally generated (i.e. paper or electronic), or as a "true copy" (8).
- Records – Records are defined as the collection of related data treated as a unit (7).
- Source data – All information in original records and certified copies of original records of clinical findings, observations, or other activities in a clinical trial necessary for the reconstruction and evaluation of the trial. Source data are contained in source documents (original records or certified copies) (9). According to the MHRA DI guideline (7), "'raw data' is synonymous with 'source data' which is defined in ICH GCP."
- Storage – A device that records (stores) or retrieves (reads) information (e-records) from any medium, including the medium itself.

By the definition of the US FDA (10), one prerequisite applicable to a CGMP record is that the data element must be recorded on the electronic storage device at the time of the creation.

Need to advise the readers that the definition of "primary data" in the ECA's GMP News initially introduced in the 201005 MHRA DI guidance document (11). This definition is no longer referenced in the most recent 2018 MHRA DI guidance document (7).

First Advice

"Raw Data Is Equated with the Generation of the First Data"

According to the definition of "raw data" and "original records" by the MHRA (above), the statement contained as a first point is accurate. The author(s) of the article published by the ECA established that: "In the CGMP environment, the raw data should be defined by the pharmaceutical manufacturer."

This last statement comes from Chapter 4 of the CGMP Medicinal Products for Human and Veterinary Use, for "electronic records regulated users should define which data are to be used as raw data. At least, all data on which quality decisions are based should be defined as raw data."

This definition by Chapter 4 of the CGMP Medicinal Products for Human and Veterinary Use takes into consideration whether the data is a CGMP data or not. For the standpoint of data management, raw data should be those records retained in the format in which they were originally generated. This characteristic is consistent with worldwide regulatory authorities. As part of the processing to the data set captured, the data set is transformed (e.g., analogue to digital), and stored in durable media. After storing the data, selected data is loaded to the CGMP records repository.

Second Advice

Figure V.1 is the same found in the ECA article and represents the data lifecycle. As noted, after filtering or selecting the data that are to be used as raw data, this data is used and then stored.

In the case of Figure V.1, the transient data is in a temporary local file before transfer to an electronic storage device (e.g., data server). After the

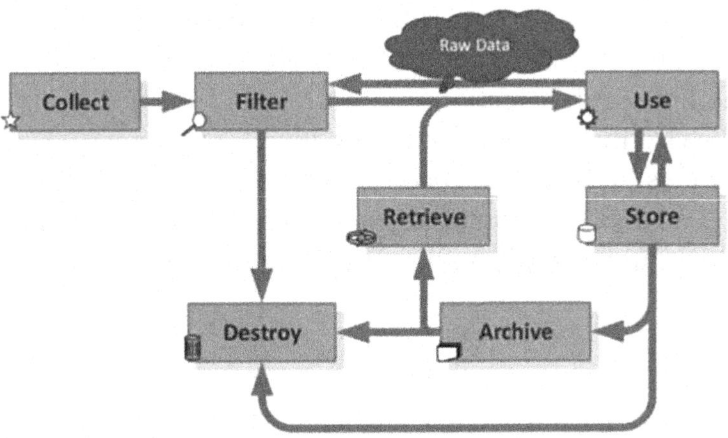

Figure V.1 Data lifecycle.

transformation from analogue to digital, there is no audit trail provision amending, deleting or recreating data. This is a data integrity risk (12).

According to the data integrity practices, transient data or data elements that have not been recorded to an electronic storage device cannot be edited by reasonable means or reprocessed by the human user, resulting in a different outcome (13). The data captured must not be altered during it is transferred to the electronic storage device because of there no technology to add an audit trail to transient data (7).

It is not acceptable to manage transient data in a manner that allows for manipulation without creating a permanent record contemporaneously.

In case the transient data cannot be immediately saved contemporaneously, the following controls are necessary: assurance that the records aren't manipulated or used on the way to the electronic storage device; the infrastructure is qualified; and built-in checks are implemented to verify the correctness of the I/Os.

Furthermore, according to Figure V.1, after the e-records are stored, these e-records may be archived. After archived, the e-records are destroyed or retrieved. The reader may note that after archived, the e-records may be retrieved. This activity is unusual. E-records are archived because these are inactive and, maybe, disabled of further modification.

A compliance solution to these situations described above, the data flow should connect "Store" with "Retrieve." A dotted line can link "Archive" with "Restore." There may be the possibility to edit e-records already disabled of modifications.

Audit trail capability must be enabled in the storage's areas.

Third Advice

Data Integrity Analytical Instruments Interface to a LIMS via a Middleware

> *Category 4: An electronic system with some limited manual adjustable input data and the generated GxP data is not stored but sent via an interface to another system, e.g. a cat 5 or 6.*
>
> **CEFIC, Practical risk-based guide for managing data integrity, March 2019**

If the data in the automated analyzer is in transient memory and there is a middleware between the analytical instrument and the LIMS, then this is considered as Category 4 in the CEFIC System categorization (3).

The data elements were captured and transformed from analogue to digital by the analytical instruments. The generated data is not stored in the analytical instruments but transferred for processing by the middleware. The middleware sends the data, via an interface, to the LIMS in which the transient data is recorded. The LIMS hosts the raw data collected at the instrument level and the LIMS is considered the processing environment.

The key CGMP records integrity controls applicable to e-records in the electronic storage device use by the LIMS to host these e-records are:

- Design reviews to verify the mapping from the middleware to the LIMS databases were the data elements will reside
- Modifications to CGMP e-records must be recorded at the time of modifying the e-records
- Monitoring of environmental conditions
- Periodic review verifying the modifications to the e-records, readability of e-records, processability of e-records, and security
- A system in place to detect modifications in the infrastructure and/or interfaces; perform an impact assessment of the modification to the e-records; proceed with the modifications appropriately
- Performing periodic full backups; and
- Security controls established to all e-record storages as a means of ensuring e-records protections

In the context of the analytical instrument and the middleware, the DI controls are those associated with the data while in transit and the qualification of the middleware. Note that the details of the processing functionality residing in the middleware were not provided. In any case, the applicable DI controls in the middleware are Built-in Checks (EU Annex 11 p5), Security (EU Annex 11 p12), and operational checks (21 CFR Part 11.10(f)). Refer to Chapter 22.

The extraction and load of data from the middleware to the LIMS must be subject to DI controls. In the context of the middleware and the LIMS, the DI controls are built-in checks. The built-in checks referenced in the EU Annex 11-5, the US FDA CPG 7132a.07 (Input/Output Checking), and US FDA 21 CFR Part 211.68(b), as examples.

Summary

1. It is important to understand that the captures of signals from instruments/equipment are not considered data until these signals are transformed to be meaningful and recorded to an electronic storage device.
2. According to the response to the inquiry after the data is captured, it is assumed to be the raw data. After the first "data" is capture in these systems, as in logic controllers in the manufacturing environment, the data is time-stamped and transformed in memory.
3. This data is called transient data because is in memory. The CGMP controls to transient data are infrastructure qualification, built-in checks, and verification of transformations.
4. After recording the transient data to the durable media or transcribed to papers contemporaneously, then it is considered data. Since the original records are retained in the format in which they were originally generated, these data can be considered raw data.
5. The DI controls associated with this setting are discussed in the earlier section in this chapter.

References

1. MHRA, "'GxP' Data Integrity Guidance and Definitions," March 2018.
2. ISO/IEC 17025:2017, "General Requirements for the Competence of Testing and Calibration Laboratories."
3. CEFIC, "Practical Risk-based Guide for Managing Data Integrity," March 2019 (Rev 1).

4. NIST, *Recommendation for Key Management, Part 1: General.* (Special Publication 800–57 Part 1 Rev 4, January 2016).
5. López, O., *Computer Infrastructure Qualification for FDA Regulated Industries.* (PDA and DHI Publishing, LLC, River Grove, IL, 2006).
6. MHRA, "Good Laboratory Practice – Guidance on Archiving," March 2006.
7. MHRA, "'GxP' Data Integrity Guidance and Definitions," March 2018.
8. ISPE/PDA, "Technical Report: Good Electronic Records Management (GERM)," July 2002.
9. ICH Harmonized Tripartite Guideline, "Good Clinical Practice, E6," Rev 2, June 2016.
10. US FDA, "Data Integrity and Compliance with Drug CGMP – Question and Answers, Guidance for Industry," December 2018.
11. MHRA, "GMP Data Integrity Definitions and Guidance for Industry," March 2015.
12. EMA, "Q&A: Good Manufacturing Practice – Data Integrity," August 2016.
13. ISPE/PDA, "Good Electronic Records Management (GERM)," July 2002.

Appendix VI

Data Integrity – EU Deviations

Company Name	*Date*		*Regulation*	*Note*
Wockhardt Limited	Jul 13	Statement of non-compliance with GMPs.	2003/94/EC (EU GMPs)	Critical deficiency: Issues were identified which compromised the integrity of analytical data produced by the QC department. Evidence was seen in data falsification. A significant number of product stability data results reported in the Product Quality Reviews had been fabricated. Neither hard copy nor electronic records were available. Besides, issues were seen with HPLC electronic data indicating unauthorized manipulation of data and incidents of unreported trial runs before reported analytical runs. (MHRA.)
Ind-Swift Limited	Oct 13	Statement of non-compliance with GMPs.	2003/94/EC (EU GMPs)	It was not possible to confirm the validity of the stability testing data. Several falsified and inaccurate results had been reported in long-term stability and batch testing. Discrepancies between electronic data and those results formally reported were identified. Established processes to verify data accuracy and integrity had failed and there had been no formal investigation raised by the company. The company provided commitments to address the data integrity concerns and initiated a wider review of quality critical data. Additional discrepancies were identified in process validation and release data. During on-going communications with the licensing authority regarding the data review, the company failed to disclose data integrity issues for all products. No satisfactory explanation was given for this discrepancy. (MHRA.)
Smruthi Organics Ltd.	Oct 13	Statement of non-compliance with GMPs.	Article 47 of 2001/83/EEC	The agency observed the manipulation and falsification of documents and data in different departments. There was no raw data available in the Quality Control laboratory for the verification of compendial analytical methods. (French Health Products Safety Agency.)

(*Continued*)

Company Name	Date		Regulation	Note
Wockhardt Limited	Nov 13	Statement of non-compliance to GMPs.	Art. 111(7) of Directive 2001/83/EC as amended.	Entries were seen to be made when personnel were not present on-site, documentation was seen that was not completed contemporaneously despite appearing to be completed in this manner. (Competent authority of the United Kingdom.)
Wockhardt Limited	Nov 13	Statement of non-compliance with GMPs.	2003/94/EC (EU GMPs)	The deficiency related to data integrity deleted electronic files with no explanation. (MHRA.)
Zeta Analytical Ltd	Nov 13	Statement of non-compliance with GMPs.	European Union's GMP guideline	The computer system being used for HPLC did not have adequate controls to prevent unrecorded changes to data. (MHRA.)
Seikagaku Corporation	Dec 13	Statement of non-compliance with GMPs.	2003/94/EC (EU GMPs)	The critical deficiency concerns systematic rewriting/ manipulation of documents, including QC raw data. The company has not been able to provide acceptable investigations and explanations to the differences seen in official and non-official versions of the same documents. (Competent Authority of Sweden.)
Punjab Chemicals and Crop Corporation Limited	Jan 14	Statement of non-compliance with GMPs.	Article 47 of 2001/83/EEC	One individual training file of an employee has been observed to be recently re-rewritten; The Batch Manufacturing record was lacking details with regards to manufacturing steps and in-process controls; The sample retention logbook for Trimethoprim had falsified entries. (French Health Products Safety Agency)
Smruthi Organics Ltd.'s	Jan 14	Statement of non-compliance with GMPs.	Article 47 of 2001/83/EEC	There was no raw data available in the Quality Control laboratory for the verification of compendial analytical methods. (French Health Products Safety Agency.)

(Continued)

Company Name	*Date*		*Regulation*	*Note*
SOMET	Mar 14	Statement of non-compliance with GMPs.	Article 47 of 2001/83/EEC Article 51 of 2001/82/EC	Complete records of raw data generated during cleanliness tests by thin-layer chromatography are missing. (French Health Products Safety Agency.)
Wockhardt Limited	Mar 14	Statement of non-compliance with GMPs.	2003/94/EC (EU GMPs) Article 47 of 2001/83/EEC	A critical deficiency was cited with regards to the data integrity of GMP records, entries were seen to be made when personnel were not present on-site, and documentation was seen that was not completed contemporaneously despite appearing to be completed in this manner. (Competent Authority of the United Kingdom.)
J P Laboratories Private Limited	Apr 14	Statement of non-compliance with GMPs.	The principles of GMP for active substances referred to in Article 47 of Directive 2001/83/EC	Quality management – integrity and security of data in the quality system. Laboratory control – integrity and security of analytical data.
Medreich Limited	May 14	Statement of non-compliance with GMPs.	Art. 111(7) of Directive 2001/83/EC as amended Art. 80(7) of Directive 2001/82/EC as amended	Data falsification.
Impax	Jul 14	483	211.68(b)	The plant has two spectrophotometers that don't have adequate controls to ensure analysts can't rewrite or delete analytical data. The systems are used in testing raw materials, stability and release. *Source:* Quality Management Network Vol 6, No 33 (August 15, 2014).
Hebei Dongfeng Pharmaceutical Co., Ltd	Aug 14	Statement of non-compliance with GMPs.	Article 47 of 2001/83/EEC	Data recording and integrity in the QC laboratory. (Competent authority of Romania.)

(*Continued*)

Company Name	Date		Regulation	Note
Renown Pharmaceuticals Pvt. Ltd	Aug 14	Statement of non-compliance with GMPs.	2003/94/EC (EU GMPs)	Record integrity and veracity: some records were made up or altered. Lack of mechanisms to ensure the integrity of analytical data. (Spanish Agency of Medicines and Medical Devices.)
Fujian South Pharmaceutical	Sep 14	Statement of non-compliance to GMPs.	Art. 111(7) of Directive 2001/83/EC	The computerized systems in the quality control department could not show whether approval of raw materials and the final API was based on valid and accurate data. (Italian Medicines Agency.)
Taishan City Chemical Pharmaceutical Co. Ltd.	Sep 14	Statement of non-compliance to GMPs.	Article 47 of Directive 2001/83/EC	Insufficient securitization of the electronic raw data in the Quality Control laboratory (no limitation of access levels, no restriction on the deleting of data, no audit trail, inadequate traceability and archiving practices). (French Health Products Safety Agency.)
Zhejiang Apeloa Kangyu Bio-Pharmaceutical Co. Ltd.	Oct 14	Statement of non-compliance to GMPs.	Art. 80(7) of Directive 2001/82/EC	The company failed to establish a procedure to identify and validate GMP-relevant computerized systems in general. Two batch analysis reports for Colistin Sulfate proved to be manipulated. HPLC chromatograms had been copied from previous batches and renamed with different batch and file names. Several electronically stored HPLC runs had not been entered into the equipment logbooks. The nature of these data could not finally be clarified. Neither the individual workstation nor the central server had been adequately protected against uncontrolled deletion or change of data. The transfer of data between workstations and server showed to be incomplete. No audit trail and no consistency checks had been implemented to prevent misuse of data.

(*Continued*)

Company Name	*Date*		*Regulation*	*Note*
North China Pharmaceutical Group Semisyntech Co., Ltd	Nov 14	Statement of non-compliance to GMPs.	Article 47 of Directive 2001/83/EC Article 51 of Directive 2001/82/EC	Manipulation and falsification of GMP documents (rewriting of records with the change of content, an inconsistency of signatures and date in many records, etc.) were observed in a different department. Lack of data integrity in the QC laboratory (no access control, inadequate traceability and archiving practices, no audit trail, no restriction on the deleting of data, etc.) and falsification of the analytical results for residual solvents. (Competent authority of France.)
Zhejiang Apeloa Kangyu Bio-Pharmaceutical Co. Ltd	Nov 14	Statement of non-compliance to GMPs	The principles of GMP for active substances referred to in Article 51 of Directive 2001/82/EC	The company failed to establish a procedure to identify and validate GMP-relevant computerized systems in general. Two batch analysis reports for Colistin Sulfate proved to be manipulated. HPLC chromatograms had been copied from previous batches and renamed with different batch and file names. Several electronically stored HPLC runs had not been entered into the equipment logbooks. The nature of these data could not finally be clarified. Neither the individual workstation nor the central server had been adequately protected against uncontrolled deletion or change of data. The transfer of data between workstations and server was shown to be incomplete. No audit trail and no consistency checks had been implemented to prevent misuse of data. (The competent authority of Germany.)

(*Continued*)

Company Name	*Date*		*Regulation*	*Note*
Sri Krishna Pharmaceuticals Ltd.	Dec 14	Statement of non-compliance to GMPs	Art. 111(7) of Directive 2001/83/EC as amended.	1. The company did not have a proper system in place to make sure that electronic raw data cannot be adulterated or deleted. Analysts routinely use the PC administrator privileges to set the controlling time and date settings back to over-write previously collected failing and/or undesirable sample results. This practice is performed until passing and/or desired results are achieved. 2. Established laboratory control mechanisms are not followed. Electronic records are used, but they do not meet systems validation requirements to ensure that they are trustworthy, reliable and generally equivalent to paper records. (Italian Medicines Agency.)
North China Pharmaceutical Group Semisyntech Co., Ltd	Jan 15	Statement of non-compliance to GMPs	Article 47 of Directive 2001/83/EC and Article 51 of Directive 2001/82/EC	No access control, inadequate traceability and archiving practices, no audit trail, and no restriction on the deleting of data. (French National Agency for Medicines and Health Products Safety.)

(*Continued*)

Company Name	*Date*		*Regulation*	*Note*
Polydrug Laboratories Pvt. Ltd	Mar 15	Statement of non-compliance to GMPs	Art. 111(7) of Directive 2001/83/EC as amended Art. 80(7) of Directive 2001/82/EC as amended	Deficient management of the computerized system. (Agency for medicinal products and medical devices of the Republic of Slovenia.) It seems that based on a deficient GMP inspection report, the Slovenian Authority caused a GMP Non-Compliance Report in EudraGMDP and the suspension of all CEPs of the company. The Inspectors have requested the marketing authorization holders using APIs from Polydrug Laboratories to change their API supplier. Health Canada and the U.S. FDA have used the GMP inspection report of the Slovenian Authority to decide on consequences for supplies to Canada and the United States. In June, Health Canada has already issued a press release in which they requested Canadian importers to voluntarily quarantine drug products with active pharmaceutical ingredients (APIs) manufactured or tested by Polydrug Laboratories, in Ambarnath, Maharashtra, India, due to data integrity concerns. Now the FDA has also issued an Import Alert. Products manufactured by Polydrug can no longer enter the U.S. market due to serious GMP violations. The EU Inspection has likely been the initial trigger for actions taken by Canada and the United States.
Minsheng Group Shaoxing Pharmaceutical Co. Ltd	May 15	Statement of non-compliance to GMPs.	The principles of GMP for active substances referred to in Article 47 of Directive 2001/83/EC	There was no procedure in place for audit trail and there was no effective audit trail in place to determine any change or deletion of the chromatographic raw data. The audit trail function, including the administrator profiles, was enabled for all the QC staff. (The competent authority of France.)

(Continued)

Company Name	*Date*		*Regulation*	*Note*
Jinan Jinda Pharmaceutical	Jun 15	Statement of non-compliance to GMPs.	Art. 111(7) of Directive 2001/83/EC as amended	Breaches of data integrity in the context of HPLC analysis. (Italian Medicine Agency.)
Parabolic Drugs Limited	Jun 15	Statement of non-compliance to GMPs.	The principles of GMP for active substances referred to in Article 47 of Directive 2001/83/EC	Falsification and Security and integrity data. Inadequate storage and control of documents and samples and material, falsification of documents and data, integrity, and security of data in the QC laboratory. (Italian Medicine Agency.)
Polydrug Laboratories Pvt. Ltd	Jun 15	Statement of non-compliance to GMPs.	The principles of GMP for active substances referred to in Article 47 of Directive 2001/83/EC and Article 51 of Directive 2001/82/EC.	Deficient management of the computerized system. (The competent authority of Slovenia.)
Wuxi Jida Pharmaceutical	Jun 15	Statement of non-compliance to GMPs.	Art. 111(7) of Directive 2001/83/EC as amended	Laboratory testing (deviation 28): some deviations were found for the IR instrument, in particular, the IR software had not controlled access via ID and password and it was not forbidden to copy and rename a file. (Italian Medicine Agency.)
Chengdu Okay Pharmaceutical Co. Ltd.	Oct 15	Statement of non-compliance to GMPs.	Art. 111(7) of Directive 2001/83/EC as amended	Computerized systems – documentation and control: There were no logins and passwords to the HPLC system and no procedure for granting permission to access to the HPLC system. There was no register of persons authorized to access to the HPLC system. On the same computer station, there were two different HPLC software. (Competent Authority of Poland.)
Hubei Hongyuan Pharmaceutical Co., Ltd.	Oct 15	Statement of non-compliance to GMPs.	Article 47 of Directive 2001/83/EC (API)	2 of 10 major deficiencies were related to Data Integrity and Computer System Validation, Change Control. (The competent authority of the Czech Republic.)

(Continued)

Company Name	*Date*		*Regulation*	*Note*
Iason Italia Srl	Oct 15	Statement of non-compliance to GMPs.	The principles and guidelines of Good Manufacturing Practice laid down in Directive 2003/94/EC	Data integrity in the context of HPLC management. (Competent Authority of Italy.)
Marksans Pharma Limited	Nov 15	Statement of non-compliance to GMPs.	Art. 111(7) of Directive 2001/83/EC as amended	The November inspection identified a critical deficiency relating to systems to Ensure Data Integrity in the following respects: (a) Evidence of destruction of multiple parts of records of prime data. (b) Overall Data Integrity management and oversight. (c) Investigations into missing and deleted data within the laboratory incomplete. (d) Procedures controlling Data Integrity within the laboratory, not in place. (Competent Authority of UK.)
Farma Mediterranea, S.L.	Jan 16	Statement of non-compliance to GMPs.	Art. 111(7) of Directive 2001/83/EC as amended Art. 80(7) of Directive 2001/82/EC as amended Art. 15 of Directive 2001/20/EC	Use in quality control non-qualified chromatography equipment, with operating faults and a with an unvalidated computerized management system. As a result, the integrity, reliability, up-to-date, originality, and authenticity of the data that are obtained cannot be guaranteed. (Spanish Agency of Medicines and Medical Devices.)
Rusa Pharma Ltd	Jan 16	Statement of non-compliance to GMPs.	Art. 111(7) of Directive 2001/83/EC as amended Art. 80(7) of Directive 2001/82/EC as amended Art. 15 of Directive 2001/20/EC	No adequate evidence that the root causes of critical data integrity issues raised at the last inspection had been addressed. The control of electronic data and laboratory systems was not adequately robust and could not assure data traceability or security. (The competent authority of the United Kingdom.)

(Continued)

Company Name	Date		Regulation	Note
Bend Research Inc.	Feb 16	Statement of non-compliance to GMPs.	Art. 111(7) of Directive 2001/83/EC as amended Art. 80(7) of Directive 2001/82/EC as amended Art. 15 of Directive 2001/20/EC	One major deficiency concerns data integrity. (The competent authority of Sweden.)
Pharmaceutics International Inc	Feb 16	Statement of non-compliance to GMPs.	Directive 2003/94/EC	Organizational data governance failures, particularly relating to generation and checking of analytical data obtained from electronic systems, and inadequate investigation into previous data integrity failures.
J P Laboratories Private Limited	Mar 16	Statement of non-compliance to GMPs.	Article 47 of Directive 2001/83/EC	Quality management – integrity and security of data in the quality system – Laboratory control – integrity and security of analytical data. (The competent authority of Italy.)
Russian Pharma Ltd	Apr 16	Statement of non-compliance to GMPs.	The principles and guidelines of Good Manufacturing Practice laid down in Directive 2003/94/EC	The control of electronic data and laboratory systems was not adequately robust and could not assure data traceability or security. (Competent Authority of the United Kingdom.)
Artemis Biotech (A Division of Themis Medicare Limited)	Jun 16	Statement of non-compliance to GMPs.	Article 47 of Directive 2001/83/EC.	Within the instrumental laboratory, the Company violated basic principles on data integrity, i.e., manual integration without justification and QA oversight. The Company's approach on the validation of computerized systems (Shimadzu LabSolutions) was considered as not in compliance with the requirements.
Nandu Chemicals Industries	Aug 16	Letter of non-compliance.	Article 47 of Directive 2001/83/EC	One observation is about data integrity: "For documentation, insufficient recording and archiving practices issues." (French National Agency for Medicines and Health Products Safety.)

(Continued)

Company Name	*Date*		*Regulation*	*Note*
Micro Labs Limited	Oct 16	Statement of non-compliance to GMPs.	The principles and guidelines of Good Manufacturing Practice laid down in Directive 2003/94/EC	There was evidence of data integrity issues within GMP documents. (The competent authority of the United Kingdom.)
EuroPharma DK APS	Dec 16	Letter of non-compliance.	Directive 2003/94/EC	The inspection found that information was deliberately hidden and falsification of the expiry date on medicinal products.
Nova DFL Industrie E Commercio, S.A.	Apr 17	Statement of non-compliance to GMPs.	The principles and guidelines of Good Manufacturing Practice laid down in Directive 2003/94/EC	The absence of data integrity guarantee (raw data management). (The competent authority of France.)
Kores (India) Limited	May 17	Statement of non-compliance to GMPs.	The principles of GMP for active substances referred to in Article 47 of Directive 2001/83/EC	Electronic and paper analytical data integrity. (The competent authority of Italy.)
Gopaldas Visram & Co. Ltd.	Aug 17	Statement of non-compliance to GMPs.	The principles and guidelines of Good Manufacturing Practice laid down in Directive 2003/94/EC	The first critical deficiency was cited with regards to data integrity, e.g., login details for the QA Manager were shared with a delegate. Employees have administrator rights to GMP related software (HPLC, stability chambers data soft system). Controlled documents were found torn in a bin where used clothes are disposed-of. (The competent authority of Malta.)
Biomedica Foscama Group S.P.A.	Oct 18	Statement of non-compliance to GMPs.	The principles and guidelines of Good Manufacturing Practice laid down in Directive 2003/94/EC and the principles of GMP for active substances referred to in Article 47 of Directive 2001/83/EC	QC equipment was not qualified and data integrity was not assured. (The competent authority of Italy.)

(*Continued*)

Company Name	*Date*		*Regulation*	*Note*
Mercury Laboratories Ltd.	Oct 18	Statement of non-compliance to GMPs.	The principles and guidelines of Good Manufacturing Practice laid down in Directive 2003/94/EC	The critical deficiency concerned authenticity of records which could not be verified, including production records and quality risk assessment records. (The competent authority of Malta.)
Kores (India) Limited	Dec 18	Statement of non-compliance to GMPs.	The principles of GMP for active substances referred to in Article 47 of Directive 2001/83/EC	Major deficiencies were found in the following areas: Data integrity and computerized systems validation. (The competent authority of France.)
Lantech Pharmaceuticals Limited	Jul 19	Statement of non-compliance to GMPs.	The Good Manufacturing Practice requirements referred to in the Agreement of Mutual Recognition between the European Union and Switzerland	Quality control showed issues in data integrity as well as equipment and reagents management. (The competent authority of Switzerland.)
Novocat Farma, S.A.	Jul 19	Statement of non-compliance to GMPs.	The principles and guidelines of Good Manufacturing Practice laid down in Directive 2003/94/EC	(b) During the period when the technical director was on sick leave, there are documents presumably signed by her in which the signature is falsified. (Competent Authority of Spain.)
Union Quimico Farmaceutica, S.A.	Oct 19	Statement of non-compliance to GMPs.	The principles of GMP for active substances (API) referred to in cc0	Evidence was found of falsified and rewritten documents, hidden products, and destroyed documentation and electronic files. (c) Failure in ensuring data integrity. In the production area, there is a systematic practice of manipulation and falsification of data related to filling the manufacturing batch records. It also affects the control in the processing unit, compromising the integrity of the data. (Competent Authority of Spain.)
Bio Plus Life Sciences Private Limited	Feb 20	Statement of non-compliance to GMPs.	The principles and guidelines of Good Manufacturing Practice laid down in Directive 2003/94/EC	The integrity of the reported data could not be relied upon. (Competent Authority of the United Kingdom.)

Index

Abstract Syntax Notation One (ASN.1), 147
Access-control entries (ACEs), 151–152
Access-control lists (ACLs), 151–152
Access controls, 151–152
ACEs, *see* Access-control entries
ACLs, *see* Access-control lists
Advanced Encryption Standard (AES), 145
Archive, 294
Audit trails, 91–92
  administration events, 179
  control, 152
  EU guidelines, 177
  product-/batch-specific data, 178
  regulators expectations, 178
  review, 176–181
    changes, 180
    guidance for, 179–180
    suspected data integrity violation, 180
  system activities, 179
  testing, 180–181
  US FDA regulatory requirements for, 177
Authentication, 152–154
Authority checks, 151–152
Automated migration, e-records, 123

Backup as a Service (BaaS), 25, 175–176
Big data
  overview, 287–288
  validation process, 288–292
    data process mapping, 290–291
    infrastructure, 289–290
    integration sequencing, 291–292
Brexit, 25
Built-in checks, 188

Certificate-based authentication, 154
Certificates of analysis, 44
Checksum, 32–33
Cloud service provider, 125–134
  e-records, integrity of
    accessibility, 133–134
    migration, 133
  periodic audits of, 133
  regulatory agencies' expectation, 134
  requirements, 126–130
    access control, 126–127
    data management and regulatory compliance, 127
    interoperability, 129
    lifecycle management, 130
    management and governance, 128
    monitoring, 127
    network access, 127
    portability and deployment, 129
    reversibility, 129–130
    security, 128–129
  selection of, 130–131
  service level agreement, 131–132
Computer systems
  access, 89–91
  access controls, 151–152
  authority checks, 151–152
  clock controls, 118–119
  and e-records lifecycles, integration between, 163–174
    archiving, 172–174
    building, testing, documenting, and installing, 169–170
    business requirements, 167–169

concept period, 165
migration, 170–172
operations periods, 170–171
risk assessment, 165–167
validation, 28–29, 164
Continued process verification (CPV), 96–97
Cryptographic technologies, 143–147
e-records integrity
application to, 149–150
tools, 160
e-records in transit, 157–159
device checks, 159
storage, e-records in, 150–157
audit trails control, 152
authentication, 152–154
computer resources, access controls and authority checks to, 151–152
electronic signatures, security of, 154–155
electronic signatures, uniqueness of, 157
signature e-records linkage, 155–156
time controls, 156
Cyphers, 145

DaaS, *see* Data as a Service
DACL, *see* Discretionary access-control list
Data, 29–31, 294
collection, 31
definition, 17
elements, 294
lifecycle, 18–20
active phase, 19
capture, 18–19
disposition/destruction, 20
vs. e-records lifecycle, 23
inactive phase, 19–20
quality, 20
transformation, 19
use, 19
migration, checklist for, 123–124
quality control, 227
raw, 30, 44
recording, 31
review and approval, 37–38
transferring/migrating, 31–33
Data accuracy, 221–222
Data as a Service (DaaS), 125
Data auditability, 222
Databases integrity, 181–182
Data completeness, 223
Data conformity, 223
Data consistency, 223
Data encryption standard (DES), 145
Data governance, 27–28
Data handling, 99
Data integrity, 224
Data integrity (DI), 1–2, 25–39, 181, 294
controls
categories of, 208–216
supporting processes applicable to, 204–208
EU deviations, 301–313
in process automation, 110
regulations/guidance, 49–50
Data integrity/quality by design (DIQbD), 142
Data provenance, 224–225
Data quality, 219–221
design, 226–227
Data steward, 7
Data validity, 225–226
Data warehouse (DW), 71–72
DES, *see* Data encryption standard
DI, *see* Data integrity
Digital notary services, 36
Digital signatures, 147–149, 154
e-records linkage, 155–156
security of, 154–155
uniqueness of, 157
Digital time-stamping (DTS), 156
DIQbD, *see* Data integrity/quality by design
Discretionary access-control list (DACL), 151
Domain integrity, 181
DTS, *see* Digital time-stamping
DW, *see* Data warehouse

EMA, *see* European Medicines Agency
Encryption, 144–145
Entity integrity, 181
E-records
archiving, 33, 172–174

audit trails, 33
automated system transactions, 37
automated system user access/system administrator roles, 38
built-in checks, 33
business requirements, 29
checksum, 32–33
controls, 29–31
copy, 36
data review and approval, 37–38
e-signatures, 33–34
file structure, 39
governance, 27
integrity, 25–39
affecting factors, 64
clauses, 45
of cloud service provider, 125–134
EMA technical requirements, 42–43
EU GMP inspectors, expectations of, 44–47
EU guidelines, 43–44
expectations, 41–42
handling and SLC, 27–39
in hybrid systems, 137–139
issues, 45, 175–189
management, 55
maxims of, 57–61
into practices, 201–216
technologies supporting, 141–147
in wireless environments, 185–189
lifecycle, 7–14, 20–22
active phase, 12
and computer systems, integration between, 163–174
creation/capture phase, 10–11
vs. data lifecycles, 23
final disposition phase, 13–14
identification phase, 9
inactive phase, 13
regulatory agencies' expectations, 14
standardization phase, 9–10
migration, 121–124, 170–172
automated, 123
data, checklist for, 123–124
process, 122–123
regulatory agencies' expectations, 124
operational checks, 34
original, 35–36
printouts/reports, 34
in process automation, 110
regulations/guidance documents, 49–50
consistencies, 54–55
differences, 52–54
elements of, 52–53
evaluation of, 50–52
reliability, 29
retention, 38–39, 182–185
documentation, 183–184
testing, 184–185
risk assessments, 83–86
risk management, 77–81
security, 34
security service, 89–93
storage, 36–39
transferring/migrating, 31–33
validation/qualification process, 33–34
vulnerabilities, 63–74
E-signatures, 33–34; *see also* Digital signatures
EU Annex 11, 201–202
as computer data integrity compliance model, 202–203
data integrity (DI) controls
categories of, 208–216
supporting processes applicable to, 204–208
European Medicines Agency (EMA), 26

File structure, e-records, 39

Handwritten signatures, 137–139
Hashing, 143–144
Hash Message Authentication Code (HMACs), 158
Heads of Medicines Agencies (HMA), 26
HMACs, *see* Hash Message Authentication Code
Hybrid systems, e-records integrity in, 137–139
handwritten signatures, 137–139
regulatory agencies' expectations, 139

Infrastructure as a Service (IaaS), 125
Infrastructure qualification, 187–188

Laboratory Information Management System (LIMS), 293–298

Maxims of e-records integrity, 57–61
  lifecycle, 57–59
  security, 60–61
  validity, measure of, 59–60
Medicine manufacturing operations, 95–105
  CGMP records, identification of, 97
  data
    exchange of, 97–99
    protection of, 100–102
    retention time, 103–104
  e-records, protection of, 100–102
    raw data, 102
    transient data, 101–102
  e-records remediation project, 191–199
    controls evaluation, 193–195
    corrective actions planning, 195–197
    execution, 198
    fundamentals, 192–193
    interpretation, 197
    new applications/application upgrade assessments, 198
    report, 199
    suppliers qualification program, 198–199
    training, 197–198
  records/e-records
    disposition of, 104–105
    retrieval of, 102–103
    storage of, 99–100
Medicines & Healthcare Products Regulatory Agency (MHRA) guidance, 25–39
  computer systems validation, 28–29
  data governance, 27–28
  requirements, 29–39
Metadata, 30–31
MHRA, *see* Medicines & Healthcare Products Regulatory Agency
Middleware, 294
Migration, e-records, 121–124, 294
  automated, 123
  data, checklist for, 123–124
  process, 122–123
  regulatory agencies' expectations, 124

Original records, 35–36, 294

PaaS, *see* Platform as a Service
Password policy, 91
PKCS, *see* Public-Key Cryptography Standards
PKI, *see* Public-key infrastructure
Platform as a Service (PaaS), 125
Processing environment, 294
Public-Key Cryptography Standards (PKCS), 147
Public-key infrastructure (PKI), 145–147

Quality control, data, 227

Race Integrity Primitives Evaluation Message Digest (RIPEMD), 143–144
Raw data, 30, 44, 294
Records, 17, 294; *see also* E-records
  definition, 17, 44
  original, 35–36
  vulnerability, 63
Referential integrity, 181
Regulations/guidance documents, 49–50
  consistencies, 54–55
  differences, 52–54
  elements of, 52–53
  evaluation of, 50–52
Reports, 44
Risk assessments, e-records, 83–86
Risk management, e-records, 77–81
  computer systems/computer-controlled equipment, 79–81
  regulatory agencies expectations, 81
  steps
    assessing risk, 78
    framing risk, 78
    monitoring risk, 78
    responding to risk, 78

SaaS, *see* Software as a Service
Secure Sockets Layer (SSL), 154
Security service, 89–93
  audit trails, 91–92
  computer access, 89–91
  password policy, 91

regulatory agencies' expectations, 93
Service level agreement (SLA), 131–132
Software as a Service (SaaS), 125
Source data, 294, *see* Raw data
SSL, *see* Secure Sockets Layer
Storage, 294
System/networked master clock, 116
controls, 118–119
regulatory agencies' expectations, 119
reliability, 116–117

Time controls, 156
Timestamps, 115, 117–119
Time zone, 118
Transient data, 109–110
controls, 111–112
in process automation, 110
protection of, 110–112
regulatory agencies' expectations, 112
Transient memory, 36, 68–69
True copy record, 36
Trustworthy computer systems, 149–150

Vulnerabilities of e-records, 63–74
in business intelligence, 69, 71–73
control measures, implementation of, 68–71
definition, 63
protection, 63–64
regulatory agencies expectations, 73
risk assessment, 68–69
security, 63–64
threats
e-records storage, 67–68
e-records transfers, 67
malware and phishing schemes, 65
old hardware, inadequate disposal of, 67
regulated users, 65
service providers/suppliers, roles of, 65–66
unrestricted access to computers, 66–67

Wireless environments, e-records integrity in, 185–189
accuracy checks, 188–189
built-in checks, 188
data integrity, 187–189
infrastructure qualification, 187–188
WLAN, 185–189

X.509 certificate, 146–147
XaaS, 125–126, 176

Printed in the United States
By Bookmasters